Wakefield Press

Foundational Fictions in South Australian History

In memory of Eric Richards

Foundational Fictions

in South Australian History

Edited by
CAROLYN COLLINS
AND **PAUL SENDZIUK**

Wakefield Press

Wakefield Press
16 Rose Street
Mile End
South Australia 5031
www.wakefieldpress.com.au

First published 2018

Copyright © this collection Carolyn Collins and Paul Sendziuk, 2018
Copyright in individual chapters remains with the respective authors

All rights reserved. This book is copyright. Apart from
any fair dealing for the purposes of private study, research,
criticism or review, as permitted under the Copyright Act,
no part may be reproduced without written permission.
Enquiries should be addressed to the publisher.

Cover designed by Liz Nicholson, designBITE
Typeset by Michael Deves, Wakefield Press

ISBN 978 1 74305 606 6

 A catalogue record for this book is available from the National Library of Australia

 Wakefield Press thanks Coriole Vineyards for continued support

Contents

	Acknowledgements	vi
1	Beautiful Lies? Foundational Fictions in South Australian History **Carolyn Collins and Paul Sendziuk**	1
2	A Contested Coast? Revisiting the Baudin–Flinders Encounter of April 1802 **Jean Fornasiero and John West-Sooby**	13
3	Wakefield Revisited Again **Eric Richards**	28
4	Born Free: Wage-slaves and Chattel-slaves **Humphrey McQueen**	43
5	True Lies: South Australia's Foundation, the Idea of 'Difference', and the Rights of Aboriginal People **Robert Foster**	64
6	George Hamilton, the Bold and Dashing Bushman: The Politics of Colonial Compassion **Jane Lydon**	79
7	Walking the Line in Historical Fiction **Lucy Treloar**	97
8	Legends of the Nineties: Literary Culture in Adelaide at the End of the Nineteenth Century **Philip Butterss**	118
9	South Australia: The Pivotal State **Stuart Macintyre**	133
10	The Great Man of History: Industrialisation and the Playford Legend **Paul Sendziuk**	150
11	Nineteenth Century Dreams, Twentieth Century Realities: Reframing the Abolishment of Capital Punishment in South Australia **Steven Anderson**	165
12	Sending Out an SOS: South Australia's Forgotten Anti-conscription Crusaders **Carolyn Collins**	177
	Notes	198
	Contributors	235
	Index	238

Acknowledgements

Paul Sendziuk and Robert Foster, the convenors of the Foundational Fictions lecture series on which this volume is based, would like to thank Professor Jennie Shaw, the Dean of the Faculty of Arts at The University of Adelaide, and Professor Jennifer Clark, the Head of the School of Humanities, for providing financial support that enabled the lectures to take place in October and early November 2017. They also greatly appreciate Mirna Heruc and Anna Rivett of University Collections for committing their time and resources to promote and attend each of the lectures, and for the generous financial contribution of University Collections. Local artist Peter Drew kindly allowed the reproduction of his work to promote the series. Deep gratitude goes to the speakers themselves for preparing and delivering such stimulating lectures and inspiring other authors to contribute chapters to this volume. Each of the lectures attracted upwards of 200 people, so we acknowledge the members of the public who, once again, demonstrated their curiosity about South Australia's past.

This book is the result of the audience's request to publish the lectures and further research on foundational aspects of the state's history. It is made possible by the support of the team at Wakefield Press, led splendidly by Michael Bollen. We thank the publisher and also the institutions that have given their permission to reproduce the images that appear within this book.

As always, we thank our respective partners and children – Roy, Bronte and Jack, Katrina, Theo and Jarvis – who cheerfully support our endeavours and who managed admirably without us while we attended the lectures and worked on producing this book.

Carolyn Collins and Paul Sendziuk, May 2018

1

Beautiful Lies? Foundational Fictions in South Australian History

CAROLYN COLLINS AND PAUL SENDZIUK

> Australian history is almost always picturesque; indeed, it is so curious and strange, that it is itself the chiefest novelty the country has to offer ... It does not read like history but like the most beautiful lies.
> – Mark Twain, *Following the Equator*[1]

When American writer Samuel Langhorne Clemens, better known by the pen name Mark Twain, visited South Australia in 1895, he was clearly impressed. In his travel log he extols the splendour of its capital, Adelaide, 'a modern city, with wide streets, compactly built; with fine homes everywhere, embowered in foliage and flowers, and with imposing masses of public buildings nobly grouped and architecturally beautiful'.[2] He heralds the colony as a workingman's 'paradise', drolly noting its abundance of public holidays, and marvels at its religious and political tolerance, where 64 different religions could be freely practised among the city's '320,000 odd' population.[3] Twain is particularly chuffed to find a fellow 'Yankee' serving as the Minister for Public Works.[4] Where else but Adelaide, he suggests, would such things ever be thought possible?

Twain paints a pretty picture of South Australia on the cusp of the twentieth century as a forward-looking society offering opportunity for all. His observations appear to reinforce South Australia's claim to its early and enlightened origins of social democracy based on its founding social, economic and political principles that were designed to set it apart from other Australian colonies. But is Twain's depiction of this egalitarian 'paradise' accurate? Earlier, during the Melbourne leg of his lecture tour, Twain wryly observes that Australian history does not 'read like history' but 'like the most beautiful lies'.[5] He makes no exception for South Australia. Arriving in Adelaide, he declares: 'There it is again, picturesque history – Australia's speciality'.⁶ While his exact meaning is open to interpretation, on closer examination his own account of South Australia's 'picturesque history' raises some questions.

Chief among them is his easy acceptance of the apparent absence of Indigenous people. Twain relates a conversation with one of the surviving first settlers attending the Proclamation Day ceremony at Glenelg. 'He thought them [Aboriginal people] intelligent – remarkably so in some directions', Twain writes, 'and he considered it a great pity that the race had died out'.⁷ Twain is quick to cast doubt on the settler's claim that Aboriginal people invented the boomerang, noting the 'toy' had been 'known to certain savage tribes in Europe in Roman times'.⁸ He makes no attempt, however, to verify the settler's other claim, perpetuating one of the earliest foundation fictions of South Australia and the fate of its original inhabitants. A falsehood, certainly, but not a 'beautiful' one.

In October 2017, in a series of public lectures at The University of Adelaide, a group of eminent historians and a writer of historical fiction were invited to examine other 'foundational fictions' in South Australia's history. The result was a sequence of provocative discussions that challenged established myths, narratives, even 'beautiful lies', about the state's past. This book is the outcome of those discussions, reproducing all of the lectures as scholarly chapters, along with other essays that we specially commissioned for the volume.

What do we mean by 'foundational fictions'? British historian John Tosh prefers the term 'foundational myth', which he defines as 'a story, usually-much treasured, about the foundation of a group of people'.⁹ This should not necessarily imply that the story is entirely untrue, he says, 'merely that it has developed into a simplistic, usually rosy version of events'.¹⁰ Some, of course, are false: beautiful lies that mask brutal realities, like colonial violence. Shaking the foundations of these narratives can send shockwaves through our own lives. In her chapter, novelist Lucy Treloar recounts the distress she felt upon learning that her family's pride in the settlement history of South Australia was based on a foundational 'lie' that hid the realities of violence against Aboriginal people: 'Part of me had believed in the dream of South Australia', she says.

Foundational narratives play an important role in society, reinforcing beliefs and a sense of identity, binding together individuals, and contributing to the process of nation-building. All societies have a collective memory, 'a storehouse of experience which is drawn on for a sense of identity and sense of direction'.[11] We see this in Australia where the ANZAC stories of mateship and sacrifice are reflected in how we view ourselves as a nation, and as people. As Tosh observes, 'For all its infatuation with the modern and the new, contemporary society continues to regard the past as a source of legitimacy and inspiration'.[12] Foundational narratives can be manipulated, however, warping our perception of the past, and the present. For history 'is a powerful discipline that can be harnessed for particular purposes', historians Paul Ashton and Anna Clarke caution, 'and each generation writes history that speaks to its own interests and concerns'.[13] In this volume, our contributors suggest different ways in which familiar narratives of South Australia's history can be reinterpreted.

While the subject matter is confined to South Australian topics, this volume taps into a wider debate concerning the nature of history, its purpose and its relationship with myth or fiction. Foundational 'myths', and efforts to update our understanding of them, have been at the heart of Australia's so-called 'history wars' that broke out in the closing decades of the twentieth century. They were flamed by former Prime Minister John Howard who objected to what he saw as the rewriting of Australia's history 'in the service of a partisan political cause'.[14] One of our contributors, Stuart Macintyre, Emeritus Professor of History at the University of Melbourne, has been at the forefront of this often-polarising public debate since the publication of his 2003 book *The History Wars*, co-authored with Anna Clark. In his contribution to the lecture series and this volume, he turns his attention to South Australia and provides an inspiring account of this state's central role in several important national events, which the former Prime Minister might well admire.

Macintyre and others worry that dominant foundational narratives can swamp alternative accounts, or cause them to be overlooked. David Stephens and Alison Broinowski most recently addressed this in their edited volume, *The Honest History Book*, arguing that Australia's obsession with ANZAC mythology, for example, has led to Australians losing their ability to look beyond war as the central pillar of their nation's history and identity. Meanwhile, alternative narratives – environmental history, multiculturalism, the role of women, settler-Indigenous relations, and immigration – have been effectively 'khaki-washed'.[15]

Ann Curthoys and John Docker argue in their book *Is History Fiction?* that the relationship between history and fiction has always been fraught. They trace what they call the 'doubleness and divided nature' of history back to Herodotus and Thucydides and their first attempts to record a 'true' history in a narrative form.[16] Not adverse to including the odd myth or hearsay in his 'histories', Herodotus is often discounted as a true 'historian' (though his account is surely more readable than Thucydides' effort). Curthoys and Docker ask, however, if we can ever know that a historical narrative is giving us a true account of what actually happened.[17] Taking up the theme, Tosh argues even the most objective historians remain fundamentally 'part of the process'. 'At every level of historical enquiry', he says, 'from the choice of materials through to the finished work of history, the present intrudes on the reconstruction of the past'.[18] The modern historian understands this; it is why historians write '*a* history' rather than '*the* history' of any particular subject. Their interpretation is but one version of perhaps multiple historical understandings of any subject, at any given point in time.

Amid the 'history wars', a conversation about the relationship between history and historical fiction has also been percolating, mostly in academic circles but sometimes bubbling over into the public domain as it did following the publication of Kate Grenville's 2005 novel *The Secret River* and the response to this book by historian Inga Clendinnen.[19] In dating parlance, the relationship is complicated, to say the least, with some on both sides of the debate declaring 'never the two shall meet'. Historian Tom Griffiths references this when he describes 'the intriguing dance of history and fiction', but he argues that 'historians and novelists do not constitute inviolable, impermeable categories of writers'.[20] Indeed, as he notes, 'some historians are also novelists and many novelists are also historians', among them Judith Wright, Thomas Keneally, David Malouf, Helen Garner and Delia Falconer. Novelists, he says, 'adopt the devices of non-fiction in their novels; historians tell stories with mystery, imagination and style. They are all creative artists who are conscious of something significant when they change genre and, thankfully, they often reflect upon it'.[21] Griffiths suggests that history and fiction are, in fact, 'a tag team, sometimes taking turns, sometimes working in tandem, to deepen our understanding and extend our imagination'.[22] History, he stresses, 'doesn't own truth, and fiction doesn't own imagination, but sometimes the differences between history and fiction are very important indeed'. However, he says it is 'incumbent on historians – on those who choose at certain times to write history – to insist and reflect on the distinction'.[23] In this volume, novelist Lucy Treloar reflects on these issues from the other side of the literary fence.

As Twain's account underlines, South Australia has its own particular set of foundational narratives. Its social, economic and political origins set it apart from the other Australian colonies; it was a free settlement established without the deliberate importation of convict labour, and planned by profit-driven entrepreneurs who were informed by liberal ideas. These foundational principles favoured the emergence of a privileged colonial elite, whose wealth and influence derived mainly from farming and mining, but it also promoted more liberal attitudes toward social and political rights. These distinctive origins, many have suggested, produced a 'sense of difference' and enabled a degree of social and political innovation that sometimes set the colony/state apart from its continental neighbours. In the political realm alone, the evidence for South Australia's distinctiveness is certainly compelling. The establishment of representative government in the 1850s, consisting of a House of Assembly elected by universal male suffrage and a (more restrictive) Legislative Council, was achieved under a Constitution that was the most liberal in Australia. South Australia was the first colony/state to have an elected town council, to accept Aboriginal evidence in court, to use the secret ballot and to grant women (including Aboriginal women) the right to vote for, and stand as, parliamentary candidates. South Australia was also among the first governments to separate Church and State, legalise trade unions, introduce industrial reforms and elect labour members to parliament. In addition, in the 1960s and 1970s, it introduced the first anti-discrimination, land rights, heritage conservation and marital rape legislation, and pioneered abortion and homosexual law reform.[24]

Yet in many respects the extent of this social and political innovation, and South Australia's distinctive trajectory, has been exaggerated, even more so in popular memory. Two examples might suffice to illustrate this point. First, South Australia's founders and early residents may have rejected the use of transported convict labour, but they participated in the transportation system by sending the colony's own convicted felons to New South Wales and Van Diemen's Land, and they were helpless to prevent large numbers of escaped and former convicts crossing the border and settling in South Australia.[25] Second, South Australian parliamentarians may have been the first in Australia to grant women the vote – some 14 years before their Victorian counterparts, and more than a quarter of a century before English and most American women gained the franchise – but they did so reluctantly, and some only pushed for the inclusion of the provision allowing women to stand for parliament in the enabling legislation because they hoped it would lead to the Bill's demise. As it was, South Australia was the last state to elect a female candidate to parliament, more than half a century after women first gained the right to stand. So while it is true that South Australians have forged a distinctive path, this was not always for the reasons that one might expect, nor with the consequences that have been commonly assumed. Examined more closely, South Australia's distinctive foundations appear more fictional than factual.

The theme 'foundational fictions' is interpreted widely by the contributors to this volume. Some debunk existing 'myths' about the origins of particular South Australian-based events, ideas or institutions. Others elect to critique some of the seminal foundational texts in the state's history, taking issue with historians as much as with historical actors. Frequently, it proves impossible to do one without the other.

In their chapter, Jean Fornasiero and John Sooby-West draw on extensive archival records to tackle three of the most enduring myths about the meeting between English explorer Matthew Flinders and his French counterpart Nicolas Baudin on 8 April 1802 in waters later named Encounter Bay. First, they question the nature of the encounter itself and whether it was 'a model of international co-operation in a time of turmoil and conflict', as it has been idealised, or something else altogether. They then turn to the proposition that both France and England were competing to settle the south coast of mainland Australia. On the contrary, they argue, South Australia may not have been considered much of a 'prize' at all. This leads to an examination of perhaps the biggest myth, 'namely that South Australia could almost have been French'. The authors conclude that while the encounter deserves to be remembered as 'the first recorded event of world significance that took place on these shores', it should not be viewed as 'a missed opportunity to be "other"'.

Eric Richards's chapter is also rooted in the time immediately before the European settlement of South Australia, when the economic principles guiding Edward Gibbon Wakefield's plan for 'systematic colonisation' were being taken up by the men who would found the new colony. For decades, South Australians learnt that Wakefield's plan was enacted as written and sowed the seeds of the colony's prosperity. More recently, historians have been much more circumspect in their assessment, proving that Wakefield was wrong in some of his calculations, and that important aspects of his plan were ignored in practice, thus diminishing his claim to the public's affection. Richards deftly outlines the arguments against him, adding his voice to those exposing a fiction of South Australia's foundation. However, he illuminates one aspect of Wakefield's scheme that was truly revolutionary and of great consequence: assisted migration, organised by the state and funded by land sales. '[T]he Wakefieldian achievement', he insists, 'is to be measured in the spectacular diversion of tens of thousands of free emigrants to the Australian colonies in a way which had appeared inconceivable in 1828. It was a revolution in the labour supply of the colonies, armed with the almost unique power of selection and control. In the process Australia received extraordinarily good-quality migrants; it was able to redesign its demography as no other society had ever done before, or perhaps since.'

It is fair to say that Humphrey McQueen takes a dimmer view of the colony's founding fathers. In many history books, the men who formed and invested in the South Australian Company and harassed the Colonial Office into supporting their colonial venture are characterised as champions of liberal, progressive ideals, disdainful of convictism, and advocating for democracy. They are heroes in a story of a place peacefully occupied by white settlers and built by the labour of free people. But before considering the *ideas* that founded South Australia, McQueen asks us to first consider the origins of the founders' wealth that made the colonisation project possible. A substantial capital investment was required before the British Government gave the colony its approval. Where did this money come from, and why was its supply, at this particular point in time, crucial? McQueen maintains that one cannot understand South Australia's foundation without first understanding the formation of joint stock companies, bank finance, and the role played by slavery in funding colonial projects (and the necessity of wage slavery in making them work). McQueen's essay is a radical departure from almost everything that has been written about the origins of European settlement in South Australia and beckons a new generation of scholars to test the assertions of its author.

In a sweeping chapter that spans colonial settlement through to the present day, Robert Foster examines the mythical claims of foundational benevolence towards Indigenous people, but also how over time the myth itself grew to provide moral legitimacy for genuine reform. South Australia has long had a reputation for being more 'enlightened' in its attitudes towards Aboriginal people. This, Foster argues, can be traced back to colony's founding documents: the Letters Patent, which seemed to acknowledge prior Aboriginal title to the land, and the Proclamation, which undertakes to place Aboriginal people under the protection of the rule of law. In fact, Foster argues, the colony's founders gave little thought to the question of Aboriginal rights when drafting the founding Act, and resisted pressure from humanitarians in Britain, making only 'modest concessions' when pressed further. Foster, an Associate Professor in the Department of History at the University of Adelaide, then proceeds to examine 20th century campaigns to establish Aboriginal reserves in the state's far north-west. As he observes, 'there is no small irony in the fact that South Australia's foundational story of its benevolent intentions towards Aboriginal people was largely a myth, yet over time, the myth itself was employed to provide the moral legitimacy for genuine reform'.

Jane Lydon looks at the ways that colonial settlement has been mythologised and incidents of violence forgotten through an examination of the life and work of prominent South Australian colonist George Hamilton. An overlander, police commissioner, horse fancier and artist, Hamilton's writings and art provide a window into the earliest years of Adelaide and South Australia. Lydon, however, argues that these mythologise the colony's origins and progress, and Hamilton's own role in it, and are coloured by his own preoccupations with class, race and masculinity. She uses his work to trace his changing views of settlement and conflicts such as the Rufus River Massacre of 1841. While Hamilton's compassion for Aboriginal people was 'conspicuously lacking', Lydon argues that he politicised and deployed emotions such as compassion in the process of narrating and mythologising the settlement of Adelaide.

Lucy Treloar brings a different dimension to this collection as a writer of historical fiction. Her critically acclaimed debut novel, *Salt Creek*, published in 2015, follows the fortunes of the Finch family and their attempts to set up a cattle farm on the Coorong. It is drawn from fragments of Treloar's own family history. In her chapter, Treloar explores how writers of historical fiction balance what is known against the demand for captivating characters and a compelling narrative arc. Drawing on her experience writing *Salt Creek*, she suggests what historians, and students of history, can learn from novelists when it comes to understanding the past. She also argues that much of the criticism of her fellow historical novelist, Kate Grenville, is based on a fundamental misunderstanding of the different roles and processes of novelists and historians. 'Writing, like history, is a big room,' she observes, 'there is space inside for us all'.

Writers also are the subject of Philip Butterss's contribution to this volume, although he is less interested in their historiographical inclinations. He challenges the myth, perpetuated in histories of Australian literature, that South Australian authors played little part in the foundational 'golden age' of Australian writing, the 1890s, when an authentic Australian 'voice' was developed by writers and embraced by readers. As Butterss recounts, when historian Arthur Jose was asked why he had neglected Adelaide in his memoir of that period, he replied: 'what was there to neglect? Adelaide was, from the literary point of view, a dependency of Melbourne, a community of appreciative audiences, not of exhilarated writers'.[26] The city's literary culture in the 1890s would be similarly overlooked in the highly influential accounts of Australian literature written in the 1950s by Vance Palmer, A.A. Phillips and Russel Ward.[27] Butterss, however, examines the situation more closely, and finds that Adelaide had strong foundations for a literary culture, such as a well-established system of schooling and an educated population, and a network of bookshops and libraries, and its writers – particularly its poets – produced a range of important, if under-appreciated, works.

Historians come under the spotlight in Stuart Macintyre's chapter in which he re-evaluates the work of his late colleague John Hirst concerning South Australia's 'distinctiveness'. Hirst, Macintyre notes, was 'just one of many gifted historians to be raised and trained in South Australia but then pursue careers elsewhere'. His doctoral thesis at the University of Adelaide formed the basis of his first book, *Adelaide and the Country* (1973), but for most of his career Hirst focused on broader, national themes in Australian history. In 2011, Hirst returned to South Australia to give a lecture that was later published in the sister title to this collection, *Turning Points: Chapters in South Australian History* (2012). In that lecture, Hirst reconsidered the distinctiveness of South Australian history and, Macintyre argues, 'took a typically contrarian approach to playing down the local characteristics and suggesting how so much happened here was determined by its position within a great whole'. Macintyre, however, does not accept that 'it is possible to dismiss South Australians' distinctiveness so readily', arguing that on a number of occasions the state played a pivotal – and distinct – role in the development of national affairs. Far from being a bit player, for example, Macintyre argues that South Australia's role in the federal movement has been underestimated. He also examines South Australia's distinctive approach to post-war reconstruction, through the formation of the volunteer association Common Cause. Nowhere else but South Australia, he argues, could such a diverse range of individuals have worked so effectively together.

Political figures are also the focus of Paul Sendziuk's essay, in particular the state's longest serving leader, Tom Playford, whose premiership spanned from 1938 until 1965. Due to the longevity of his political career, and character traits that have seen him described as a 'shrewd, persistent and persuasive ... ruthless and cunning',[28] Playford is often credited with being the primary agent of South Australia's industrial transformation in the middle of the twentieth century.[29] That South Australia's economic base was transformed is beyond doubt; factory employment grew by 168% during Playford's period in office, coal mines and power stations were developed in the north of the state, and tens of thousands of new homes were built as the suburbs and smokestacks of Adelaide multiplied, and new industrial cities and towns were forged. Sendziuk accepts that the Premier's determination and political skills were crucial in some respects, but argues that the foundations of this transformation were set in place by other people and enabled by forces and institutions beyond his direct control. 'Playford', he suggests, 'played his part by recognising when others had good ideas and by trusting them, even if this placed him at odds with his previously held views and the *laissez faire* liberals in his own party'.

While Playford is lauded by historians for facilitating the state's economic development, the other dominant political figure of the twentieth century, Don Dunstan, is credited with instigating policies and legislative reforms that transformed social relations and cultural life. Among other things, Dunstan and his governments are attributed with recognising Aboriginal land rights, decriminalising homosexuality, enacting consumer protection and anti-discrimination laws, and implementing electoral reforms that made voting a much more democratic process. Dunstan is also remembered for abolishing capital punishment in 1976, after first campaigning for its abolition – and establishing his reputation for reformist zeal – as a member of the Opposition in parliament in the late 1950s. In a fascinating contribution to this volume, Steven Anderson shows that while Dunstan played a key role, the rationale for the abolition of capital punishment, and the origins of this movement, had been established more than one hundred years earlier, when men such as David McLaren and William Burford argued against the death penalty. Anderson reminds us that ideas, as well as people and events, have histories, and that these histories can be long.

During his premiership, Dunstan found himself in the uncomfortable position of personally opposing the war in Vietnam, yet leading a state whose population appeared to be in general support. The conscription of men to fight in the war was the most contentious issue at this time, particularly after a young South Australian man, Errol Noack, became the first national servicemen to be killed in Vietnam in 1966. While narratives of protest in this period traditionally focus on student activism and Labor party politics, Carolyn Collins argues in our final chapter that the important efforts of other dissenters have been overlooked. She turns her attention to the Save Our Sons (SOS) group, one of the earliest anti-conscription groups formed in Adelaide, challenging assumptions about the class and political backgrounds of its members and their contribution to the wider protest movement, which is often portrayed as marginal at best. On the contrary, Collins argues that, together with their interstate counterparts, SA SOS played an important role, not least in broadening the appeal of the anti-war movement, thus reaching segments of society that did not relate to the more radical student protestors. Perhaps most importantly, the movement provided those new to activism, particularly women, with a safe, non-political vehicle and supportive collegiate environment through which they could register their dissent. As Collins reveals, many found the experience life-changing.

The lectures that were presented at the University of Adelaide as part of the Foundational Fictions series proved unsettling for some in the audience. One of us, as the co-convenor of the series, received a telephone call from a particularly aggrieved attendee who took issue with one of the interpretations that was presented. The lecturer, they argued, had strayed from 'the facts' and thus merely constructed a fiction over that he was claiming to demolish; the phrase 'beautiful lies' might have been mentioned. The caller was asked to consider what constitutes 'the facts' of any event, and who brings them to light, and how might subjectivity and context influence this process. And they were reminded, as we remind you, that the lecturer's view need not be taken as the final word on the subject.

2

A Contested Coast? Revisiting the Baudin–Flinders Encounter of April 1802

JEAN FORNASIERO AND JOHN WEST-SOOBY

The meeting between French navigator Nicolas Baudin and his English counterpart Matthew Flinders on 8 April 1802, in the waters that Flinders later named Encounter Bay, has engendered a number of enduring myths. With the increasing availability of important archival records, however, just how much longer can the mythology surrounding this event persist? Historians have long been aware that significant elements of the encounter narrative invite further scrutiny, and we have identified three of these as our focus here. The first concerns the nature of the encounter itself, which has been idealised as a model of international cooperation at a time of turmoil and conflict. A close examination of the various witness accounts, including documents recently brought to light, will serve to highlight a more troubled underlying narrative and help us to move closer to determining the true nature and the full consequences of the encounter.[1] The same approach can be applied to a second, countervailing myth, which derives from the political analysis of the event. Since the charting of the south coast of mainland Australia had become a priority for both France and Britain, the encounter itself has long served as a marker of their rivalry in the Indo-Pacific region. But beyond the glory of geographical discovery, just how much of a prize was this southern part of Australia for the British and the French at that time? A detailed study of this issue will enable us to address perhaps the most persistent myth of all, namely that South Australia could almost have been French. Such a proposition has long invited us to see the encounter as a reflection of what might have been rather than of what was to come, namely the quickening of the pace of British settlement. This in turns begs the question as to whether we should remember the encounter primarily as a decisive moment, after which nothing was ever the same, or as an 'if' of history, a more desirable outcome, and hence a source of endless nostalgia.[2]

Before turning to these questions, let us commence by recalling the encounter itself and explaining how it came to represent a founding moment in South Australian history. Essentially this was a chance meeting between two navigators from rival European nations that served to put the contours of what would become South Australia on the map. The combined cartographic achievements of the two captains were indeed of great significance. Before they set out on their voyages – Baudin in October 1800, Flinders some nine months later – no European had sailed further east along mainland Australia's southern coast than the Nuyts Archipelago, off present-day Ceduna.[3] The coast of what is now Victoria had begun to yield some of its secrets, thanks to the combined efforts of James Grant and John Murray in the *Lady Nelson*. However, their surveys of the Bass Strait area in 1800–1802 were far from definitive. They extended no further west than Cape Banks and Mount Gambier, which Grant had simply sighted when he sailed east through the recently discovered Bass Strait in December 1800, on his way to Port Jackson. The south coast thus remained a source of speculation and mystery until Baudin and Flinders, sailing from opposite directions, met in the waters of Encounter Bay and jointly filled in what had previously been a cartographic blank.[4]

The importance of solving the geographical puzzle of this section of coastline was made clear to both captains in their respective instructions. As the Comte de Fleurieu pointed out in the itinerary he compiled for Baudin's voyage: 'This section of coast has not yet been discovered: no navigator has seen it, and Citizen Baudin must apply himself to […] drawing up an accurate chart of the whole that will show its development'.[5] The Admiralty likewise enjoined Flinders to 'be very diligent in your examination of the said coast, and to take particular care to insert in your journal every circumstance that may be useful to a full and complete knowledge thereof'.[6] The similarity in their instructions and the coincidence of their meeting have led many to portray the two captains as being engaged in a race – a view reinforced by the more general context of Franco-British rivalry, which had been given fresh impetus by the Revolutionary wars in Europe and was playing out in other theatres around the globe.[7] Although Baudin, having left Europe first, had no inkling that he had acquired a rival and that the 'discovery' of the south coast had become a race against time, there was certainly a sense of urgency on the part of the British. Sir Joseph Banks, who had arranged for Baudin to be granted a passport by the Admiralty, was well aware of the threat posed by the French. In a letter to Earl Spencer, First Lord of the Admiralty, recommending that Flinders be appointed to lead a surveying expedition to Australia, Banks quite clearly stressed the need to 'anticipate the French' so as to 'ensure to him [Flinders], & to the English nation, the honor of the discovery'.[8] In the light of this imperative, the encounter between the two navigators could only have been an unwelcome moment for their commanding authorities, thereafter obliged to share the coveted honours. But how did events transpire for the captains themselves?

The story of the encounter has been told many times, but in order to determine just how cordial – or otherwise – the meeting really was, a close examination of the full range of archival and published records from both expeditions is warranted. At five o'clock on the afternoon of 8 April 1802, the lookout on the *Investigator* announced the appearance of what looked like a white rock on the horizon, but which was soon identified as a sail. On board, opinions regarding the possible identity of this ship were divided. As Flinders noted in his log, Baudin's expedition had 'frequently furnished us with a topic of conversation; but when we first ascertained that it was a ship seen ahead, it was much doubted whether it was one of the French ships, or whether it was an English merchant ship examining along this coast for seals or whales'.[9] As Flinders well knew, the establishment of a colony at Port Jackson in 1788 had opened up a lucrative business for British sealers and whalers in the region. It was therefore entirely plausible that their fishing activities might by then have extended to this part of the Australian coast. If the discussion centred around those two possibilities – an English merchant ship or one of the two French ships engaged in discovery – then it is Flinders' next manoeuvre that invites questions. In his re-telling of the encounter in *A Voyage to Terra Australis*, published 12 years after the event, Flinders reveals an attitude that appears more suspicious than welcoming: 'On approaching nearer, it [the white rock] proved to be a ship standing towards us; and we cleared for action, in case of being attacked'.[10] Whatever his suppositions about the ship's identity, Flinders was taking no chances. He would have had nothing to fear from an English merchant ship, nor would he have considered that a French ship on a mission of scientific discovery, and bearing a British passport, represented a serious risk. It is thus unlikely that Flinders seriously envisaged taking on the larger ship – he was no doubt being prudent rather than belligerent – but his attitude did stand in contrast to that of Baudin, who was clearly not moved to take similar action.[11] Even when Flinders had established the identity of the French ship, he 'veered round as *Le Geographe* was passing, so as to keep our broadside to her, lest the flag of truce should be a deception'.[12] The extent of these manoeuvres clearly tells us that Flinders was in a wary frame of mind as he prepared to meet his French counterpart.

On board the *Géographe*, meanwhile, the announcement from aloft of an approaching ship was likewise the source of some speculation. Baudin and his companions first thought that this could be their consort ship, the *Naturaliste*, from which they had become separated during a storm off the east coast of Tasmania one month earlier. They soon saw from her colours, however, that the approaching ship was not French but British. When the two vessels drew alongside one another, the French were surprised to hear the British captain ask whether their ship was the *Géographe*, under the command of Nicolas Baudin. On receiving confirmation of this, Flinders, putting his apprehension – but not his formality – to one side, doffed his hat in salute and his officers followed suit.[13] Flinders then had a boat hoisted out and went across to meet his counterpart.

As Flinders could not speak French, he took his naturalist Robert Brown with him to serve as interpreter. In the event, the meeting in Baudin's cabin, Flinders noted, was 'mostly carried on in English, which the captain spoke so as to be understood'.[14] Brown, for his part, was less flattering in his assessment of Baudin's linguistic skills, commenting in his journal on the 'extreme badness of his English'.[15] Problematic though communication may have been, the two captains managed to spend a little under an hour together in conversation.[16] Everything suggests that on this first occasion their attitudes were markedly different. Flinders adhered strictly to formal protocols whereas Baudin had a more relaxed demeanour. Flinders, according to midshipman Hyacinthe de Bougainville, presented himself 'in full uniform'; we do not know how Baudin was attired, though the same

Bougainville described him as 'dressed like a robber' when he received Flinders the following morning.[17] Given Bougainville's animosity towards Baudin, we may take this with a grain of salt. It is nevertheless plausible that, on that first afternoon, after a long and difficult day of surveying, the French captain did not see the need to don his full regalia for a chance meeting with an unknown British captain. The meeting began with Flinders, still in formal mode, asking to see the passport Baudin had been granted by the Admiralty. When Flinders in turn presented the safe conduct issued to him by the French Minister of Marine, Baudin apparently handed it back without inspecting it. We can surmise from this that he had no inkling of the *Investigator*'s mission – Flinders was certainly mute on that point – and that he must have taken this English vessel to be on a run from Europe to Port Jackson, or perhaps engaged in commercial activities. He was in any case so far from suspecting that Flinders was engaged like himself in a voyage of discovery that he felt it unimportant and unnecessary to examine the British captain's credentials.

The records on both sides suggest that the French captain did most of the talking during this first encounter. Baudin wrote in his journal that Flinders 'expressed great satisfaction at this agreeable meeting, but was extremely reserved on all other matters'. The captain's log on the *Investigator* likewise indicates that most of the time was occupied by Baudin's answers to Flinders' questions about his discoveries in Tasmania and Bass Strait. Flinders, still on his guard, was playing his cards close to his chest. Baudin, on the other hand, was quite forthcoming about his explorations, enthusiastic even. As Flinders wrote in *A Voyage to Terra Australis*: 'It somewhat surprised me, that captain Baudin made no enquiries concerning my business upon this unknown coast, but as he seemed more desirous of communicating information, I was happy to receive it'.[18] For Baudin, this encounter presented a rare opportunity to share his story and achievements with an outsider who might be interested and even impressed. In similarly frank spirit, Baudin made some criticisms of a chart of Bass Strait published in England in 1800, of which he had been given a copy before departure. He was particularly critical of its representation of the northern side, but had evidently not noticed a disclaimer on the chart indicating that this coast had simply been seen by Bass from an open boat. When Flinders pointed this out, Baudin expressed some surprise. He would have been even more surprised to learn that this chart had been drawn up by none other than the man to whom he was speaking, but he had not looked at Flinders' passport and, according to Bougainville, Flinders, in keeping with his reserved attitude, did not volunteer to name himself.[19] As it was growing dark, Flinders suggested that their ships keep company overnight and that they meet again the next morning, promising to bring Baudin a more detailed version of the chart of Bass Strait.

At daybreak on 9 April, Flinders returned to the *Géographe* and this time the conversation took on a different tone. As Flinders noted, 'Captain Baudin was much more inquisitive this morning concerning the *Investigator* and her destination than before, having learned from the boats [sic] crew that our business was discovery; and finding that we had examined the south coast of New Holland thus far, I thought he appeared to be somewhat mortified'.[20] The atmosphere at this second meeting was indeed tenser. Knowing now that he was dealing with someone engaged like him in a voyage of discovery, Baudin informed Flinders of all he had done on the western coast of Australia, in Tasmania and in Bass Strait. He was clearly determined to establish his credentials and to make an impression on his young British counterpart. Flinders in turn informed Baudin of what he had found on this southern coast, notably the harbour he later named Port Lincoln, the two adjacent gulfs, and the island he had named in honour of the kangaroos that had furnished him and his crew with a much needed source of fresh food. These were significant finds: Baudin may have felt he had played some winning cards but Flinders had convincingly trumped him, at least on this part of the coast. According to the zoologist François Péron, Flinders indeed had a competitive motive for showing his hand: in giving the French commander 'several maps of his work', his intention was 'to put us in the position where we would be unable to contest his discoveries or to fail to recognise them'.[21]

As they parted, at around eight o'clock in the morning, Baudin, according to Flinders, thought to ask him his name, 'and finding it to be the same as the author of the chart which he had been criticising, expressed not a little surprise; but had the politeness to congratulate himself on meeting me'.[22] Irrespective of whether Baudin was indeed asking Flinders his name or was merely seeking to confirm it, his politeness could not conceal his disquiet. As Flinders noted somewhat laconically in his log,

'I did not apprehend that my being here at this time, so far along the unknown part of the coast, gave him any great pleasure'.[23] This sense of gloom was shared by all on board the *Géographe*. While the encounter between Baudin and Flinders signalled the end of their respective discoveries, the British navigator had claimed the lion's share, depriving the French of their sense of purpose. The spirit was summed up by Péron:

> According to what he told us, there remained nothing of any importance for us to do on that coast and what is unfortunate in all of this is that we are now bereft of any hope of doing anything remarkable since everything has been done on that coast, and if he had had several days more this indefatigable navigator would have bestowed names on the section of coastline that we had observed after leaving Western Port.[24]

In summary, while the two captains behaved in a way that was polite and even gracious, their encounter could hardly be labelled as friendly. It is true that, on the first occasion, Baudin's relaxed demeanour and effusiveness in communicating his discoveries betrayed a certain pleasure at meeting a fellow traveller, but this was not reciprocated by Flinders, who maintained a formal attitude and remained guarded throughout. Their second meeting the following day appears to have been more than a little strained, with both captains engaging in a game of one-upmanship. The mood on both ships was similarly far from joyous. The news of Flinders' discoveries cast a shroud of gloom over the French ship, while conversely, Baudin's own discoveries, albeit more modest, had deprived Flinders of the opportunity of claiming exclusive rights for Britain over the southern coast. For the participants, then, the famous encounter was more fraught than genuinely friendly. To return to the narrative of two national rivals virtuously ignoring what separated them, we can see that the differences remained intact and the vexations ran deep. Baudin and Flinders were simply constrained to play the roles mapped out for them as commanders of voyages of discovery, locked in their prescribed diplomatic neutrality.[25]

This brings us to the second question, which concerns not the nature but the impact of the encounter, and notably what it suggested regarding the significance of the 'unknown' coast in geopolitical terms. If our first myth arose because the two captains were seen as cordially transcending intense national rivalries, our second is concerned with the exact terms of that national rivalry. If the meeting of two cartographic missions is seen on the political level as the confrontation of imperialistic designs on the Indo-Pacific region, then the previously uncharted south coast of mainland Australia could logically have acquired the status of a contested site. But was this portion of the south coast in itself an object of colonial rivalry? And, if not, why was the encounter a source of profound disappointment in terms of geopolitical ambitions?

There is no doubt that, from a scientific point of view, great prestige was attached to the resolution of the geographical mystery of the south coast. The 'Terre Napoléon' controversy stands as a testament to its symbolic importance. When François Péron published the first volume of his account of the Baudin expedition in 1807, in collaboration with Louis Freycinet who was working on the maps, he attributed French names to all the features of this coast, which he labelled 'Terre Napoléon', conveniently glossing over the fact that much of it had been discovered by Flinders. He and Freycinet evidently still found it difficult to come to terms with this lost opportunity. Flinders generously but erroneously presumed that Péron had been forced to adopt this nomenclature by the French authorities and that what he wrote 'smote him to the heart'. The only explanation for this act of 'aggression', in Flinders' view, was that it 'may have originated in the desire to rival the British nation in the honour of completing the discovery of the globe'.[26] As the language here shows, the stakes were high.

Reactions to the encounter on both sides also illustrate the prestige attached to being the first to chart the south coast. The encounter clearly rankled with the French officers. It is well known that, when they later caught up with Flinders in Port Jackson, Henri Freycinet, Baudin's lieutenant on the *Géographe*, reportedly said to him: 'Captain, if we had not been kept so long picking up shells and catching butterflies at Van Diemen's Land, you would not have discovered the South Coast before us'[27] – a 'fatuous' and deeply disloyal remark, as Frank Horner has noted, but one that points directly to frustrated political objectives.[28] Flinders too would suffer from the consequences of the encounter. Charting the 'unknown' south coast was the first priority for his expedition, and accordingly his instructions had directed him to begin his survey at Nuyts Archipelago.[29] But Flinders chose instead to commence his reconnaissance at Cape Leeuwin, thereby surveying a vast length of coastline that had already been laid down, albeit imperfectly, by earlier navigators. In so doing, he allowed Baudin time to begin his survey of the south coast and lost the opportunity for Britain to claim exclusive rights of discovery over it. Despite all that he had discovered, he had ultimately failed in this key part of his mission.

This was important because the glory of discovery not only fed national pride, it also held the prospect of strategic, territorial or economic advantage. But did this prospect attach itself to the site of this shared discovery, to the 'unknown' coast itself? It is instructive in this respect to compare the interest generated by the future South Australia with the attention paid to other contested sites around Australia during that period of European exploration and discovery. Historian Alan Frost has long argued, for example, that Britain's decision to found a colony at Botany Bay was motivated less by the need to rid itself of unwanted criminals than by the desire to gain a strategic foothold in the Pacific.[30] Documentary evidence confirms that this was certainly how France and Spain, Britain's rivals in the region, viewed the settlement.[31] Correspondence between the governor of New South Wales, Philip Gidley King, and the authorities in London indicates that strategic as well as commercial interests were likewise the spur for early plans to establish settlements in Port Phillip and Bass Strait. As Lord Hobart wrote to King on 14 February 1803:

> It seems to be fully ascertained by the vessels that have already passed those streights that the sea abounds with the seal and the sea elephant, and the attempts that have already been made to fish there have been sufficiently successful to afford encouragement to prosecute that pursuit. It is also evident that the attention of other European powers has been drawn to that quarter of the world, and it need scarcely be observed that the establishment of any foreign power on that part of the coast might, in the event of hostilities, greatly interrupt the communication with Port Jackson, and materially endanger the tranquility and security of our possessions there.[32]

Towards the end of the previous year, Baudin's extensive operations in Tasmania and Bass Strait had fuelled rumours about French settlement plans in the area. Though King doubted the veracity of these rumours, he nevertheless sent a ship after Baudin to advise him that he was now proceeding with his own plans for a settlement in the south. In the latter part of 1803, these plans began to materialise, with small colonies established on the banks of the Derwent River and in Port Phillip Bay, though the latter would prove short-lived.

Subsequent French interest in other parts of Australia similarly served as a prompt for the British to extend their settlements. Following the fall of Napoleon in 1815, the French resumed exploration in the Indo-Pacific region. The western third of Australia was at that point still unclaimed by European nations, so it naturally fell under the gaze of the French authorities. The Restoration government contemplated the possibility of setting up convict settlements along the Swan River and in King George Sound. It also dispatched a series of navigators to western Australia. Louis Freycinet, during his round-the-world voyage in the *Uranie*, spent some time in Shark Bay in 1818. Both Louis Duperrey in 1822 and Hyacinthe de Bougainville in 1824 left France with orders to visit south-western Australia, though neither ultimately called there. Nevertheless, it was clear to the British that the French were circling, so in 1826 the governor of New South Wales, Ralph Darling, sent a small contingent of soldiers and convicts headed by Major Edmund Lockyer to King George Sound. On 21 January 1827, at the site of what is now the town of Albany, he hoisted the Union Jack and took formal possession of the western third of Australia for Britain. Three years later, a colony was established on the Swan River. As in Tasmania and Bass Strait, the need to forestall the French was the motivation for British settlement plans in the west.

In contrast, it is striking that no such scenario played out in what is now South Australia. After the encounter between Baudin and Flinders, it would take more than 30 years for the British to renew their interest in this isolated part of the world.[33] The French did not display an immediate interest either: in the decades following the encounter, the succession of French voyagers in Australian waters bypassed the region completely. Louis Freycinet, for example, who had conducted detailed surveys of Kangaroo Island and the two gulfs behind it in 1803, did not feel compelled to return to the scene of his earlier cartographic exploits during his 1817–1820 circumnavigation of the globe. He preferred instead to visit Port Jackson in the east and Shark Bay in the west. In short, the geographical contest of 1802 did not subsequently translate into a political competition between the British and the French. South Australia was a long way from being put on the map, in the figurative sense.

There are several explanations for this waning of interest in central southern Australia in the wake of the Baudin and Flinders expeditions. For the French, of course, circumstances did not lend themselves to any serious new colonial undertakings. When the Baudin expedition returned to France in 1804, Napoleon, who had just crowned himself Emperor, was preoccupied with other projects, chief among them his plans for an invasion of England. He had neither the resources nor the inclination to send another expedition to the Antipodes, especially given that Baudin's detractors had convinced him that his voyage had been a complete failure. But even if Napoleon had wanted to follow up on Baudin's discoveries, it is highly unlikely that he would have chosen to do so in the area where Baudin and Flinders had met. As noted above, when the French resumed exploration in the Indo-Pacific following the end of the Napoleonic wars, it was south-western Australia that attracted their attention.

This points to one of the key reasons why neither the British nor the French sustained their interest in central southern Australia: its location, which was not considered to have any particular strategic importance. This stands in contrast to Tasmania and the recently discovered Bass Strait. Settlements in and around Bass Strait were vital in order to control the shipping lanes and the lucrative fisheries of the area. It is also not difficult to see why a foothold in the south-western tip of the continent soon became desirable, not just from a territorial point of view but in terms of facilitating – or disrupting – the passage of ships between Port Jackson and Britain, or between Port Jackson and India. With the south-western and south-eastern extremities secured, there was no strategic need for a base in an area whose indented coastline put it at some distance from the main shipping routes.

The barren appearance of the future South Australia also suggested that it did not have the resources or the commercial potential offered by other parts of Australia. It is true that, once the south coast was known, and perhaps even before then, sealers were quick to make their way westward. A small community soon grew up on Kangaroo Island, with others similarly emerging on the islands off Eyre Peninsula. As profitable as these activities may have been, however, they were an insufficient base on which to build a sustainable and fully developed settlement. As far as the mainland was concerned, nothing that Baudin or Flinders reported would have encouraged their governments to consider colonising the area. Flinders' description of the land around Port Lincoln, for example, is punctuated by the word 'barren'. This harbour was an interesting discovery in geographical terms, and offered protection for any passing vessels, but it appeared too arid and sterile for settlement:

> Port Lincoln is certainly a fine harbour; and it is much to be regretted that it possesses no constant run of fresh water [...]. Our pits at the head of the port will, however, supply ships at all times; and though discoloured by whitish clay, the water has no pernicious quality, nor is it ill tasted. This and wood, which was easily procured, were all that we found of use to ships; and for the establishment of a colony, which the excellence of the port might seem to invite, the little fertility of the soil offers no inducement.[34]

Flinders and his men were similarly unimpressed with what they found as they proceeded up Spencer Gulf. They were disappointed to find no major river flowing into it, and when Flinders explored the inlet at the head of the gulf he found it 'mortifying' that the water there was nearly as salty as that where the ship was anchored.[35] Nor was the hinterland any more promising: an excursion to the top of Mount Brown undertaken by the botanist, Robert Brown, with a party including the two artists, Ferdinand Bauer and William Westall, afforded extensive views of the land but revealed neither lakes nor rivers: 'In almost every direction the eye traversed over an uninterruptedly flat, woody country'.[36] In his rough log, Flinders wrote 'dead uninteresting flat country', which is presumably what Brown originally reported.[37] Flinders did find some sections of the South Australian coastline pleasant and fertile-looking, principally on either side of Gulf St Vincent, and the supply of kangaroos and seals on Kangaroo Island held some attraction, despite the difficulty of finding water there. With these few exceptions, however, there was very little in Flinders' account of the area that invited thoughts of settlement. Indeed, as maritime historian Geoffrey Ingleton has noted, the spur for Wakefield's subsequent settlement plans was not Flinders' account of his travels but Charles Sturt's book: *Two Expeditions into the Interior of Southern Australia*, published in 1833.[38]

French assessments of the South Australian coast were similarly unfavourable. As Baudin completed his survey of what we know today as the Coorong, he summed up the mood on board: 'The entire stretch of coast that we have examined since yesterday consists solely of sand-hills and inspires nothing but gloom and disappointment. Quite apart from the unpleasant view that it offers, the sea breaks with extraordinary force all along the shore'.[39] This sentiment was echoed by François Péron in his official account of the voyage, in which he described the 'sad picture of sterility, of monotony' that they had formed of most of New Holland and that was exemplified by this coast.[40] Baudin found the hinterland of Kangaroo Island to be 'rather pleasant' and considered there was 'enough greenery for the view to be attractive',[41] but this contrasted with what he saw of the mainland as he headed north from Cape Jervis: 'Most of the mountains were treeless; others had some that had shed their leaves, and the majority had nothing but arid ground with dry, straw-coloured grass'.[42] His impression did not change as he sailed further up Gulf St Vincent. Working then up Spencer Gulf, he noted that the coast was 'dreary-looking' and offered 'few features of any importance'.[43] There was nothing here to inspire feelings of covetousness or excite visions of colonisation. The French authorities, like the British, would hardly have been enticed by such descriptions to consider returning to these shores.

To put these observations into context, we need to recall, as historical geographer Paul Carter has noted, that such reports by early Australian explorers were not particularly well informed as they represented very one-sided impressions taken from on board a ship or, at best, during brief shore excursions.[44] Nevertheless, it is sobering to read these unflattering descriptions of the future South Australia by those who first surveyed its coast. They certainly relativise the price placed on the 'discovery' of this last uncharted section of the Australian coastline and the level of curiosity it generated in Europe before Baudin and Flinders set out on their voyages. In any event, the inauspicious observations from both expeditions provide further explanation as to why the governments of France and Britain were not moved to send further voyagers to these shores in the decades that followed the encounter. This once hotly contested site was of no further interest.

This conclusion should also serve to put to rest the myth – or perhaps more the fantasy – that regularly surfaces as a topic of conversation and debate: that South Australia could almost have been French. While it can be entertaining and even instructive to engage in speculation about what this might have meant for everything from the co-existence with Indigenous peoples or the advent of republicanism to our linguistic and culinary heritage, the evidence suggests that there is nothing on which to base such a hypothesis when it comes to South Australia. The myth has a stronger foundation with respect to Tasmania, Western Australia or Sydney, where thoughts of settlement had been discreetly or even formally canvassed in French government circles.[45] In contrast, the attraction of South Australia as a destination was not evoked in France until well after settlement. For example, Adelaide was famously touted by French novelist Jules Verne in 1891 as representing the acme of desirability, largely because of its climate, described as:

> the most salubrious in the continent, in the midst of territories which are afflicted neither by consumption, nor endemic fevers, nor any kind of contagious epidemic. Sometimes people do yet die there; but as Mr D. Charnay wittily observes, 'this may possibly be an exceptional event'.[46]

In 1807, however, when the French public was first introduced to the 'unknown' coast, the region inspired no such utopian fantasy. On the other hand, the atlas accompanying it may have engendered another form of wishful thinking. The nostalgia around South Australia's putative French origins might well have been fostered by Péron and Freycinet's cartographical coup of naming part of the south coast 'Terre Napoléon', a coup that was repeated in various forms on maps for much of the nineteenth century, and not just by the French.[47] As an exercise in self-promotion, it exceeded all expectations, since Péron and Freycinet's proprietorial act continues to draw commentary today. However, if this were an exercise in seduction, it has a classic ending, in that the coveted object was ultimately spurned.

Whatever the causes of the unrequited nostalgia for French beginnings, and however ill-founded the mythology may be in historical terms, the sustained interest in the meeting between Baudin and Flinders itself is readily understood and fully justified. The encounter of 1802 was the first recorded event of world significance that took place on these shores. As a major cartographical event, it must remain a fixture on the historical calendar – but by virtue of its historical context and not by reason of the mythology that has long enveloped it. This memorable event stands as a turning point in our geographical understanding of the globe and of the place that is now South Australia, but not as a missed opportunity to be 'other'.

3

Wakefield Revisited Again

ERIC RICHARDS

Edward Gibbon Wakefield's influence upon Australia began with an elaborate anonymous fiction. His *Letter from Sydney*, written in Newgate Prison in London in 1829, sought to revolutionise the way in which Britain colonised and it installed a new mechanism of emigration. He claimed to invent a means of 'systematic colonisation' and to create a blueprint for the first trial of his system, namely the Province of South Australia, founded in 1836. As a fiction, as a theory and as a practical plan, Wakefield's legions of critics have never ceased to question the credibility of its author.

Yet until 1957, with some notable exceptions,[1] Wakefield was widely celebrated as 'the Father of South Australia' and the true progenitor of the theory of systematic colonisation. Typical of the older, reverential interpretation was that of Archibald Grenfell Price, who said that 'in the procreation of South Australia, no one can dispute Wakefield's place, even if the colony had to be rescued from disaster by his disciples'. The local Pioneers' Association accorded Wakefield the highest rank in the 'local hierarchy of pioneer deities'.[2] This view prevailed even though Wakefield disconnected himself from the South Australian project.

At the hands of later historians, Wakefield was an enigma, his reputation in serious disrepair. The vigorous debunking found in Michael Turnbull's *New Zealand Bubble* was matched, blow for blow, by two of South Australia's most prominent historians. The most acerbic of Wakefield's critics was Douglas Pike, whose indictment was comprehensive. First, Wakefield was 'capricious, unscrupulous, avid for influence and fame'.[3] He was also a plagiarist: at critical times in Wakefield's literary career, Robert Gouger was at least his unacknowledged co-author, and Gouger was a much more substantial figure in launching the new colony of South Australia. Second, Wakefield was a model of inconsistency, always performing intellectual somersaults. He constructed his own biography to deceive posterity, and, according to Pike, had been sanctified 'into a stained glass window', all his defects concealed. Thus Pike set about the necessary demolition: Wakefield was 'emotionally unstable, mercurial, erratic, hungry for power, appreciably amoral, a practised hypnotist and so intense a manipulator of "puppets" that he undermined his own health'.

Pike's indictment went even further: Wakefield had wickedly traduced Wilmot-Horton, who had pioneered the cause of colonisation in the 1820s. Wakefield's own theory was primarily propaganda because South Australia, from its inception, was 'a land job'. It was highly successful for a few speculators like Torrens and Angas, but disastrous for many others. Pike scorned the subtitle of Paul Bloomfield's biography: Wakefield was never a 'Founder of Empire'; he had not even built a colony. All the major principles of his system failed. Wakefield's influence on land policy was grotesquely exaggerated: the substitution of land sales for land grants – a critical axiom of Wakefield's system – was already part of Colonial Office policy even before the Ripon Regulations of 1831.

Equalling Pike in vehemence was Peter Howell, who regarded the entire South Australian project and the idea of systematic colonisation as a Wakefieldian confidence trick: Wakefield was a sham, a 'mountebank', 'an amazing charlatan'. Howell concluded that the South Australian record was a history of incompetence, stupidity and cupidity.[4] The early immigrants arrived at the new colony without preparation; the land surveyors were understaffed and the land purchasers could not get onto the land; labour was unemployed and resources bottled up; then the special surveys allowed the biggest investors 'to pick the eyes out of the country'.[5] The sale of all the land at the same price, regardless of its potential, was absurd and 'meant that the colony's most valuable asset was squandered'. The central idea of a balance between land, labour and capital was undermined by the fact that more than half the land was sold to absentees 'who had no idea of migration there, and had no interest in employing labour'. Many of the new colonial proprietors simply held the land for speculative capital gains. Indeed, one-acre blocks in Adelaide bought for £1 were sold, within two years, for between £500 and £2000. Nothing was done for the relief of the sick or the unemployed. Howell remarks that 'the utopianism and the rhetoric of the systematic colonisers were essentially concoctions to attract the gullible of one sort or another'. The surveyors were inadequate in numbers, experience and equipment; the inflow of labour was totally unsynchronised. The financial collapse of South Australia in 1841–2 brought the colony to its knees. Its subsequent recovery and success had nothing to do with Wakefieldianism: South Australian prosperity was a consequence, not of Wakefield's theory, but of a run of better seasons, the success of wheat production on the fertile soils of the Adelaide Plains, and the spectacular rewards from the great copper mines at Burra.[6]

According to Howell, Wakefield's system was based on notions about reproducing the type of agricultural settlement found in southern England: concentrated, civilised and rural. This vision was attractive to the respectable English prospective migrants as it fed their own arcadian assumptions. But most colonial conditions were intrinsically and inevitably better suited to large-scale and widely dispersed wool-growing in the hands of great capitalistic graziers, occupying as squatters vast acreages in the outback. This was the contradiction at the centre of Wakefield's vision. In New South Wales it was not possible to restrain the logic of colonial geography, as colonial governors realised, most of all Gipps. Wakefield had little appreciation of the character of squatting in the Australian context.[7]

Emigration was at the centre of Wakefield's scheme: he had diagnosed the original problem of pre-Wakefieldian colonisation in terms of the ineffective supply of free labour to the new colonies. But his original emigration provisions were essentially ambiguous. In his *Letter from Sydney* (1829) he was brief and undogmatic: land sales were essential in order to concentrate settlement;[8] the revenue might be used to send out emigrants, but this was not accorded any priority. It is clear that Wakefield and his supporters eventually diverged on the emigration question. Most of the South Australian Wakefieldians – the Adelphi Planners – undoubtedly made a vital principle of the equation of land sales and emigration subsidies. But Wakefield himself abandoned the imperative even before the Province of South Australia was begun. In his evidence before a House of Commons Select Committee in 1836, he said explicitly that:

> The Object of the price is not to create an emigration fund ... There is no relation ... between the price required for land and immigration.[9]

This statement made a mockery of the notion that there would be a perfectly balanced mechanism that spontaneously co-ordinated the supply of land, labour and capital in the new colony. Wakefield, however, was characteristically variable on this matter.

Wakefield's own heresy did not prevent the incorporation of the emigration idea in South Australia, nor in New South Wales and New Zealand. Land sales revenue was indeed employed to deliver working immigrants to the colonies under the systematic formulae. But policy and practice diverged seriously. The Wakefieldian planners specified that the land-fund should be used exclusively to assist emigration. However, in the outcome, only a third of the £300,000 raised in South Australian land sales by 1839 was spent on emigration. As Pike put it, 'the balance was frittered away in London on publicity and less worthy purposes'.[10] Thus the indictment is compounded: first the land was sold at very low prices; then the revenue was spent very wastefully with extraordinary 'evaporations' from the fund;[11] and finally the labour force which arrived (according to several Australian historians after Madgwick) was at best mediocre in quality. Some said that the emigrants brought to Australia under the Wakefield system were the refuse of British society.[12] Typically, Pike encapsulated these root and branch criticisms of Wakefield in a phrase: the Wakefieldians, he said, had 'squandered the great national asset of Crown lands in order to lure inexperienced labourers'.[13] All in all, Wakefield's critics represented his ideas as figments of fiction and deception.

Anti-Wakefield opinion was not confined to the South Australian story. The economic historian J.W. McCarty declared that the imposition of a uniform and minimum price for land of different qualities and locations was unequivocally wrong. Wakefield, he said, had bamboozled contemporaries by a clever misuse of theory, but conceded that he may have exerted a temporary but positive influence on the flow of migration and investment.[14] Wakefieldian land policy is dismissed by Burroughs as 'administratively impracticable and economically unrealistic';[15] Clarke contended it may have helped to reinforce the more conservative approach to colonial land disposal, but the systematic colonisers were not able to control the dispersion associated with squatting.[16] As Governor Gipps declared, they did not understand the imperatives of pastoralism in Australia: 'As well might it be attempted to confine the Arabs of the desert within a circle, traced upon the sand.'[17] Wakefield himself, in one of his many intellectual gyrations, equivocated on the idea of concentrated settlement in the 1840s.[18]

The weight of Australian historical judgement is that Wakefield was mainly irrelevant to colonial evolution. His most obviously inappropriate notion was the model of dense population located in evenly spaced villages, which was based on an English model and never likely to suit Australia. Most economic opinion says that Wakefieldian policy did not transcend the common effects of supply and demand, and that profit levels determined most elements of the colonial economy, including the crisis of 1841–2. These remained the ruling forces.

The artillery fire directed at Wakefield by Australian historians faced few defenders. Some commentators will allow that Wakefield was a remarkably effective propagandist on behalf of the colonies,[19] and a few will allow that Wakefieldian ideas exerted a positive influence in South Australia. Thus Michael Williams asserted that the planned settlement of the Adelaide Plains created an authentically concentrated pattern in tune with the theory: 'The original Wakefieldian ideal of a self-supporting peasant agriculture and freehold farms, worked by a sturdy middle class yeomanry, was all but achieved in these early years.'[20] Other commentators even defend the much-derided special surveys. These 4000-acre sales, in some instances, did not create 'injurious dispersion' but, rather, the nucleus of a new village centre in the hands of enlightened proprietors on the English model.[21]

It is not difficult to identify a patrician strain in Wakefield's outpourings. He generally regarded redundant labour in the British economy as a social problem[22] for which he offered a cheap and elegant solution by way of subsidised emigration. Helen Taft Manning long ago pointed out Wakefield's anti-proletarian leanings.[23] Wakefield's labour-value theory was seized upon, with glee, by Marx, who believed that it exposed once and for all the transparently exploitative nature of the capitalist system.[24] Both T.A. Coghlan and Ken Buckley believed that the theory was designed to maintain a 'colonial proletariat'.[25] Wakefield's original diagnosis of colonial failures was based on the notion of labour shortage induced by the excessive alacrity with which immigrant labourers had been able to settle themselves on the land.[26] The basis for this claim has long since been demolished: labourers generally did not obtain land quickly and access to land was constrained much more by the economies of scale and the capital requirements of pastoralism.[27] Wakefield may have nurtured neo-aristocratic, Olde Englishe fantasies in the minds of suggestible prospective migrants, though he implored the managers of South Australia to 'make the working people happy'.[28]

Despite the deluge of criticism, two of Wakefield's central prescriptions remain relatively intact, saving a vestige of his credibility as a coloniser. Both relate to the activation of un-coerced emigration to the antipodes in the twenty years before the gold-rushes. The first involved the commitment by the colonies of very considerable financing to generate inflows of migrants. This represented an unprecedented channelling of a society's current revenues to this crucial priority. The second entailed the recruitment and selection of specific immigrants for very long-distance destinations.

In his original formulation, Wakefield made no provision for immigration, assuming that market forces would somehow manifest themselves and supply the colony with its needs, presumably paid for by colonial employers using indentures. Yet Wakefield already knew that indenturing was doomed so far as British emigration was concerned. He did not oppose the introduction of coolie labour to the colonies,[29] but he soon shifted his position, specifying that land revenues should be used exclusively for labour imports. Land was to be sold, and the money would provide the buyers with employable labour.

Wakefield, at first, equivocated on the issue of subsidising immigration.[30] He accorded much more importance to the mechanism of the sufficient price for land, designed to concentrate settlement and create the conditions of civilised society, the division of labour, and the development of a nascent colonial economic structure. These fundamentals would automatically produce a society so attractive that emigrants would flow naturally to the new Eden. The use to which the resulting land fund was put was, initially, immaterial. Wakefield took a decidedly cavalier approach to the question – so long as concentration was achieved, the land sales monies could as well be poured into the ocean.³¹ This was a rhetorical flourish that a propagandist like Wakefield simply could not resist. In reality, he quickly connected his main proposition with the idea of subsidising immigration.

The money raised for the land fund could pay for the imported labour, the supply of which, in the systematic coloniser's formulation, had been the critical problem in all previous colonisation. Better still, and more cleverly in theoretical terms, the sale of land would become proportional to the import of labour: the whole mechanism would be spontaneously synchronised, operating like a beautifully designed machine. It would use the one great resource of the new colony, its land, to sponsor the introduction of the key scarce resource, labour. It was a thing of theoretical sophistication, worthy of the classical economists whom (with mixed success) all the colonisers sought to impress.

This germinal idea was not entirely new but it became the *sine qua non* of antipodean emigration, and the distinct contribution Australia made to the history of international migration. In the 1820s the cost of a passage to Sydney from England was between five and eight times that to eastern Canada. As Wakefield's grandmother said, New Holland was 'terribly out of the way'.³² Wakefield's system would overcome this impediment to immigration.

The most obvious beneficiary of Wakefield's subsidisation idea was the British Exchequer. The use of colonial land revenue released the British taxpayer from the responsibility for funding the emigration of its redundant population. This had been the great weakness of Wilmot-Horton's policies, which always threatened heavy, and politically unacceptable, commitments from the Treasury. Wakefield's system solved the financial problem of state-aided emigration by diverting colonial land revenues into the subsidisation of passages. Wilmot-Horton had been reviled for allegedly advocating that paupers be 'shovelled out' to the colonies. But Wakefield also assumed that the main candidates for assisted emigration would be redundant labourers, 'the poor' if not actually 'paupers'. His theory was expressly designed to act as a safety-valve in the ostensibly explosive political conditions into which British society had fallen in the late 1820s.

Wakefield's idea was so simple and operational that it might be argued that the connection would have been made anyway. When land revenues flowed handsomely in the mid-1830s, the colonial governments, inevitably, would have used the financial windfalls to meet and finance this crying need.[33] Much of this is plausible, but Wakefield's practical impact should not be underestimated. His cobbled theory gave the policy the imprimatur of economic science; it provided theoretical justification for government intervention, in the teeth of the *laissez-faire* doctrines of the times. Wakefield's disciples persuaded hard-nosed capitalists and idealistic colonists alike that almost every penny of land sales revenue should be earmarked for the exclusive purpose of emigration. It was, in both theory and practice, a hazardous commitment precisely because it channelled a very high proportion of state revenue away from other government uses. Eventually, in New South Wales, it caused Governor Gipps to commit almost £1 million to emigration.[34] South Australia also committed its land revenues (despite leakages into administrative expenditure) to an immigration fund. In 1841 land sales collapsed and the new colony, which had previously flaunted its financial independence, was bankrupted. It was rescued by the British Treasury, which imposed new constraints on the colony's operations.

The broad context, of course, was the sheer improbability of un-coerced emigration to Australia. Though free emigration from the British Isles accelerated after Waterloo, it flowed almost exclusively to North America. In 1826, the *Westminster Review* openly doubted that 'emigration to New South Wales, on a large scale, can ever become expedient, or even practical'. William Cobbett strongly advised against it, and the influential political economist J.R. McCulloch said that 'Whatever may be the advantages of New South Wales in respect of open country and climate, it is removed by distance beyond the natural sphere of European connexion; its future commerce must be Asiatic.' Marx was to call Australia 'a United States of deported murderers, burglars, ravishers and pickpockets'.[35] Wilmot-Horton had bored Parliament and the nation with the idea of colonies, and the government was resistant to intervention in emigration, even in the regulation of safety aboard ships. Wakefield changed this attitude in remarkably short time.[36] As Brian Fitzpatrick observed, his ideas were 'the first major impulse to British colonisation in the nineteenth century'.[37] He persuaded the likes of Dickens, Bentham and Harriet Martineau that emigration was a civic responsibility.[38] He created a vision of civilised society, possible even in the barbarous antipodes; he persuaded 'the uneasy classes' that emigration was a feasible and respectable option, a new social and economic ladder beyond Britain.[39] And, most of all, he persuaded the government, against the tide of contemporary doctrine, to intervene in the commerce of emigration – in the great people trade.

Most surprising of all, Wakefield prevailed on colonial employers to pass to the colonial state the responsibility for recruiting, funding and delivering the colonial labour supply. This transfer of function from the private sector to the state was remarkable (though practically prefigured by the convict system). It entailed the adoption of a quasi-collectivist function, whereby the state would tax employers (i.e. land buyers and land leasers) in order to create the means of immigration on behalf of the entire colony. In the process the individual employer lost all control over the labour for which he/she had paid. This radical proposition was not swallowed without resistance by colonial opinion, nor were the results greeted with unanimous acclaim. Nevertheless, Herman Merivale, a penetrating commentator on colonial matters, remarked that the 'staple interest of the colony' demanded a supply of labour to colonial employers. He said that without 'an immigration system' the labour situation 'would have been utterly hopeless'.[40]

The prevailing emigration flows from the British Isles had operated without co-ordination by either commercial interests or the government. Emigration was indeed often unpredictable, and migrants behaved atomistically, impulsively, even capriciously. The emigrant trade and its shipping networks did not extend as far as Australia before the mid-1830s. All the existing forms of emigration – slave, convict, indentured and volitional migration – were unsatisfactory in various ways, but most notably because their compositions were dominated by single male emigrants. None of them matched the requirements adopted by post-convict transportation Australia (convict transportation being in sharp decline by 1841). Private enterprise had not woken up to the needs of the antipodean colonies.[41]

The Australian system of assisted immigration eventually combined bounty, government and mixed methods and entailed the direct involvement of the state in the actual enterprise of recruiting and shipping emigrants. It soon required an elaborate apparatus, the Colonial Land and Emigration Commission (CLEC, established in 1840), which employed and contracted a substantial body of agents and shippers. It licensed ships' surgeons, appointed agencies and inspectors, requisitioned, provisioned and supervised much of the complicated shipping business. It also established extraordinarily high standards of safety and welfare on the ships, which rapidly reduced shipboard mortality. In other words, Australian emigration became big business and to a large extent a great government enterprise in the age of *laissez-faire*. It was a paradox of the times, a genuine measure of the power of Wakefield's persuasion on government policy. To some, it was regarded as an unnatural practice, foisted upon them by the 'Cockney Colonization doctors'.[42]

T.F. Elliot, of the CLEC, who presided over much of this enterprise, had no doubt where origins of the system lay:

> The Merit of suggesting the Scheme of selling Lands and applying the Proceeds to Emigration, was due to Mr Wakefield. What the Government did was, within less than Two Years of the very first Hint of the Theory in his earliest Publication, and indeed in less than a Twelvemonth after it was proposed in any formal Shape, heartily to adopt and carry out these Suggestions.[43]

While some colonists complained of high land prices and waste of revenue, it was a mark of Wakefield's influence that many of them became angry when the land fund was diverted to non-immigration purposes. For two decades the Australian colonies continued to dedicate a very high proportion of this revenue to immigration. Wakefieldianism had established immigration as the great colonial priority, and produced the mechanism that satisfied that priority. It was peculiar for any society to adopt so clear-cut a vision; Wakefield supplied its intellectual and political rationale.[44]

At the same time, Wakefield helped persuade British investors to sink large amounts of capital into untried, unexplored colonies, and this enabled the government to use almost the entire sum on collectivist immigration programs. In its first years the province of South Australia sold more land than New South Wales, even though the latter colony was far better known in terms of geography and natural assets.[45]

The mechanism for migration, in Wakefield's schema, was designed to be 'a bridge without toll'.[46] What was the outcome?

Before answering this question, we should observe that one general circumstance favoured both Australia and Wakefield. The late 1820s saw the advent of an age of mass emigration, when the propensity to emigrate from the British Isles increased decisively.[47] In Ireland, where previous emigration had been mainly confined to the Scotch/Irish of Ulster, emigrants began to emerge in large numbers from the Catholic peasant fastnesses of the south and west. The Irish became the most migratory people in Europe, and this contained large implications for the peopling of Australasia.

Emigration from the British Isles at the time of Wakefield's *Letter from Sydney* was dominated by two flows: from Ireland to mainland Britain, and from Britain to North America. These streams had two main contributors: first, substantial families with capital; and second, single men, increasingly from the mobile urban populations. Rural English labour was, ostensibly, less mobile. As the cost of getting from Liverpool to Canada fell, the possibility of the poorest joining the emigrant flows increased. Wakefield and the emigrationists (as well as the British government) anticipated that the bulk of Australia's immigrants would be not only proletarian, but also poor. James Macarthur described the new incoming migrants arriving in New South Wales in the late 1830s as mainly 'indigent families'.[48]

The rise in the propensity to emigrate in the British Isles was affected by a number of factors, most notably the reduction in passage cost across the Atlantic. Simultaneously there was a great increase in information and propaganda positively encouraging the emigrants to leave the country, and short-term circumstances in Britain created a climate of discombobulation – in terms of the increased amplitude of the trade cycle, recurrent unemployment and political disturbance which made these years appear close to revolution according to some commentators. The rural sector in particular was passing through a structural change that created great anxieties in all strata of the countryside.

In this complicated context Wakefield and his associates had little chance of affecting most of the conditions in the British Isles – save for two. One was the image of the new Australian colony which was subject to extraordinary puffery and persuasion – effective enough to cause substantial investment. The other was the sheer cost of conveying poor people across the globe. This was the most fundamental impediment to emigration. For the new colony the decisive issue was how to tap into the new potential, how to divert a flow away from the overwhelmingly attractive influence of North America? Wakefield produced the answer and it was decisive.

The outcome, in terms of actual emigration to Australia, was remarkable, and largely unsung, in the received accounts of Australia's colonial story. Within ten years, emigration grew from a few hundred per annum to 28,000 in 1841. In that year, Australian numbers began to have an impact even on the North American currents. As a consequence of the Wakefieldian program, Australia joined the big league of emigrant destinations. The intensity of this development was unprecedented. In its first four years, South Australia received 15,000 migrants (New South Wales received 40,300 free immigrants in the years 1830–1840). This sudden creation of large migrant intakes required a level of government supervision which, outside the conduct of war, the British government had rarely undertaken. No government, perhaps not even a private agency, had ever organised so large a body of free emigrants in the history of migration. It required the mobilisation of contractors, shippers, agencies, surgeons, inspectors, and, most of all, thousands of proletarian emigrants. Much of this work was contracted out, semi-privatised, but this should not obscure the scale of intervention, nor the sophistication of bureaucratic enterprise, activated in the name of the Australian colonies and originally inspired by Wakefield.[49]

Within a few years, the colonies decisively reduced their reliance on convict labour intakes, and critically avoided a switch to Asian indentured labour (which some colonists regarded as the most practical preferred alternative to the expensive Wakefield system). The difficulties facing Australian recruiters should not be underestimated: emigration to Australia was impeded not only by distance and expense. The convict colonies were, in the minds of British working people, fearful places. Australia was a hopelessly distant place of banishment. The British working people, no less than the petty capitalists of the day, were resistant to the idea.[50] Large-scale un-coerced emigration to Australia had been an improbable project. It is against this resistance that the success of the new emigration should be measured.

South Australia, merely a figment of theory until 1836, was able to recruit large numbers of working migrants, notably in southern England.

This was attributed to its successful propaganda campaign, to the substantial investment poured into the scheme, and to the fact that the colony was regarded as a *tabula rasa*, uncontaminated by convictism. Even so, it was astonishing that South Australia could gather together an almost perfect immigrant population in terms of age, family structure, occupational structure and gender balance. Wakefield and his disciples convinced capitalists to provide the funds, and emigrants to provide their lives. Between them, they set in motion an unprecedentedly long-distance migration which was strikingly different, not only in its geographical direction, but also in its composition and organisation, from the prevailing modes of international migration in the first third of the nineteenth century. The Australian schemes yielded a selection of emigrants that was better equipped for Wakefield's ambitious society-making purposes than any contemporary migrant flow. Compared with the flows of people crossing the Irish Sea, and the Atlantic, between 1830 and 1850, the Australasian intakes were probably healthier, better balanced, younger, with fewer dependants, and more literate.[51]

The Wakefieldian immigration systems yielded a perfect balance of the sexes, which was in total contrast with all other flows in the world of nineteenth-century international migration. Given the low propensity to migrate among single women, that was a substantial achievement in its own right. The age structure was also ideal for an immediately employable labour force. It contained rather more children and women than colonial employers sought, but this was imposed by the colonial regulations. These were people in their prime, for production and reproduction, and for the construction of colonial society. Their occupational status was better than the colonies had bargained for. Moreover, if we treat literacy as a measure of their skills, education and status as human capital, then these immigrants were, demonstrably, a cut above the populations whence they came, and into which they were received. They were probably better equipped than concurrent emigrants to North America. Though they were selected from the lowest occupational strata of the British and Irish populations (primarily agricultural labourers and domestic servants), they were more literate than the national average of all occupations. All the available indicators suggest that these people were remarkably good selections from the working population of the British Isles.[52]

The first emigrant flows often sustain further rounds of emigration: by means of chain migration, and the passage of migrant letters and intelligence, emigration to particular destinations becomes cumulative. This was one of the functions performed by the Wakefieldian emigrations before the 1850s: providing the vital spark to populate the antipodes. The gold-rushes altered this decisively and made Australia an automatic destination for almost a decade; but afterwards there was a return to Wakefieldianism in various guises. Eventually it became less doctrinaire. But the first twenty years were pivotal in the peopling of Australia, and here Wakefield's peculiar achievement can be registered.

For Australia, therefore, the Wakefieldian achievement is to be measured in the spectacular diversion of tens of thousands of free emigrants to the Australian colonies in a way which had appeared inconceivable in 1828. It was a revolution in the labour supply of the colonies, armed with the almost unique power of selection and control. In the process Australia received extraordinarily good-quality migrants; it was able to redesign its demography as no other society had ever done before, or perhaps since. It avoided large-scale coolie immigration. The colonies were thereby able to sustain the unlikely dream of a British Pacific and to control most of its composition.

There was, however, a central irony in this achievement. Wakefield had promoted emigration – in tune with the Hortonian and quasi-Malthusian assumptions of the 1820s – as a vital relief mechanism for Britain. It would remove the dangerous labour surpluses, drain the radical cesspools, counter the effect of a population growing faster than agriculture or manufacturing could absorb.[53] Yet, in the outcome, the emigrants for Australia were not drawn from the black holes of agriculture and industrial unemployment in England. Only a small proportion came from the 'huddled masses'. There were, it is true, orphans, prostitutes, a few handloom-weavers, some peasantry, some famished and some broken, among the emigrants to Australia. But, overwhelmingly, the Wakefieldian emigrants derived from the middle rungs of proletarian life. It is doubtful that the great flow of emigration to the Antipodes did much at all to relieve Britain of its critical social and economic problems.[54] Nevertheless, it evidently created a new series of potential destinations for the mobile youth of Britain, and this was a fillip for national morale, both at home and in the colonies.

Wakefield was a prophet of his times. As Bell and Morrell remarked many years ago, he saw, 'and in his strident voice proclaim[ed], the great fact of the ages, the movement of the peoples of Europe to new homes overseas'.[55] For Australia, indeed, he made this great fact a reality by designing a mechanism which, despite all its defects, conveyed great numbers of ordinary people across the oceans.

* This chapter draws liberally in an earlier paper, 'Wakefield and Australia', in *Edward Gibbon Wakefield and the Colonial Dream: A Reconsideration*, Wellington: Friends of the Turnbull Library, 1997, pp. 89–105, but redirects its focus to the context out of which the early emigrants were recruited to South Australia.

4

Born Free: Wage-slaves and Chattel-slaves

HUMPHREY MCQUEEN

> Direct slavery is just as much the pivot of bourgeois industry as machinery, credits, etc. Without slavery you have no cotton; without cotton you have no modern industry. It is slavery that gave the colonies their value; it is the colonies that created world trade, and it is world trade that is the precondition of large-scale industry. Thus slavery is an economic category of the greatest importance.
>
> – Karl Marx, 1847[1]

> In the new anti-imperialist world which began in the forties, emphasis shifted, where empire had to be maintained, from islands to continents, from tropical to temperate climates, from plantations of blacks to settlements of whites.
>
> – Eric Williams, 1944[2]

No sooner had I been invited to participate in the Foundational Fictions lecture series than my thoughts unscrambled to come up with a foundational myth: 'South Australia had been born capitalist', or, indeed, 'born free', as South Australians have typically regarded their state's origins. In challenging these assumptions, three streams of my thinking merged. The first goes back to Ken Dallas and whether Botany Bay began as a Trading Post or a Penal Colony; the second has been obsession with the origins of capitalism since the 2008 implosion in its expanded reproduction; and the third spur is the up-hill battle to get *soi-disant* Marxists to pay attention to Marx's *Capital* in its sesqui-centennial year of 2017.

These three backdrops to my choice of foundational fiction come together in Marx's final chapter, 'The Modern Theory of Colonisation', which is amusing, brief, and records the lessons that Edward Gibbon Wakefield drew from Thomas Peel's failure on the Swan River in 1829 where the immigrant labourers, upon regaining possession of the productive resource needed to sustain themselves – namely, land – had declined to sell their capacity to add value.[3] Henceforth, they were free to 'abstain' from enriching the would-be capitalist, Mr Peel, who had 'provided for everything except the export of English relations of production to Swan River!'[4] To succeed as a capitalist, Peel needed to ship out not only things but also power relationships to drive the accumulation process. Thomas needed uncle Robert's Peelers. Chapter 33 of *Capital* encapsulates the critical analysis that Marx presents throughout his previous 800 pages:

> Wakefield discovered that, in the colonies, property in money, means of subsistence, machines and other means of production does not as yet stamp a man as a capitalist, if the essential complement to these things is missing: the wage-labourer, the other man, who is compelled to sell himself of his own free will.

Without those attributes, Marx adds, 'capitalist accumulation and the capitalist mode of production are impossible'.[5] To make sure that those needs could be met, advocates of Systematic Colonisation proffered a method for reproducing wage-slaves without resort to the violence overt in convictism and chattel-slavery.

Among the reasons why no one questions the foundational mode of production in South Australia none is more widespread than the assumption that, since Britain had been capitalist before 1836,[6] its white settlement colonies could not be otherwise. This conviction can be called 'capitalism as cargo', by which the convicts unloaded capitalism along with Governor Phillip's pre-fabricated house. The failure at the Swan River in 1829 demonstrates its fallaciousness.[7]

Given the preeminence of the United States among today's corporate warfare imperia, it may come as a surprise to find that dating the triumph of the capitalist mode there remains similarly in contention. Alertness to those debates should reduce the strangeness of asking parallel, if never exactly comparable, questions about South Australia. In the US case, the disputants take two lines: first, how to deal with the slave South;[8] and second, when does the economy move beyond simple commodity production? Some scholars are content to place the switch as early as the 1790s, relying on an extension of the areas across which goods were traded, despite a scarcity of ready money.[9] Their opponents highlight the Jacksonian counter-revolution, stressing the demolition of a regime of credit after the 1837 crisis.[10] In 1867, Marx notes that the US economy 'must still be considered a European colony'; in preparing the fourth German edition in 1890, Marx's collaborator, Friedrich Engels, adds that its 'industry holds second place in the world, without on that account entirely losing its colonial character'.[11] Marxist Professor of Accounting Rob A. Bryer deduces that simple commodity production held its own into the 1900s.[12]

How does this debate play in Australia? Try this thought experiment. It is January 1788 around Botany Bay. The French arrive before Phillip's fleet, lay claim to New Holland, and beat off the British. France is still feudal, hence its latest acquisition is also feudal. Within two years, that feudal order has been overthrown. Hence, its antipodean possession now has a different mode of production. This chain of assertions is not only obviously a daft way to proceed but assumes what has to be analysed: which mode was dominant in Britain and which in France? If it is arguable that Britain was not capitalist in 1788 and France no longer feudal, both were indisputably capitalist by 1836, albeit with peculiarities etched on each because the revolution inside capital 'assumes different aspects in different countries, and runs through its various phases in different orders of succession, and at different historical epochs'.[13] Marx dismisses the attempt to impose a single-factor explanation on human experience as 'a very rewarding method – for stilted, mock-scientific, highfaluting ignorance and intellectual laziness'.[14]

Spasmodic debate among historians and political economists about which mode dominated the initial areas of incursion and occupation along the east coast of Australia ranges across the 70 years to 1860–61.[15] Ken Dallas wrote about the convict system as a sub-species of slavery.[16] Liz Humphries sails around the shoals of handling the mode of production as cargo by making a putative British capitalism determine the mode in the Australian colonies.[17] Ken Buckley relied on quantitative determinants to conclude that Botany Bay had become capitalist within a couple of decades.[18] The only non-Marxists, G.J. Abbott and Margaret Steven, suspended the starting date until sufficient wealth had been totalled up by 1821.[19] Their approach fails to distinguish *initial* accumulations of money-capital from the application of at least some of those hoards to *initiate* the self-expansion characteristic of capitalism, as distinct from the forms of capital in every other mode.[20] Michael Dunn emphasised the political level to conclude that the end of transportation to New South Wales in 1841 marked the dominance of a capitalist mode.[21] Drawing on Lenin, D.W.A. Baker re-interpreted the 1861 Crown Lands Acts (NSW) as the victory of urban capital over the 'squattocracy', a view challenged by J.N. Connolly, but lately endorsed by Joe Collins drawing on Marx's concept of rent.[22]

Irrespective of the correctness of any of these claims, the disputes serve to clarify and to contextualise the concepts required to think through the question closer to home. In seeking the nature of the early years of invasion, we shall locate South Australia against these approaches for other places and within the 250-year expansion of capital-within-capitalism as a global system. Historical Enterprises Inc. got over its prejudice that Australia had no history, or that the little it did have should be hitched to the Course of Empire. An over-correction in the 1970s severed the local from the global; in a negative feedback, we shall re-tether the South Australian Company and its banks to that wider world.

'Capital' refined

To ask whether South Australia was capitalist from Proclamation Day makes sense only through two other lines of inquiry. First, what is meant by 'capitalist'? Marx defines a capitalist as the 'personification of capital'.[23] That answer requires taking a further step back to ask 'what is capital?' If the former is rarely scrutinised, the latter is first cousin to the unicorn.[24] The concept of capital-within-capitalism is called for to distinguish the hoards that had been present across the millennia from the relationships and processes required to install a form of capital that must expand in order to persist. How that revolution inside capital was accomplished is largely beyond the compass of this chapter, which provides little more than a contextualised conspectus of the concepts required to deal with the new mode; their workings will need to be taken far beyond the margins of the Province's good earth.

By contrast, and in what Marx appreciates was 'a wonderful feat of logical acumen', Captain Robert Torrens asks us to believe that the accumulation of capital began when an Aborigine first picked up a rock to throw at a kangaroo.[25] Such vulgar economists obliterate the differences between a mode of production based on the casting of stones and the one that extracted, processed and marketed ore bodies at Moonta, with that undertaking's financial, mechanical, and commercial ramifications. In like vein, apologists for capitalism extrapolate Adam Smith's remark about 'the general disposition to truck, barter, and exchange'[26] into an eternal, natural and universal condition, thereby drying up an ocean of differences between the bartering of ochre from Bookartoo and the global marketing of paints by Dulux.[27]

Crises

My sorting through of these approaches to capital and its cognates flows from an invitation in 2012 to address the Blackheath History Forum on 'The Two Depressions', meaning the 1930s and the crisis that erupted in September 2008. The memory that there had been Depressions before the 1930s intersected with an awareness that capitalism is unique in as much as it has to expand in order to exist, leaving the system prone to crises of over-production. These characteristics suggest a novel way to think about the origins of capitalism. To identify the first crisis of over-production is to have a benchmark as to when a revolution inside capital had resulted in a new form of capital, capital-within-capitalism. Let me be very clear: the date of the first crisis can be fixed to a particular year – 1825 or 1857. Dating that crisis turns a searchlight back into a period during which the revolution must have occurred but cannot deliver equivalent exactness for its triumph. There is no 1770, no 1492, no 1066. The revolution inside capital came later than we think, certainly not much before 1800.

At the crux of this chapter is linking the puzzles around the origins of capital-within-capitalism with how and when that form came to dominance in the Province of South Australia. What is beyond dispute is that both were forged – if not produced – during the financial upheavals of 1825–6 and their aftermath. Changes in the global economy shaped the options for South Australia, notably those consequent upon Britain's protracted adoption of 'freer trade', permitted by its dominance of world commerce. In 1828 Britain reduced tariffs on Australian exports, and in 1833 deprived the East India Company of its trading monopoly, opening opportunities for South Australian venturers.

Marx mentions 1825 as the first 'general crisis' and 1832 as the year from which capitalism attained dominance at the political level.[28] The disruptions were in part the backwash from adjusting the economy to peacetime conditions after 23 years of world war.[29] The proximate sources included defaulting loans to the new South American republics, including Poyais, a non-existent country. If 1825 were a crisis from overproduction, rather than another upset to the financial system, then any doubts about the dominance of the capitalist mode in Britain at the time of the establishment of the Province of South Australia disappear. Even so, conditions in the United Kingdom do not explain all those in New Holland. Time, manner and place apply. Despite the exchanges between Britain, China, the East India Company and the Australian colonies, each node demands its own account.[30] What seems beyond doubt is that the legislative and business responses to the 1825–6 upheavals secured dominance for capital-within-capitalism in Britain by the mid-1830s.

The historical materialist analysis employed here is predicated on the transitoriness of social practices, structures and mentalities. For instance, conditions in 1829 need not have held sway until 1836. During those seven years, Britain underwent political-economic transformations more profound than those after the Glorious Revolution of 1688, as witnessed by the Whig victory of 1830, the *Reform Act* of 1832, the *Poor Law Amendment Act* of 1834, and a displacement of chattel-slavery across the empire by a new kind of bonded labour. On top of those changes came commercial developments from a return to the gold standard between 1819 and 1821, and a relaxation of the laws governing joint-stock companies and banks, while holding a line against usury.

Those dislocations and reforms had multiple impacts, both direct and indirect, personal and institutional, on the establishment of South Australia. For instance, the driving force behind the South Australian Company, George Fife Angas, almost went under, preserved by his father's £10,000 overdraft.[31] Without that guarantee, it is an open question as to whether he could have redeemed his fortunes and reputation by 1834 to take a hand in financing the South Australian Company. As a personification of capital, he faced the limited choices laid out by Max Weber:

The belief in 'freedom of his will' is of precious little value to the manufacturer in the competitive struggle or to the broker on the stock exchange. He has the choice between economic destruction and the pursuit of very specific maxims of economic conduct.[32]

The lessons that Angas took from his peril over the seas were to give up furniture making for general merchandising, followed by a move into banking.

As keenly as E.G. Wakefield's writings revealed the actualities required for capitalist exploitation and accumulation, it took action by Angas for the Province of South Australia to come into being. As 'Mr Philanthropy at 5 per cent', his career opens up two elements pertinent to our knowing whether the Province was capitalist from the July 1836 landing on Kangaroo Island. The first is a school of thought, which by taking a mentalist rather than a materialist line, sees capitalism as the product of an 'Idea', an approach blamed on Max Weber. As a closet Marxist, however, Weber bases his understanding of '*Geist*' ('Spirit') on rational calculation and 'free labour';[33] he shows further how, well before 1600, the calculating ethic of capitalism had vanquished the ascetic spirit of Calvin. To adapt a footnote from Marx: Cornish miners could no more live on Methodism or bonded Germans on Pietism than the Ancient world did on politics or the Middle Ages on Thomism. The task before an historical materialist is to track the transitory expressions of each ideological form as it becomes predominant for a specific time and in particular locations.[34]

The second characteristic of Angas as a personification of capital comes closer to the substance of Weber's analysis of capitalism in terms of rational calculation by drawing us into the institutions and instruments required for capital to become the production of its own reproduction.[35] Abstinence ran a poor second to the capitalists' ability to pass on their accumulations from the labour by others, eased by the emergence of joint-stock companies and banks, though in hazard until the granting of limited liability after 1856.[36]

The joint-stock company
Accounts of the colonisation of South Australia traverse four joint-stock companies starting from the South Australian Land Company in 1832,[37]

before Angas took a hand in the others, the South Australian Company (1835), the Bank of South Australia (1836) and the Union Bank (1837–8).[38] Neglect of the accumulation that characterises capital-within-capitalism[39] has meant never querying the status of the joint-stock company. Instead, scholars are content to read backwards from what the firm has come to be, not what it could be prior to 1825. In a belief that the *Bubble Act* of 1720 had made joint-stock companies illegal, almost none on the scale of the East India Company was formed across the next 105 years. Needless to say, the need to bring together more funds than most individuals or families could muster obliged undertakers to find ways around, or through, the prohibitions supposedly flowing from the Act. After the 1760s, incorporation had been bestowed on specific purposes over limited periods, for instance, to construct canals and turnpikes, with Crown charters for the provision of other public goods. Co-partnerships of up to six were the usual method to finance slaving ventures.[40] Meanwhile, the *Bubble Act* was looking like a dead letter until 1808 when Lord Chancellor Eldon (1751–1838) led the courts towards his interpretation of the Common Law in order to stymie stock-market speculation as a threat to funding the national debt through the sale of shares (consols) in the national debt, which all sound thinkers understood underwrote the fiscal-naval state that kept Britain on top.[41]

Only 150 joint-stock companies were operating before 1825, mostly in transport and insurance, few of which had been incorporated by the Crown.[42] Without the business papers for G.F. Angas & Co., we cannot know how its funds had been assembled, since '& Co.' was being applied without indiscrimination to partnerships, and to the incorporated or unincorporated alike. At that time, his enterprise could have been only either a family trust or no more than a six-person partnership, both of which left all participants equally liable for the sum total of a bankrupt's debts, 'to the last shilling and the last acre'.[43] When Angas senior provided that £10,000 overdraft he could have been saving the fortunes of his extended family and not just that of one son.

Venturers like Angas might have hoped that the 1825 repeal of the *Bubble Act* would free businesses from these dodges. Not so. The trading of shares in an unincorporated joint-stock company remained dubious, and perhaps illegal under Common Law.[44] Railways broke the nexus since those joint-stock companies were admixtures of both securities and real property in land but also in rolling stock so that, ineluctably, the Law Lords learnt to tell a house from a horse.[45]

So what was a joint-stock company before then, and how was it regarded? Only in Scotland was it legal. The Scots preserved their legal system, based on Roman Law and not the Common Law, allowing judicial interpretation there to be more favorable than its English counterpart to the collective enterprises essential for the expanded reproduction of capital.[46] In a world where unincorporated joint-stock companies, protected by limited liability, have been the order of the day for 150 years, it takes some effort to think our way into a time when they were deemed diabolical. Adam Smith thought them another conspiracy against the public.[47] Even after they became lawful from 1825, *The Times* and the Law Lords continued to condemn them as threats to the natural order, a grievance and a public mischief to 'licence every species of fraud'.[48] Yet, as Marx observes, had the world 'had to wait until accumulation had got a few individual capitals far enough to be adequate for the construction of a railway', Engels would still have been visiting him by coach in 1867. 'Centralisation, however, accomplished this in the twinkling of an eye, by means of joint-stock companies.'[49] Centralisation of funds in joint-stock firms and banks did much the same for South Australia.

Allegations of Republicanism against the Company's promoters were not, as is often assumed, a reaction to the method of government proposed for the Province, but were being hurled at every attempt to set up joint-stock companies without a Charter from the Crown. The failure of historians to appreciate the context for the accusation of 'republicanism' against one company exemplifies the misunderstandings that must follow from addiction to parliamentary and court reports as revealed truth.[50]

Banks
Writings about the institutions and instruments that supported the foundation of the Province still focus on the Association, the Company, the Commissioners and the Governors, shadowed by the hand of the British empire-market-state. No less significant were the Bank of South Australia, in both manifestations, and the Union Bank. The Province's success depended on them.[51] The Company needed to garner the

initial investments, transmit funds back and forth, conduct government business,[52] and to pay wages in the colony.[53]

To understand what banks could and could not do for the South Australian Company requires purging our expectations of the sprawl of functions that financial institutions now perform. In the 1830s, banks might accept deposits, discount bills of exchange or issue their own notes, although the latter two were often accepted only within the area where their issuers were known personally.[54] Routine business required traders of every scale and kind to discount bills of exchange and accept promissory notes. The integration of producer, merchant and financier became part of how capitalists taught themselves how to personify capital-within-capitalism.[55] With every trader acting as some sort of money-lender by extending commercial credit to customers, Angas's turn to banking was predictable for a trans-Atlantic shipper. He learned the delights of joint-stock banks from his pamphleteering cousin, Thomas Joplin (1790–1847), with whom he became a co-founder of National Provincial Bank, an association of country banks, scheduled for 1829 but delayed until 1833 because of Reform-era uncertainties.[56] Just as the South Australia Act was sneaking through Westminster, a mania for joint-stock banks saw sixty-one conducting 472 branches by March 1836, with thirty-eight more banks to open that year.[57]

Differences between Chartered banks and those with an Act of Incorporation proved more significant on paper than in practice. Of the imperial banks in Australia, only the Bank of Australasia obtained a charter, the others being authorised by local Acts.[58] To operate in the Province, the directors of the Bank of South Australia required only an Act to facilitate local legal proceedings. Accordingly, Governor Hindmarsh contented himself with publishing the regulations 'for general information', and with securing returns from the Bank by agreement.[59]

The Act confined the Bank of South Australia to within the Province, and to dealings with the United Kingdom, while the invaders had to deal with neighbouring colonies, as could the Bank of Australasia. At first, Angas hoped that it would service the Province, possibly because cousin Joplin had been spoken of as its first manager.[60] When the Bank of Australasia declined, the Company had to set up its own bank to carry out transactions in the Province and between it and London. The directors also had to establish the means to deal with businesses in the other colonies. To that end, Angas led fellow London capitalists to support the Union Bank as a rival for the Australasia, while insisting that the newcomer keep out of South Australia.[61] As the name 'Union' implies, its directors expected to merge with existing institutions, but only the Tamar Bank in Van Diemen's Land did so,[62] proving a valuable connection once Launceston became a principal source of imports to Adelaide.[63]

With new banking regulations under discussion in the U.K. in late 1830s,[64] Angas worried lest the success of the Bank of South Australia stand in the way of the Company's obtaining a charter. Ever 'fertile in expedients', as his hagiographer has it, he had arranged by early in 1841 to put the Bank under a separate board but with the same set of Directors as for the Company.[65] The Bank remained an English concern after separating from the Company in 1842, gaining a charter in 1846.[66]

Primary communalism

Having placed the South Australian Company and its financial institutions in the context of the legal obligations and commercial conventions of the Reform Era, which confirmed the triumph of the capitalist mode of social reproduction, we must now consider what mode its personifications and agents encountered as they came ashore.

The fictions we are being invited to challenge in this lecture series and volume of essays were not conjured of the air. Conventional wisdoms draw upon the need that propertied classes have to nourish narratives supportive of their interests. Such are the culture-history wars. No red-armband view need apply. That imperative is keenest in a reluctance among the invaders to recognise an Aboriginal mode of production. If no mode of production were being practiced here, the Company could grab the lot. Yet, the people with most reason to be alarmed at the replacement of one mode of production by another were also the least likely to formulate their dispossession in those terms; they knew their own practices as integral to their survival and as central to beliefs about their place in the world, but they had no experience of other modes – no chattel-slavery or feudal-serfdom – against which to suppose that their ways of doing and imagining could be displaced.[67]

The teleological shadow cast over the mode known as 'primitive communism' should be erased by a coinage such as 'primary communalism', a mode more different from capitalism than capitalism is from slavery and serfdom since, unlike that trio, it has neither classes, nor a state, nor nation except in the archaic sense of tribe. Similarly, to recognise that the first peoples might have created multiple modes of production across 80,000 years without ever having had an 'economy', or a 'market' in current Western terms, is to celebrate difference, not to denigrate the other.[68] As a category, 'mode of production' is too readily equated with large-scale machinery when each mode embraces the social reproduction of every element in human existence. To archaeologist Gordon Childe's way of reasoning, the Arunta saw themselves as producing food as much as through their ceremonies as by seed gathering or hunting: '"Our magic rites," an Arunta would say, "are just as necessary and efficacious in keeping up the supply of emus and grubs, as the digging and weeding done by wretched cultivators."'[69]

Alien creatures had been advancing westwards on a broad front for more than twenty years with smallpox as their advance party. Explorer Charles Sturt reached the Darling in February 1829 and two years later his party rowed across Lake Alexandrina. The Hentys were at Portland from November 1834. Well before then, word had spread of the collapse of the 'pillars holding up the sky'.[70] Spatially, indigenous social relations of reproduction dominated until the 1860s; demographically, they did so for a shorter period – only until the number of settlers went above 15,000 in the 1840s. Politically, which is to say, militarily, it is not silly to suggest that they had lost before 1836. Across the continent, the armed might of the invaders amounted to a monopoly of violence. They had won the 'Black War' in Van Diemen's Land after outlaying sums as great as the Company raised to establish the Province of South Australia. The prospect of a new guerilla war encouraged an early gubernatorial prospect, Colonel Napier, to stress military preparedness.[71] Modes of social re-production extend to the means for the application of violence, with rifles as tools for killing, while the training of killers in the police and the army adds one more social division to labour.[72] The Province exemplifies 'property-as-theft' as a *pre*condition for the capitalist mode of exploitation, which, as Marx recognises, comes into the world 'dripping from head to toe, from every pore, with blood and dirt'.[73]

Once the Colonial Office realised that, unlike all the instructions to governors of other colonies, the 1834 Act had not spelt out protections for the prior occupants, the law officers sought to bring the projectors back into line by adding stipulations to the Letters Patent, and by extracting promises to protect animals if they were the locals' food source.[74] In that spirit, two-thirds of the Proclamation set out those commitments.[75] Yet, the first peoples would retain title only if found to be settled, which the un-settlers understood to mean 'cultivated'. Would Torrens have accepted fisheries as cultivation? Even the Ngarrindjeri, who shifted around inside quite small territories, could seem nomadic to a Dorsetshire villager, or 'altogether homeless', as Hodder would have it sixty years later.[76]

And so it was that the so-called settled districts became the unsettled ones, unsettled by the invaders.

The failure of the 1834 Act to acknowledge prior occupancy is indicative of more than absent-minded prejudice. No document setting limits on the avarice of the investors could regulate a land-grab taking place 20,000 km away from the reach of the Crown, as had been shown by the failure of the 1831 Ripon Regulations to draw a line in the sand against squatters in New South Wales.[77] Moreover, the authorities imported the faith that the enclosure of 85 per cent of England had seeded wastelands with virtue.[78] It was no surprise, then, that the Province proved to be a 'job' run, as the editor of the *South Australian Gazette and Colonial Register* noted, by the 'veriest set of buggers' headed by Governor Hindmarsh.[79] The mess that the invaders made of their own land dealings highlights how preposterous was the thought that a delineation of native lands could have been made to work, or game preserved in their interest. Torrens's son, also Robert, came up with a novel title-transfer in 1858,[80] which conveyed how the promoters had always seen land as just another marketable commodity, a radical viewpoint then edging towards acceptance in the British courts, out from under much feudal learning that had cared not to distinguish realty from personalty.[81]

Freed labour

No fiction remains more fundamental to the self-image of South Australians than that their patch was conceived and born free from the 'hated stain',[82] with the founders inscribing 'No convicts!' into their promotions.

Lop-sided views of 'free labour' disable analyses of capitalism since a foundational fiction among vulgar Marxians is that the mode's determining characteristic is 'free labour', in contrast to the slave or serf kind. Marx's own critique of the capitalist mode is never mono-causal. Moreover, the multi-faceted operations of each of its dynamics[83] are rendered opaque by using the phrase 'free labour' for a power relationship better rendered as 'freed labour', freed, that is, from possessing the means of production which would otherwise allow labourers to remain self-sustaining. Setting labour free compels its owners to sell their capacity to add value, making freed the antithesis of self-emancipatory. Indeed, freed labour guarantees wage-slavery. To be a freed labourer, warns Marx, is a misfortune, not a stroke of luck.[84]

By selling wastelands at a price sufficient to prevent immigrant workers from becoming self-sustaining before they had repaid more than their passage fee, Wakefield's systematic colonisation looks like a device for reproducing freed labour. However, the agents of capital can extract the maximum of value from labour-power only after disciplining its application. The Wakefieldian promise of a measure of independence after seven years of enriching one's Master could be an indirect means to internalise the sought-after diligence in order to save up the purchase price.

However, that carrot could not spirit away the stick. Even though all 420 of the South Australian Company's workforce were indentured for three years, other employers needed to make it a crime for freed labour to quit before even an implied contract expired. Within weeks of arrival, a *Masters and Servants Act* came into force. Workers could be imprisoned for six months and forfeit their wages. Because there was no gaol, offenders were chained to trees. On paper, the Act protected both parties. In practice, as a water carrier declared in 1838, it had been 'framed for the benefit of the rich alone'.[85] After the Colonial Secretary, Lord Glenelg, found its provisions more suited to a penal colony, the Act lapsed for two years to be replaced in 1841.[86]

Masters can discipline their servants only for as long as the latter must sell their labour power in order to live. Even then, the Masters need state apparatuses to marshall that commodity. Adam Smith records how '[t]he masters ... never cease to call aloud for the assistance of the civil magistrate, and the rigorous execution of those laws which have been enacted with so much severity against the combinations of servants, labourers, and journeymen.'[87] Max Weber drew on 140 more years of developments in capitalism to recognise that

> [t]he industrialist takes into account the fact that people exist who are hungry, and that those other people in the spiked helmets will prevent them using physical force simply to take the means where they find them which could serve to allay their hunger ...[88]

The fiction that the state is an umpire, the neutral arbiter, is the foundation of all apologists for class rule. To know which mode of production is dominant it is essential to discern which class or fraction has control at the political level. For South Australia in the 1830s, that search extends from Adelaide to London and back again. Yet, the existence of classes means that the state is always one more site for conflict. The long arms of Whitehall and the Admiralty made themselves felt in the disallowance of the first *Master and Servants Act*; while the replacement of governors Hindmarsh and Gawler fused the local with the imperial. There is no doubt who held state power in regard to the Indigenous people. There is no doubt about which class held state power in the Province, though with more restraints on its exercise over immigrant labourers than upon the original occupiers.

To reduce unrest at home at the time of rural riots, the 1831 Regulations on the occupancy of land in New South Wales were, in part, to encourage emigration. Three years later, the Tolpuddle Martyrs were transported for resisting a further cut in their wages. More significant was the campaign through the Owenite Grand National Trade Union Confederation which won them free pardons in March 1836. By reversing that 'injustice within the law', organised workers taught the British state and the South Australian Company that they could not rule over labour in their old ways. The relative strengths of the contending classes were shifting, and did so faster in Australia where the crew of the Company vessels struck for higher wages as soon as they reached Kangaroo Island.[89] As the lash and the gallows lost out to the anti-transportation leagues, the agents of capital sought to maintain their authority through ideological apparatuses.[90] Public hangings, transportation and such consolations no longer sufficed to ease emigration to a better world.

In deciding which mode of production dominated here from 1836, the fiction about the freedom of its indentured labourers needs to be located in the relations between capital and labour across the globe. For Britain's propertied classes to import a million 'ghost acres' from the Americas and Australasia,[91] they had to export millions of chattel slaves out of Africa, hundreds of thousands of convicts and millions of freed labourers from the UK, and, with the ending of chattel-slavery,[92] to dispatch contract labourers from the Indian sub-continent under 'a new system of slavery',[93] forging a supply chain that brought Gandhi to South Africa, but only a handful of coolies to South Australia.[94]

One could be forgiven for supposing that the distinction between systematic colonisation and contract labour had something to do with the colour of one's skin. The 1832 proposal from the South Australian Land Company had spoken of drawing its 'labour force from foreign countries in the belief that such workers would be more docile'; indeed, its promoters planned 'to discriminate against British subjects when awarding assisted passages'.[95] The risk with 'docile' labourers was that they were unlikely to be clock-trained and, therefore 'as every employer knows', according to Weber,

> the lack of *concienziosita* of the labourers of such countries, for instance Italy as compared with Germany, has been, to a certain extent still is, one of the principal obstacles to their capitalistic development. Capitalism cannot make use of the labour of those who practice the doctrine of undisciplined *liberum arbitrium* ... [96]

Angas could redeem his fortunes after 1841 by relying on the parsimonious probity of his bonded German Pietists.[97]

So many other arrivals, however, had set up farms for themselves by 1842–3 that bumper crops, the shortage of labour and consequential wage demands made crops too expensive to harvest, causing Governor Grey to send officials and 150 soldiers from New South Wales into the fields.[98] More widely, grains were grown on what Dunsdorf calls a '[n]on-capitalist basis', meaning that farmers employed little or no outside labour.[99] Rather than coolies or convicts came machinery in the shape of the Bull-Ridley stripper, with fifty of them in use by 1850.[100] Marx recognised in machines a means for producing relative surplus-value, for strike-breaking and for cutting labour costs.[101]

The foundational fiction of free labour in South Australia persists because of the measure of independence that immigrant labourers won as small farmers, as tradesmen or as unionised wage-slaves. To invert the concluding paragraph of Marx's chapter 33:

> Since we are concerned here with the condition of the Province, the principal thing that interests us is how the political economy of the Old World exposes the actualities of the New, despite being veiled by its chroniclers.

Upon reading *Capital* in 1888, the future Chief Justice Sir Samuel Griffith concurred: 'In short, the rule of the strong, which is one form is slavery, or the practical ownership of men by men, has by no means disappeared from our social system. We have abolished its most objectionable outward and apparent manifestation, but it still exists as part of the practical rule of life.'[102] Fifty years earlier, a spectre was haunting Adelaide, the spectre of chattel-slavery.

Checking a detail regarding George Fife Angas, I returned to his entry in the *Australian Dictionary of Biography*:

> By 1822, Angas was carrying the main burden of his father's large establishment at Newcastle, with branches in British ports, the West Indies and Spanish America. In 1824 he moved to London to form the shipping business of G.F. Angas & Co. Next year he nearly overreached himself in bubble speculations, but recovered with his father's help.[103]

Here were foundational facts that I had failed to interrogate: how could Angas contribute to the South Australian Company? Part of his investment derived from his family's wage-slaves who crafted furniture out of Honduran mahogany harvested by chattel-slaves,[104] while a portion came from participating in the Atlantic trades that equipped the slave economies, as he could boast in September 1822: 'probably we have sent as great a quantity of British goods out during the past year as any of the Bay merchants, one excepted'.[105] Two years later, he became a 'shipper', going deeper into that triangular trade. Because his father had accumulated a hoard from like sources, he was able to rescue George Fife from ruin after 1825. My tardiness in catching sight of the slave-hewn mahogany through the footnotes, and thus of pursuing the source of the founders' funds in 1834–6, are extensions of the want of learned interest in how the development of commercial institutions and instruments in Britain allowed the Company's directors to get about their business across the globe.

Like every venture, the invasion of South Australia was weaned on the slave system.[106]

Edwin Hodder's praise for Angas's 1822–3 campaign to free 200–300 Indian slaves along the Mosquito Coast[107] gives no hint of the Africans for whose emancipation Angas would receive £6,345 in compensation after 1833, an enormous sum of money at the time.[108] Without company files and private papers we can but guess why his concern for the Indians did not preclude his ownership of as many Africans. Did the logging methods of the Indians' 'owners' threaten his profits? Did he expect to convert the Indians more readily than his own chattels? Whatever the reasoning, his conscience did not run to manumission.[109]

Angas was not the only beneficiary from dealing in 'living tools' to promote the Company. Two Montefiore brothers involved themselves with the early years of the Province: Jamaica-born Jacob (1801–95) and Joseph Barrow (1803–93).[110] The surviving third of the Barbados Naval Office Records between 1781 and 1806 show that their father, Eliezer, had traded 211 slaves to Demerara and Belize.[111] The brothers signed compensation claims as trustees for three children of a tenant in tail; No. 2374 for £386 was granted but no. 2029 for £514 was not. (Sir) Moses Montefiore recorded in his diary on 7 May 1835 that he had

> called at Downing Street on the Right Hon. Spring-Rice, Chancellor of the Exchequer. I was immediately admitted and received by him in a most friendly manner. I thanked him for having, at my request, appointed Jacob Montefiore one of Her Majesty's Commissioners for the Colonisation of South Australia. The Chancellor spoke of the many new schemes now afloat of Companies of small capital, and said he would always be glad to see me.[112]

As he was on 23 August 1835, when Montefiore returned with his regular partner and in-law, Nathan Rothschild,[113] to contract for the £15 million loan, equivalent to 40 per cent of the British budget, which the government needed to compensate the slave-owners.[114] Jacob visited in June 1843 and again in 1854.[115] Joseph spent thirteen years in New South Wales until his 1841 bankruptcy, which saw his return to London, before taking up residence in Adelaide between 1846 and 1860.[116]

Following the South Australian Company's money trail also leads to the retired financier and Dissenter, Samuel Mills, who had put up most of the £23,000 contributed by early November 1835, and who could offer £120,000 in 1841 to take over the Company debt. Mills had made his millions from the London Assurance Co.,[117] which flourished on marine insurance for slave goods and against fire in the sugar refineries along the West India Dock.[118]

Other South Australians to receive compensation included the poet Fidelia Hill, who inherited an estate in Jamaica where she lived with her husband, Robert, between 1830 and 1835, from whence, flush with compensation, they moved to Adelaide on the understanding that Robert would be given a position.[119] The Creole Edward Stirling (1804–73) arrived with a remittance of £1,000 in 1838 to cut a huge figure in mining and pastoral endeavours, serve in the Legislative Council, take a hand in the colony's constitution, father Sir John Lancelot and Sir Edward Charles, and have a small municipality named after him in the Adelaide Hills. With compensation funds, the two sons of Neill Malcolm set up Poltalloch cattle station after 1838, expecting to resettle tenants cleared off the Clan estates in Argyllshire. Sir Robert Dalrymple Ross (1828–87), an inheritor from his father's slaves in St Vincent, became treasurer and Speaker in the House of Assembly from 1881 until his death. The sixth governor, Sir James Fergusson, inherited from absentee slave-owners.[120] By way of contrast, a West Indian seaman, James Gordon, convicted at Port Adelaide in 1837 of stealing a watch was transported from the free colony to serve his seven-year sentence in the penal one across the border.[121]

Less directly, but more pervasively, financing the trade in slave-produced goods, more than the slave trade itself, called forth the regime of credit pivotal for the revolution inside capital.[122] For like the Tobacco Lords of Glasgow before 1778,[123] and like Jane Austin's Reverend father, gentlemen did not need to trade in human cargoes or to own slaves – as did the Gladstones and the Barings – in order to benefit from the system.[124] That bloodline explains why the free-trade British cotton-millers had to support the slave-holders revolt in the early 1860s.

The Faustian bargain struck by capitalists between indulgence and accumulation[125] allowed space for slave-based fortunes to endow the theological *Hibbert Journal* and the Codrington Library, All Souls College, Oxford, as well as many a stately home besides Fontill Abbey and Bromley Hill Place. As Walter Benjamin remarks: 'There is no document of civilisation which is not at the same time a document of barbarism.'[126] The 'glory that was Greece and the grandeur that was Rome' were paid for out of dehumanising toil, from which the Athens of the South was not to be exempt.

The latest front to open in the culture-cum-history wars is the Right's promotion of Western Civilisation, underwritten by $15 million from medical over-servicing billionaire Paul Ramsay to fund degrees and scholarships in study of the history of Western Civilisation at several Australian universities.[127] Often as not, the case for Western Civilisation rises on the plethora of commodities, or slides into defending the bad against the worst: the benign Britisher against Kipling's 'lesser breeds without the law'.[128] There is no denying the existence of Western Civilisation or gainsaying its worth, both of which are the outcome of struggles against the forebears of the people who now have the lucre from their expropriating the surplus-value of wage-slaves to fund a further closing of the Australian mind.

For such civilisation as the world now enjoys has been won by men and women who broke bad laws. Slave revolts pricked consciences before the abolitions of 1807 and 1833.[129] The secretary of the Builders' Labourers Union, Samuel Champ, explained to a Domain crowd in Hobart in 1916:

> British liberties had not been won by mining magnates or stock-exchange jobbers, but by genuine men of the working-class movement who had died on the gallows and rotted in dungeons and were buried in nameless graves. These were the men to whom we owed the liberates we enjoyed today. Eight hours and other privileges in Australia had been won by men who suffered gaol and persecution.[130]

Freedom of the press owes somewhat more to Richard Carlile and the printers who followed him into prison in the 1820s by defying the four-pence duty on newspapers than to 'The Thunderer' (*The Times*), or to 'Mass' Murdoch. The engine behind the Abolitionists' victory in 1807,

Thomas Clarkson, kept a brick from the Bastille on his desk while William Wilberforce promoted Acts to criminalise working-class resistance to wage-slavery.

To adapt Marx's linking of cotton and slavery with capitalism to the civilising enterprise of the South Australian Company:

> Without chattel slaves, the Angases have no mahogany to import and no market for their exports; without those profits they have no hoard. It is chattel-slavery which gives the South Australian Company its founding philanthropist. Thus, slavery is an economic category of the greatest importance for free settlement.

Not every bluestone in Adelaide is mortared with the blood of a slave as is charged against the bricks of Bristol and Liverpool,[131] yet the fine particles that cemented the City of Light's Proclamation Tree were mixed with the blood of West Indian slaves and Kaurna bones, since plastered over with an insouciant scholarship.

5

True Lies: South Australia's Foundation, the Idea of 'Difference', and the Rights of Aboriginal People

ROBERT FOSTER

On 28 December 2007, I attended the annual Proclamation Day ceremony at Glenelg. Official guests were seated on a podium beneath the iconic Old Gum Tree which of course marks the place where South Australia's first Governor, Sir John Hindmarsh, witnessed the reading of the Proclamation symbolically inaugurating the colony in 1836. As the current Governor walked through an honour guard of men dressed in the uniforms of colonial police, a pair of modern-day mounted police rode forward to shield a small group of Aboriginal protesters who waited on the footpath opposite the entrance gate. Once all the dignitaries had taken their places, the event began, as it had begun for generations, with the reading of the Proclamation. As the Chief Executive Officer of the Holdfast Council read the passage of the Proclamation that promised 'to punish with exemplary severity all acts of violence and injustice ... against the natives', an Aboriginal protester called out: 'what justice?' The protesters carried placards calling for a treaty, and stood before a banner that read:

> 'Aborigines were wrongfully deprived of their just dues.
> We must, as far as we can, right those wrongs.'
> Hon D.A. Dunstan, Minister for Aboriginal Affairs
> 13 July 1966

These were words spoken by Don Dunstan in the South Australian parliament. Implicit in his words, and the protesters' use of them, was a belief that South Australia had a historical obligation to do justice to Aboriginal people. The philosopher Janna Thompson has written on the theme of historical obligations in her book, *Taking Responsibility for the Past.* 'Injustices', she writes, 'cast a long shadow', and a community's moral responsibility for them is not easily diminished by the passage of time.¹ That responsibility, she argues, lies in the fact that we live in an 'intergenerational community' whose 'institutions and moral relationships persist over time and through a succession of generations'. Further, it 'depends for its moral and political integrity on its members accepting transgenerational obligations and honouring historical entitlements'.[2] For me, Thompson's conception of society as an intergenerational community played out in all the resonances of the events that morning: the reading of the 1836 Proclamation with its promises of justice, contested in 2007 by the words of Don Dunstan spoken in 1966.

South Australia has long had a reputation of being more 'enlightened' in its attitudes toward Aboriginal people, and the reforming years of the 'Dunstan decade' are sometimes pointed to as proof of this claim. This idea of 'benevolent intentions' toward Aboriginal people has been one of a suite of qualities that, historically, were seen to set the State apart: it was established as a free colony, free of convicts; it was a planned colony, built on Wakefield's theory of systematic colonisation; and it was a colony predicated on ideals of religious and political freedom, including a more liberal approach to Aboriginal rights and protection.[3] It is this idea of 'difference' in the colony's attitude to, and treatment of Aboriginal people, that I want to explore in this chapter. The origins of this claim can be traced the colony's founding documents; especially the Letters Patent, which seemingly acknowledged prior Aboriginal title to the land, and the Proclamation, which undertook to place Aboriginal people under the protection of the rule of law. These were genuine points of difference in the history of Australian settlement.[4]

Foundational undertakings?

What were the foundational undertakings contained in those documents? The Letters Patent, issued on 19 February 1836, gave royal authority to the establishment of the colony, and defined its boundaries. In doing so, it included the following caveat:

> PROVIDED ALWAYS that nothing in those our Letters Patent contained shall affect or be construed to affect the rights of any Aboriginal natives of the

said Province to the actual occupation or enjoyment in their own persons or in the persons of their Descendants of any lands therein now actually occupied or enjoyed by such Natives.[5]

Another document, less well-known, set out the colonists' plans regarding Aboriginal people, and this was the *First Annual Report of the Colonization Commissioners*. It was published in London on 28 July 1836, just as settlers were coming ashore on Kangaroo Island, and detailed, among other things, how those rights to land, which Aboriginal people 'actually occupied or enjoyed' were to be dealt with. Regarding their treatment, the report stated that the

> following objects should be aimed at: to guard them against personal outrage and violence; to protect them in the undisturbed enjoyment of their proprietary right to the soil, wherever such a right might be found to exist; to make it an invariable and cardinal condition in all bargains and treaties made with the natives for the cession of land possessed by them, in occupation or enjoyment, that permanent subsistence shall be supplied to them from some other source.[6]

The report went on the stress that only lands voluntarily ceded would be offered for sale, and that it would be the responsibility of the Protector of Aborigines to ensure that any 'bargains or treaties' entered into were 'faithfully executed'. Finally, the Commissioners wrote that they had 'under consideration' a plan whereby those lands that were 'ceded by the natives', would be sold on the condition that, after a term of years, one fifth of every 80-acre section sold, 'would be resumed as a reserve for the use of the Aborigines'. Such a scheme, they suggested, would benefit both parties: settlers would get the gratuitous use of 16 acres for a term of years, while the moneys generated would 'constitute a permanent fund for the endowment of schools and establishments for the benefit of the Aborigines'.[7]

The other key founding document was Governor Hindmarsh's first Proclamation, which was read out to an assembly of the colonists on 28 December 1836. The Proclamation, while having no legal force, nonetheless spelled out an ideal of Aboriginal protection. It called upon the colonists to respect the laws, conduct themselves with industry and sobriety, practise a 'sound morality', and 'prove themselves worthy to be the FOUNDERS of a great and free Colony'. Most of the Proclamation, however, was devoted to the rights and welfare of the Aboriginal people:

> It is also at this time especially, my duty to apprize the Colonists of my resolution, to take every lawful means for extending the same protection to the NATIVE POPULATION as to the rest of His Majesty's Subjects, and of my firm determination to punish with exemplary severity, all acts of violence or injustice which may in any manner be practised or attempted against the NATIVES who are to be considered as much under the Safeguard of the law as the Colonists themselves, and equally entitled to the privileges of British Subjects.[8]

The sentiments expressed in this document, while making no reference to the issue of land, nonetheless offered the protection of the rule of law, and the privileges of British subjects. This would be a colony where, to quote the earlier report of the Colonization Commissioners, 'the virtuous settler' would displace the 'lawless squatters' and 'runaway convicts'.

Whose ideals?

The ideals expressed in these documents, full of rhetoric about rights and protections, were not, or at least not fundamentally, the ideals of the colony's founders. What they reflected were the ideals of the evangelical reformers who now dominated the new Whig government of Lord Glenelg. These were humanitarians who had won their campaign against slavery in 1833 and who were now shifting their attention to the protection of Aboriginal people in British colonies. The entrepreneurial planners of the South Australian colony had given little thought to the Aboriginal people who were known to inhabit the region. The Act of Parliament establishing the colony, which they had drafted and had been passed by the British parliament in 1834, described the region as 'waste and unoccupied' and 'fit for the purposes of colonisation'.[9] None of its provisions addressed the question of Aboriginal rights or welfare.

Their minds were turned to the question *only* after Governor Arthur in Van Diemen's Land, who had heard of the proposed settlement, wrote to the Colonial Office expressing his concerns. Reflecting on his own experiences, he thought it 'a great oversight that a treaty was not' made with the Aborigines and compensation given them as a fair equivalent for what they had surrendered. Such an approach, he thought, might have reduced the 'feeling of injustice' they felt and averted the 'warfare so long waged' between them and the settlers. He encouraged the colonists of this newly proposed colony to avoid his mistakes by 'coming to an understanding with the natives of Southern Australia' before settlement commenced.[10]

In response to this letter, the Colonial Office now pressed the South Australian Colonization Commissioners to explain what provisions were being made for the Aboriginal people in the colony. It stressed that it was not about to 'sanction any act of injustice', and demanded that the Commissioners 'not proceed any further than those limits within which they can shew, by some sufficient evidence, that the land is unoccupied, and that no earlier and preferable title exists'.[11] The Emigration Agent, John Brown, reported that Col. Torrens, Chairman of the Commission, was 'exceedingly depressed by the Communication', and 'very nervous'.[12] Their first response was to push back and point out that they were operating on the same assumptions that guided the acquisition of land in other Australian colonies, where land, they pointed out, was daily being brought and sold without the least consideration being given to the question of Aboriginal proprietary rights. The Colonial Office did not back down, it continued to demand that the Commissioners detail their plans regarding Aboriginal rights and welfare. At one point, Lord Glenelg suggested that the settlement be postponed until the Act was amended.[13] On hearing this news, Torrens is reported to have said that he thought 'the Colony was pretty well ended'.[14] The Commissioners then went on the offence, Torrens threatened that the Board would resign if these changes were insisted upon. At this point the Colonial Office backed down.

It was as a consequence of these exchanges that the undertakings spelled out in those foundational documents took shape, and there is a strong sense that they were framed to satisfy the humanitarian sentiments of the Colonial Office, without unduly compromising their scheme. We get an insight into this in the writings of the Emigration Agent John Brown. He sneers at the concerns of the Colonial Office. He made it clear that he did not believe Aboriginal people 'actually occupied' land in a manner that accorded with European notions. On another occasion, he complained that the Colonial Office 'wish to bind us before we start to some plan for the protection of the natives in order to satisfy the saints in the House of Commons'. One of those leading saints, of course, was Thomas Fowell Buxton who Brown personally visited to convince him of colonists' goodwill. Brown even offered to be the colony's first Protector of Aborigines. The founders of the colony regarded these undertakings, squeezed out of them by humanitarians in the British government, as bothersome interventions, and did what they could to circumvent them.[15]

When the colonists finally got on the ground, the undertaking that they might negotiate for lands was seemingly forgotten. When interim Protector William Wyatt approached the Resident Commissioner in 1837 (the Resident Commissioner had authority over land sales) and asked that some lands be reserved for the Aborigines, he was bluntly told that the Act admitted of no such thing. The issue of rights to land was not seriously addressed until 1840. At this time, the Act had been amended, Governor Gawler had been given the powers of the Resident Commissioner, and the Crown-appointed Protector of Aborigines had finally arrived in the colony. In the middle of 1840, Gawler directed the Protector, to set aside reserves of land in the recently completed Special Surveys for the 'future use and benefit of the Aborigines'. When those who held preliminary land orders to these surveys discovered that first choice to land in these districts had been given to the Protector, they protested. They demanded that these choices be annulled, and that they be given first choice. This then led Gawler, who was trying to do justice to his instructions as Resident Commissioner and Governor, to voice what, on the surface, seemed a powerful defence of Aboriginal land rights. Speaking through his Assistant Commissioner, Charles Sturt, Gawler told them that Aboriginal people had the right to 'reasonable portions of the choicest land, for their especial use and benefit, out of the very extensive districts over which, from time immemorial, these aborigines have exercised distinct, defined and absolute rights of proprietary and hereditary possession'. Despite the powerful rhetoric, Gawler made clear that he would not enter into 'treaties and bargains' and merely agreed to reserve small portions of land, which would be held in trust, for the 'future use and benefit' of Aboriginal people.

This, then, was the government's 'land policy' regarding Aboriginal people. Over the course of the 19th century, the few areas of reserve land given to Aboriginal people were all granted on the basis that they would assist in their assimilation. Grants were sometimes made to Aboriginal women who married European men. They were occasionally made to Aboriginal men who expressed a willingness to farm. While more extensive grants were made to missionary organisations, to assist them in their task of civilising and Christianising.

The founders of the colony gave little thought to the question of Aboriginal rights when they drafted the founding Act. When humanitarians in the government pressed them to act on these issues, they resisted. Pressed further, they came up with promises that were so conditional and open to interpretation that they carried little force. Once on the ground they continued to resist even modest concessions such as the reservation of a few sections of land. Eventually the Imperial government stopped bothering them. It is ironic that the humanitarian principles that they went to great lengths to resist would, over time, become emblematic of the colony's 'benevolent intentions' and would be invoked increasingly over the course of the 20th century to give moral legitimacy to campaigns for Aboriginal rights, especially rights to land.

20th century campaigns

The first of those campaigns I want to look at is the campaign to establish an Aboriginal Reserve in South Australia's far north-west. By the late 19th century there had been something of a paradigm-shift in European understandings of Aboriginal society and culture. The influence of Darwin's theory of evolution, with its focus on the question of humankind's origins, led scientists to regard so-called 'primitive' peoples as living 'relics of the dawn of time'. As a consequence, Aboriginal communities still living traditionally were regarded as historically, and scientifically, unique. For scientists who wished to know about the evolution of man, these were people who deserved to be protected.

This was certainly the view of Herbert Basedow, son of a prominent, German-born settler and parliamentarian. In 1903, Basedow Jnr travelled through South Australia's north-west as part of a prospecting expedition. He wrote effusively about the Aboriginal people he encountered, and the purity of their culture, reporting that the region was 'practically unexplored, from an ethnological point of view'. Not long after this expedition, Basedow travelled to Germany to study medicine and anthropology. After he came back to Australia, he served briefly as Chief Protector in the new, federally-controlled Northern Territory, before returning to Adelaide. Over those years, he had not lost his interest in the north-west. In 1914, he approached the influential Methodist preacher, Henry Howard, asking for his help in securing protection for what he described as the 'primitive, uncorrupted, and uncontaminated' tribes of the region. In June 1914, they wrote to the government asking it to set aside extensive reserves in north-western ranges, saying there was still time to save 'at least a few tribes' from the fate that had befallen their brethren in other parts of the country. The Premier was receptive and wrote to the Western Australian and Commonwealth governments to see if they would establish contiguous reserves in their jurisdictions. However, with the outbreak of war a couple of months later, the idea fell by the wayside. Basedow, being of German ancestry, understandably kept a low profile.

The campaign was revived a few years later by the ornithologist S.A. White. Between 1913 and 1918, White undertook several expeditions into the outback, one of them to the north-west. Like Basedow, he admired the Aboriginal people he met. In his published account of the expedition he described them as the 'honest owners of the soil' who had 'yet to come into contact with the white man', writing that it was a pity it could not be assured 'they would never do so'. In 1917, he joined up with Methodist minister J.C. Jennison and they resumed the campaign for a 'Reserve for Aborigines in the North-West corner of this state'. They led a deputation to present their plan for 70,000 square miles to be set aside 'for the sole use of the Aborigines in that part of the country', to protect them from 'unclean civilization'. The minister agreed to approach the Western Australian and Commonwealth governments to ask if they would agree to set aside similar reserves. In August 1918, the Western Australians agreed, but by this time the South Australian Premier had had a change of heart and decided not to proceed with the plan. Nonetheless, the campaign continued. In 1919, White and Jennison again led a deputation to the Premier, and on this occasion Basedow was back on board. In the arguments presented, some of the speakers pointed to sorry impact settlement has had on Aboriginal people, despite the assurances of 'goodwill' and 'protection' in Hindmarsh's Proclamation. Adding that these 'pledges can be honoured in the letter and the spirit only by giving attention to the welfare' of the Aboriginal people.[16]

Their lobbying was finally successful, and the reserve was proclaimed on 16 February 1921. Basedow is usually the person given credit for the establishment of the North-West Reserve but while he certainly initiated the campaign, it was S.A. White, who brought it to fruition, and importantly, shaped the nature of reserve itself. When Basedow had originally floated the idea, he contemplated the establishment of Christian mission in the reserve, but that proposal had fallen away by the time the Reserve was declared. White's idea was to achieve a sort of protective isolation and to secure them from the 'contamination' of civilization. The North-West Reserve is important in the history of land rights because it was one of the first Aboriginal reserves set aside not to facilitate the assimilation of Aboriginal people, but to protect them from assimilation. The rhetoric of foundational promises and historical obligations, while present in the North-West Reserve campaign, was not dominant. However, it grew louder in the 1920s and 1930s, and was especially prominent in the campaign of the Aborigines Protection League, for what they called a 'Model Aboriginal State'.

This campaign was initiated by Col. J.C. Genders in 1925. Genders was no young firebrand; he was a 66-year-old businessman, freemason, head of the Justice's Association, and editor of his own newspaper, called *Daylight*. In 1924, he joined the Aborigines Friends Association. In 1925, Genders put the following resolution to a meeting of the General Committee:

> That a petition be presented to Federal Parliament praying for the creation of a separate state in Northern Australia to be called the Australian Black State, the Australian Zion State, or some other appropriate name, citizenship in which to be restricted to Australian natives ...[17]

The Committee politely deferred discussion of the matter. John Henry Sexton, the influential Secretary of this very conservative Association, later described the scheme as 'fantastic' and Genders as an 'impractical dreamer'. Genders resigned and set about promoting his idea. He set up a series of roundtable discussions to work out a manifesto and drum up support. By the end of 1926, the Aborigines Protection League was established: Herbert Basedow was elected President, Genders was Honorary Secretary, and the committee included the natural scientists

S.A. White and T.P. Bellchambers, members of the Women's Non-Party Association, including Constance Cooke, and the Aboriginal polymath, David Unaipon. By March of the following year, the League had published its manifesto and had begun circulating a petition which they planned to present to the Commonwealth parliament. The core element of their proposal was the establishment of a 'Native State' to ultimately be managed by a native tribunal. Except for 'authorized missionaries, teachers and agricultural instructors' no one was permitted to enter the State without the authority of the tribunal, but Aboriginal people were permitted to come and go as they pleased. They also requested that the state have representation in Federal Parliament, along New Zealand lines. The manifesto elaborated the details of the plan, explaining that this was to be a 'Model Aboriginal State' and if it was successful others 'would surely follow' and that 'the growth of a sense of nationhood would be a great incentive'.

In this conception, the Aboriginal State was imagined as developing toward an equivalent status to the existing States of the Commonwealth, enjoying its own constitution, with its citizens governing themselves in their own country. The precise location of the first State was not specified, but it was imagined to be an existing tribal territory somewhere in Arnhem Land. As the campaign progressed, its supporters endeavoured to clarify the details. Given that these 'States' were imagined as essentially the territories of existing tribal groups, it was proposed that Government Residents would be appointed, and federal resources be provided, to assist in the inevitable growth of the States toward the conditions of modern life. Furthermore, they thought that educated Aboriginal people like David Unaipon could be engaged to 'assist' in their founding. In consideration of Aboriginal people who had already been dispossessed of their land, it was suggested that they be granted land in southern Australia to develop their own States.[18] As utopian as this must have sounded at the time, there were two core principles that set the League's agenda apart; the demand that Aboriginal people be given their land, and that they be allowed to manage their own affairs. What we would call today, land rights and self-determination.

In the literature of the League, and the speeches given by its members, it is clear that their agenda was driven by a deep sense that Aboriginal people had been subject to an historical injustice that had to be corrected. In a statement for the League, Genders wrote that after 'one hundred and fifty years, elementary justice had not been done'. The leading plank of the League, he wrote was 'that the legal ownership of suitable land be transferred from the Crown to the Aborigines without power of alienation'. Aboriginal people, he added, were 'landless proletarians' whose hunting grounds had been over-run, and who 'wanted some of the land back which has been stolen'. He reminded his readers that early governors, like Governor Gawler in South Australia, 'had definite instructions' that 'land was not to be taken' from Aboriginal people 'without their consent'. This was a 'sacred trust' that had 'been greatly neglected'.[19] Although the petition, signed by 7,000 people, was tabled in federal parliament in October 1927, it was hardly debated. But the League persisted with its campaign.

In 1929, there was a meeting of societies and associations interested in Aboriginal welfare. Called by the Commonwealth Minister of Home Affairs, and held in Melbourne, it was an opportunity for Genders to put forward the following motion:

> That to the nomadic tribes who still have their tribal governments intact, land, taking the Aboriginal boundaries, be allotted in perpetuity, and that they be allowed to govern it as far as they are able with the assistance of teachers and others, and that no white person be allowed in the territory without a permit.[20]

Constance Cooke seconded the motion, but no one else supported it. For most of those in the room, it ran directly counter to the assimilation policies that were being developed at the time. The Minister commented, 'I think you are a little ahead of your time, Mr. Genders'. Genders himself later responded, 'with due respect to the Minister, I was 100 years late'.[21] For Genders, the recognition of land rights and the extension of self-government were not radical innovations; they were the belated recognition of what he called a 'time-honoured policy'.

Although the campaign for the Model Aboriginal State gradually petered out, the idea that the State should honour foundational promises continued to be a feature of the rhetoric of the era. Later that year, Basedow gave a talk in the Adelaide Town Hall in which he outlined his efforts to provide 'relief' for Aboriginal people in Central Australia who were suffering from a severe drought. To underscore the importance of these efforts he reminded his audience of the colony's first Proclamation in which the Governor 'promised justice to the blacks and bespoke for them the kindly consideration of the white invaders'.[22]

In 1929, a correspondent in the *Advertiser,* protesting the poor treatment of Aboriginal people, quoted extensively from the Proclamation, emphasising particularly the pledge to punish with 'exemplary severity' any acts of injustice against them. 'Is it not an irony', he went on,

> to speak of the rights of the natives being equal to those of the colonists, and can anyone point out how or where the privileges of British subjects have been allowed the blackfellow? It appears to me that the humane and generous intentions of Governor Hindmarsh have been studiously ignored, rather honored in the breach than the observance.[23]

The idea of the State's moral responsibility toward Aboriginal people also became a prominent sub-theme of preparations leading up to the State's centennial celebrations of 1936. Calls for ideas about how to commemorate the event led a number of citizens to suggest that it could be best accomplished 'by improving the condition of our aborigines'.[24] In November 1934, the anthropologist J.B. Cleland addressed the Royal Society and began by suggesting 'that South Australians could not mark the centenary of their State in a better way than by honouring some of their obligations to the Aborigines'. Speaking particularly of the people living in the remote north-west, he called for adequate funds to be made available for 'rescuing them as far as possible from the fate of extermination'. He, like Basedow before him, underscored his demands by pointing to Hindmarsh's proclamation which 'dealt with the rights and protection of the natives, and only one-third dealt with the affairs of the white inhabitants'.[25] Others picked up on this theme, one correspondent wrote of 'enforcing' the Proclamation of Governor Hindmarsh: 'our vaunted chivalry, our sense of British fair play, our Christian conscience, and love of justice, must be so aroused as to compel evasive politicians to face this problem'.[26]

The Women's Rights campaigner, Constance Cooke, took up the same challenge during the State's preparations for the centenary celebrations. A Women's Centenary Committee was formed to determine how they could best contribute to the event and Cooke participated as a representative of the Aborigines Protection League. As historian Marilyn Lake has argued, she lobbied not just for the recognition of Aboriginal women in the celebrations, but for the return of land. On behalf of the Aborigines Protection League she put forward a resolution:

> That a portion of the land that has been taken from the Aborigines should be allotted to them in perpetuity so that they may become self-supporting and enabled to work out their own destinies in their own communities.[27]

Such a 'return of land', she suggested, would be 'a small step towards redressing the "wrongs of a century"'. When her proposals were rejected she resigned from the Committee. Tellingly, the arguments put forward to recognise Aboriginal rights and to advance Aboriginal interests were not just underpinned by humanitarian concerns but by a deep sense of addressing historical obligations.

'Wrongfully deprived of their just dues'

The 1960s in South Australia were a time of genuinely radical reform in the area of Aboriginal policy, primarily under the stewardship of Don Dunstan. In 1965, the *Aboriginal and Historic Relics Preservation Act* was introduced with the intention of protecting Aboriginal heritage. In 1966, Dunstan introduced the *Prohibition of Discrimination Act*, which had the effect, among other things, of making illegal what had been socially enforced 'colour-bars' within the community. In 1967, further amendments were introduced to the *Aborigines Affairs Act*, which provided additional powers for Aboriginal people to administer their own reserves, because it was 'considered desirable that the Aboriginal people should be encouraged to run their own affairs'.[28] One of the most significant reforms of this era was the passage of the *Aboriginal Lands Trust Act* in 1966, which gave control of Aboriginal reserve lands to a board made up entirely of Aboriginal people. It is generally regarded as the 'first legislative acknowledgement of Indigenous rights to land in Australian history'.[29]

Significantly, when Dunstan introduced the Bill to parliament he reached back into history to give, if not legal authority, then at least, moral legitimacy to the changes he was proposing. This Bill, he said, was a significant step in the treatment of Aboriginal people not only in this

State but in Australia. 'The Aboriginal people of this country are the only comparable indigenous people who have been given no specific rights in their own land'. 'It is not surprising', he went on, 'that Aborigines everywhere in this country have been bitter that they have had their country taken from them, and been given no compensatory rights to land in any area'.[30]

Like Basedow, Genders, Cleland and Cooke before him, Dunstan made clear in his speech that the nature of the State's very foundational ideals gave South Australia a moral obligation to address this issue. In introducing the Bill, he said, 'I intend to trace the history of Aboriginal land rights in South Australia because on examination it is clear that Aborigines were wrongfully deprived of their just dues. We must as far as we can, right the wrongs done by our forefathers'. He then quoted in detail the passage from the Letters Patent with its reference to Aboriginal prior title to the land. He outlined the principles that were to guide the Commissioners in their negotiations for Aboriginal land, and he pointed out that it was the duty of the Protector 'not only to see that such bargains or treaties were faithfully executed ... but also ... to protect the natives in the undisturbed enjoyment of their lands of which they should not be disposed to make a voluntary transfer'.[31] He cited the instructions given to the Resident Commissioner regarding the proper process of negotiation, before noting that, with the exception of a few small areas, Aboriginal rights to land were not protected. The least that could now be done was to ensure that Aboriginal rights to the little land they had been granted were recognised in law and given over to their control.[32] 'These were matters', he concluded, that went to 'the moral stature of the Australian people as a whole'.[33]

Provisions in one section of the Bill made it clear that Dunstan's intentions went beyond making a moral gesture and encompassed an idea of compensation on the basis of historical entitlement. Historian and political scientist John Summers has argued that one of the most significant provisions of the Bill was a section that 'sought to grant to Aborigines pre-eminent mineral rights for the land held by the Trust, a right which does not go with ordinary title to land in South Australia'.[34] The founders of the colony, Dunstan claimed, had subverted the British Government's original intention so granting these rights to minerals 'would be some small compensation for the failure to provide Aboriginal people of South Australia with the land which ... they were to be provided with on the founding of the province'.[35] Dunstan evoked a similar argument when he introduced the *Pitjantjatjara Land Rights Bill* in 1978. It was 'an act of simple justice' to provide for 'the restitution of the comparatively little land remaining to its original owners' in light of the 'massive' land alienation that had occurred since first settlement.[36] In his memoir, Dunstan reflected on his battles to reform Aboriginal policy and to further the case for Aboriginal land rights, actions clearly informed by a consciousness of the State's foundational undertakings: 'The Letters Patent to the Governor at the time of the founding of the colony', he wrote, somewhat conflating the Letters Patent with the Proclamation, 'had required protection of the rights of the indigenous inhabitants'.[37]

Conclusion

In 2008, I again attended the Proclamation Day ceremony. In the intervening 12 months, the Kaurna Heritage Committee and the Holdfast Bay City Council had negotiated to develop an inclusive ceremony. An Aboriginal 'welcome to country' performance began the formalities, and the formal ceremony closed with two Kaurna elders rising to speak about the ongoing importance of reconciliation.

As Janna Thompson has so eloquently put it, we live in an 'intergenerational community' whose 'institutions and moral relationships persist over time and through a succession of generations', a society that 'depends for its moral and political integrity on its members accepting transgenerational obligations and honouring historical entitlements'.[38] The rhetoric of historical obligations toward Aboriginal people that evolved in South Australia, associated particularly with the state's founding Proclamation and Letters Patent, powerfully demonstrates the force of this intergenerational nexus. There is no small irony in the fact that South Australia's foundational story of its 'benevolent intentions' toward Aboriginal people was largely a myth, yet over time, the myth itself was employed to provide the moral legitimacy for genuine reform.

* This chapter is a significantly revised version of a paper first published as '"His Majesty's Most Gracious and Benevolent Intentions": South Australia's Foundation, the Idea of "Difference", and Aboriginal Rights', *Journal of Australian Colonial History*, vol. 15, 2013, pp. 105–20.

6

George Hamilton, the Bold and Dashing Bushman: The Politics of Colonial Compassion

JANE LYDON

In this essay I examine the life and work of a prominent South Australian colonist George Hamilton (1812–1883) over the course of his long career as overlander, police commissioner, horse fancier, and artist. Hamilton arrived in Adelaide during its earliest years, and his narratives, as well as his prolific art, constitute a fine-grained historical record – a 'foundational fiction' – that tells us much about the colonisation of South Australia. By the time of his death Hamilton was remembered as both 'a fine type of the bold and dashing bushman of the colony's early days', and 'no mean judge of a good painting'.[1] Hamilton's prolific art works and reminiscences mythologise the colony's origins and progress, and his own role within it, inflected by his concerns with class, race and masculinity. Here I explore these preoccupations and Hamilton's representations of frontier violence, which express his changing views about settlement and conflicts such as the Rufus River Massacre of 1841. As Hamilton's work shows us, emotional narratives and images are a powerful way of defining our relations with others, and especially effectual are those narratives that define whose lives are valuable and therefore worthy of compassion. Hamilton sought to elicit compassion for horses as 'sentient beings, with ends, preferences, and a capacity to suffer harm and experience well-being'. However Hamilton's compassion for Aboriginal people was conspicuously lacking. This paper examines why this was the case, and how Hamilton politicised and deployed emotions such as compassion in the process of narrating and mythologising the settlement of Adelaide.

Many scholars have explored the way that narratives, images and political discourse make some lives appear more distinctly human than others.² Philosopher Judith Butler reflects on the practices through which American audiences comprehend the human costs of war by differentiating 'the cries we can hear from those we cannot, the sights we can see from those we cannot'.³ The emotional narratives deployed by colonists were powerful means of creating 'affective communities', and constructing social relationships in imperial scope. So, for example, historians Jane Haggis and Margaret Allen have shown how Anglo-Indian missionary texts aimed to elicit the 'right feeling' and construct social relations amongst missionaries, bible women and converts – however unequal those relationships may have been.⁴ This process is also fundamental to modern global warfare, as Judith Butler argues in her analysis of war journalism. It can be seen at work wherever interests and rights compete: whether those of Aboriginal people, white men, or even horses.

Hamilton is well known for his concern for horses. In 1864, he published *The Horse: Its Treatment in Australia*, and in 1866 he published *An Appeal for the Horse*.⁵ Hamilton and the treatment of horses in Australia during the nineteenth century was the focus of an exhibition hosted by The National Museum of Australia, which is still accessible online.⁶ He was very good at drawing horses and the natural world – but less skilled in his depictions of human beings, perhaps an expression of his interest in these different subjects.

Hamilton sought to elicit compassion for horses as living beings with feelings, and the capacity to experience both pain and pleasure. One technique he used was to place them in familiar domestic human categories. They are 'faithful servants', companions, and frequently more dear than wives or children.⁷ He notes of the 'desert Arab' that he 'bestow[s] more affection on his horse than he does on the wife of his bosom, or the child of his loins' and 'is heard saying "Uncover his back, and satisfy thy gaze! Say not he is my horse, say it is my son; he is pure as gold"'.⁸

Hamilton's works critique his own society's devaluation of the horse, and intriguingly, he turns to a less 'civilised nation' for an exemplar of humane treatment, arguing that the British need to learn from the Arab 'of the desert' – carefully distinguished from degenerate urban Arabs.⁹ Primarily, the Arab's 'kindness to and his consideration for his horse is, in [his] opinion, a shining virtue of the very first quality' and a caution to Europe and Australia.¹⁰ Hamilton argued that we can learn from the less

Figure 1. George Hamilton, 'He is thoroughly broken in', from *The Horse: Its Treatment in Australia*, Adelaide: J.T. Shawyer, 1864. Courtesy of the National Museum of Australia.

Figure 2. George Hamilton, 'He descends to a jaunting car', from *The Horse: Its Treatment in Australia*, Adelaide: J.T. Shawyer, 1864. Courtesy of the National Museum of Australia.

'civilised nations' because British culture has 'neglected to recognise the claim the horse has upon our sympathies, and treating him as a machine, they have forgotten the higher attributes of his nature, and considered only his bone and muscle'.[11] While he seeks to persuade on the grounds of common sense, efficiency and financial advantage, he appeals to the moral virtue of kindness, hoping to 'live to rejoice over the triumph of kindness, and to witness the decline and fall of cruelty'.[12] At one level, Hamilton's critique is an attack on secular modernity and industrialisation itself, nostalgically turning to a vision of a pre-industrial harmony between human and animal.

Although Australian anti-cruelty laws were passed as early as 1837, more specific prohibitions against cruelty to animals were not introduced until the 1860s. Hamilton was therefore a trailblazer in making this argument, and his challenge to the boundary we have constructed between humans and animals anticipated considerable recent research that questions this divide. Contemporaries also acknowledged his position, one review noting of Hamilton's love for the horse that

> There be some who term the love of the brute creation a mere hobby; if so, it is a hobby which often bespeaks a nobler character than showy philanthropies, or spouting on the general reform of the universe. He who renders the life even of a horse more comfortable does good in the best sense of the term, and amid the many institutions which appear to need reform the stable is not by any means the least important.[13]

However, Hamilton's compassion for Aboriginal people was conspicuously lacking. Here I explore why this was, and how Hamilton politicised and deployed emotions such as compassion – but also anger and fear – in the process of narrating and mythologising the settlement of Adelaide. Between the 1830s and 1880s his experiences were transformed into a colonial triumphalism that celebrated pioneer achievement.

First, who was Hamilton? Hamilton's biographer J.H. Love tells us that Hamilton was born in March 1812 in England, and attended Harrow School between 1823 and 1826. He served in the navy as a midshipman.[14] He arrived in Sydney in 1836, as indicated by his dated drawings and narratives, and in 1847 helped to organise the first exhibition of South Australian artists' works at the Council Room, Adelaide.[15] Hamilton became a clerk in the South Australian Treasury in 1848, and inspector of mounted police in 1853. In 1867, he became commissioner, surviving public criticism and two parliamentary inquiries.[16]

Hamilton was an 'overlander', a colonist who participated in 'opening up' the land for colonial transport between Sydney, Melbourne and Adelaide during the late 1830s and early 1840s. The term 'overlander' itself implies a cartographic, colonial, perspective that sees history as a process of mapping territory and connecting settlements, erasing its impact upon the Indigenous occupants. In 1841, fellow overlander George Grey noted in his own published journals that the name was only coined after Adelaide had been reached in 1838, first by Joseph Hawdon from the Goulburn and followed shortly afterwards by Edward Eyre from Port Phillip, describing how

> The first step taken by the Overlanders was the connexion of Port Phillip with Sydney, and they thus, as it were, established a great base line from which their subsequent operations could be carried on ... In February 1838 Mr. [Joseph] Hawdon moved from the Goulburn and Mr. [Edward] Eyre from Port Phillip. In April 1838 Mr. Hawdon arrived in Adelaide and shortly afterwards was followed by Mr. Eyre. In the remaining portion of 1838 and in 1839 the energies of the Overlanders were fully employed in supplying South Australia with stock; and during this period several new and shorter lines of route were struck out, the last great improvement of this kind being made by the adventurous C. Bonney, Esquire, who connected Port Phillip with Adelaide by a direct road running nearly parallel to the coast.[17]

We have five distinct accounts by George Hamilton of overland journeys between Sydney and Melbourne, and between Melbourne and Adelaide, from 1836 to 1846, ranging from day-by-day journal entries, to factual transcriptions, to a fictionalised reminiscence.[18] Grey went on,

> The Overlanders are nearly all men in the prime of youth ... they have overcome difficulties of no ordinary kind, which have made the more timid and weak-hearted quail ... almost every Overlander you meet is a remarkable man.[19]

Hamilton was friends with Grey and Eyre, and closely followed behind Bonney in travelling from Port Phillip to Adelaide, setting forth in May

1839.[20] As his obituary stated, 'He first made his appearance in Adelaide in October 1, 1839, three years after the foundation of the colony, coming over with a mob of cattle from Port Phillip'.

But he had already seen a lot of the country before he got to Adelaide, having undertaken his first journey in early 1837, from Sydney to Melbourne, inspired by Mitchell's 'discovery' of 'Australia Felix' in 1836. In his journals, he wrote,

> Being young, ardent, and sanguine, I soon resolved to transport myself to this favoured land, the very name charmed me and in Australia Felix I fancied that the happiness I had sought for through life, was to be found ... there is not a more exciting employment than preparing for a journey; every article, as it is placed on the dray, seems to forebode some eventful crisis. The flour bags are bursting with hope, the matted and glazed bags of sugar speak of comfort, the beef tierce has its voice, the tea chest its whisper.[21]

He described the drunken departure of the expedition (Figure 3), the search for water, and the bliss of finding a pond in which all members of the party plunged, humans and animals (Figure 4) – wonderfully conveyed by his drawings. Several of these have a humorous air, perhaps enhanced by his lack of skill in rendering the human figure.

In this first account, Hamilton's encounters with Aboriginal people are shaped by stereotype, but are also relatively open to experience. Some of his accounts of Aboriginal people were distancing – for example, he was disparaging about Aboriginal women. However, there are descriptions of the harmony and peace of traditional Aboriginal life, such as an idyllic scene on a cold but beautiful day in which Aboriginal men gather 'muscles' by the banks of the river, and children play in the water. He writes,

> The black women kindled their fires and many columns of white smoke rose through the clustered trees, the black children were laughing, screaming and playing in the river little urchins who hardly knew how to use their legs on dry banks were splashing plunging and diving in the cold current.[22]

These idealising moments are complemented by descriptions of amicable encounters, with curiosity on both sides. Hamilton camped together with a party of Aboriginal people, and noted aspects of culture such as a drink made by dunking banksia cones in water to make honey, and a skirt they

Figure 3. George Hamilton, 'Starting on an expedition' [c. 1840], from the series *Journeys in New South Wales and South Australia from 1836 to 1845*. Courtesy of the National Library of Australia (PIC Drawer 632 #T1604 NK705/2/nla.obj-135139418).

Figure 4. George Hamilton, 'The postponed ablutin [i.e. ablution] in the wilderness' [c. 1840], from the series *Journeys in New South Wales and South Australia from 1836 to 1845*. Courtesy of the National Library of Australia (PIC T1607 NK705/5 LOC 635/ nla.obj-135140923).

had never seen before made of strips of kangaroo hide (see Figure 5). Although he set a double watch, he also talked to them and learned and wrote an 'irregular vocabulary'.[23] They 'sang their wild songs until the night was far advanced'.[24] This mutual curiosity and friendliness is expressed by Hamilton's drawings illustrating these encounters.

While there are hints of threat from Aboriginal people, Hamilton's narratives instead emphasise conflict among convicts. He described how three convicts took arms and ammunition and deserted in the night, only to be murdered by deserters from other expeditions.[25] Aboriginal people were easily managed by the Overlander's firm hand – and he ridiculed the convicts' constant and exaggerated fear of Aboriginal people. When Hamilton's overseer saw 'heaps of muscle shells' his horror was registered by a 'pallid face' and he exclaimed,

> By G – sir the blacks are here; let us turn back –
> Pooh! Pooh! I see no blacks, but only the fragments of their suppers or dinners, which they may have discussed months ago, besides have we not our trusty guns with us, and shall we fear a black fellows wooden spear, when we can send him a leaden shower beyond his spear's range?[26]

This is complemented by the Hamilton's humorous drawing – illustrating a moment where the party thought 'there are the natives at last!' but they were only emus.[27]

Representing frontier violence

Hamilton's 1837 account downplayed the menace of frontier violence, and his encounters expressed curiosity and relative friendliness. However by 1839, and especially during the 1840s, Hamilton's views of Indigenous people hardened and became more hostile. Hamilton's first overlander journey from Port Phillip to Adelaide commenced in May 1839, following the route established by Charles Bonney via the Grampians and parallel to the coast rather than along the Murray.[28]

He seemingly avoided conflict, although the threat of attack is ever present, and he later recounted a tense confrontation with two Aboriginal men, in which he drew and cocked his pistol, ready to fire. The moment passed, but he explained that

Figure 5. George Hamilton, 'Meeting natives on the Campaspi plains, Victoria, June 1836', from *Three Scenes around the Campaspi River and Plains, Victoria, 1836*. Courtesy of the National Library of Australia (PIC Volume 1186 #PIC/20001/2/nla.obj-321140428).

Figure 6. George Hamilton, 'Basaltic rocks at the Campaspie River near Port Phillip', from *Three Scenes around the Campaspi River and Plains, Victoria, 1836*. Courtesy of the National Library of Australia (PIC Volume 1186 #PIC/20001/3/nla.obj-321248810).

there was no bloodthirsty feeling actuating me in my conduct towards these fine specimens of savages. No person (not even the benevolent Exeter-hallers) could have felt more kindly towards these niggers than I did, but although they were 'men and brothers' and all that, yet I was not inclined to lose my cattle and become ruined because a 'man and a brother' insisted on a course of conduct which would seriously injure me. Let me confess, however, that although it was my intention to fire upon my black relations, it was with no desire to kill them. No 'most reverend and pious signiors of Exeter Hall', they would have been merely winged, shot through the leg or arm, or in some place not vital.[29]

Hamilton contrasted his willingness to harm, if not kill, Aboriginal people with what he saw as the hypocrisy of those 'pious persons' who cared more about 'ignorant pagan black monsters' than 'their white brethren who are, from poverty, neglect, and vicious teaching, fast falling into a savagedom far more frightful'. Like many at this time, he pitted the rights of Indigenous people against those of poor whites, whether in Britain or in the colonies. His shifting views express the broader pattern of worsening frontier violence across south-eastern Australia during the late 1830s and early 1840s. In NSW, following the notorious Myall Creek Massacre of June 1838 in north-western NSW, seven white men were hanged for the murder of 28 Wererai people, outraging white colonists and increasing racial tensions over subsequent decades.[30]

Closer to Adelaide, the Maraura people defended the Murray River route throughout 1840, especially around the Rufus River junction, and in August 1841 the 'Rufus River massacre' saw between 30 and 40 Aborigines killed and four taken prisoner (including two women and a boy). Amanda Nettelbeck, Rob Foster and Rick Hosking have traced the ways that the Rufus River conflict was represented in texts, first by contemporaries, and then thirty years later by historian John Wrathall Bull's *Early Experiences of Life in South Australia*, which became a template for later histories. They show that the event was seen in competing ways at the time, while by contrast Bull's later version had a simpler moral outcome and celebrated colonial success.[31]

In 1841, the Adelaide *Register* expressed moral uncertainty about the legitimacy of the massacre, and cautioned readers not to be led 'away by any harsh and unnecessary feelings of hostility to the Natives'. Officials also worked to counter its sensational and terrifying effects: a few months later, Edward Eyre was sent to the area with the view, if possible, 'of establishing a friendly intercourse with the Aborigines'.[32] He reported that the numbers of Aboriginal people were much reduced, and noted that 'At first the natives were very much alarmed, but by degrees overcame this fear', and near the Rufus he

> observed many women in deep mourning for their husbands, who had been shot in some of the conflicts with Europeans. Many children were pointed out to me as being fatherless from the same cause, and I have no doubt that the loss of life in these districts has been considerable from such affrays.[33]

Eyre's account humanised the fearful spectres of settler imagination, emphasising their shared humanity – and the losses suffered by Indigenous families. He sought to evoke sympathy for the Aboriginal victims of the clash. He recommended establishing a post managed by 'someone who had a knowledge of the manners and customs of the aborigines' to prevent 'those fearful scenes of retaliation and bloodshed which have heretofore so frequently occurred in the district'. Eyre was subsequently appointed Resident Magistrate and Protector of Aborigines on the Murray, and a police station was established at Moorunde.[34]

Hamilton's detailed and delicate drawings of conflict produced around 1846 sometimes showed conflict in relatively objective terms, such as his ink drawing 'Overlanders Attacking the Natives' (Figure 7). Even 'Natives Spearing the Overlanders' Cattle' (Figure 8), while showing Aboriginal people as aggressors, remains relatively neutral. Neither of these, produced soon after the Rufus River clash, shows Aboriginal people as aggressors against whites – although obviously they are provoking settlers by dispatching their cattle. Indeed, 'Overlanders Attacking the Natives' suggests an even-handed view of this exchange. However, perhaps we could also see Aboriginal people made the equivalent of the cattle in the first image. Just as the cattle are rendered abject and helpless under Aboriginal attack, so are the Aboriginal people shot down like animals.

However, during the 1840s, Hamilton began to produce less sympathetic images. A series of lithographs from the late 1840s have a nastier edge, losing their quality of realist observation and descending into caricature.

Figure 7. George Hamilton, 'Overlanders attacking the natives', 1846. Courtesy of the Mitchell Library, State Library of New South Wales (V/89).

Figure 8. George Hamilton, 'Natives spearing the Overlanders cattle', 1846. Courtesy of the Mitchell Library, State Library of New South Wales (V/88).

Figure 9. George Hamilton, 'The harmless natives' [lithograph], published by Penman and Galbraith, Adelaide, 1846–56.
Courtesy of the Mitchell Library, State Library of New South Wales.

Figure 10. George Hamilton, 'The persecuting white men' [lithograph], published by Penman and Galbraith, Adelaide, 1846–56.
Courtesy of the Mitchell Library, State Library of New South Wales.

These show Aboriginal people in stereotypical terms as aggressive and savage, attacking peaceful settlers, with ironic titles such as 'The Harmless Natives' (Figure 9), or 'The Persecuting White Men' (Figure 10). Here Hamilton directs our sympathy from black to white.

Perhaps Hamilton's direct experience during his three overlander trips between Melbourne and Adelaide from 1839–1846 prompted a change to a more hostile stance. This shift in tone aligned with broader social and political developments, as the humanitarian sentiment of the 1830s underwent profound challenge both in England and in the colonies during the 1840s and 1850s, pitting popular and political figures such as Thomas Carlyle and Charles Dickens against the (British) humanitarian lobby, sneeringly referred to as 'Exeter Hall'. In 1839, Hamilton lamented that

> The Chadbands of Exeter Hall, after having greased their wheels with ham and eggs and buttered toast, will set their sympathetic benevolent heads together and weep over the sorrows of the black brute, who, by-the-bye, has no sorrows except those he himself creates; and turn their backs upon their white brethren who are, from poverty, neglect, and vicious teaching, fast falling into a savagedom far more frightful, but not so sentimental, as the ignorant pagan black monster who creates so much sympathy in certain civilised societies.[35]

In this tirade, Hamilton is directly quoting the argument made by Charles Dickens in his 1853 novel *Bleak House* that evangelicals are hypocritical because their 'telescopic philanthropy' focuses on faraway blacks at the expense of those deserving and neglected closest to them.[36] In *Bleak House*, the smarmy Chadband preaches at the starving waif, Jo the crossing-sweep, instead of helping him, a caricature of hypocrisy and misdirected philanthropy. So here we see a colonist applying 'telescopic philanthropy' to the colonies, to argue for racial loyalty, and against what he suggested was misplaced sympathy for Indigenous people.

His 1845 journal stated 'tonight we have to be on the alert on account of the blacks in this neighbourhood having a propensity to spearing horses and my friends are loading their firearms'.[37] In a plea for sympathy for the white victims of black violence, Hamilton wrote,

> The aggregate number of murders committed by the natives of Australia since 1836 would astonish many persons in England who advocate the Black

man's cause. I cannot at present place before my readers the number of the bloody deeds during that time but they may conceive what it is likely to be when in some instances the crews and passengers of ships have been slaughtered wholesale when wrecked on the coast and I will venture to assert that there is not a tribe of blacks from Moreton Bay to Swan River but what is guilty of some wanton act of bloodshed on the unoffending white man.[38]

By the time Hamilton's fictionalised account was published in 1880 as *Experiences of a Colonist Forty Years Ago*, he had made some significant changes to the original texts, held in the National Library of Australia. In its exaggerations and additions, Hamilton's fictionalised 1880 reminiscences express a retrospective, idealising vision of relations between black and white, and between different social classes; they reflect significant shifts in race relations that had taken place during the intervening years. We can see this later account as a textual re-enactment, set in the past, yet coloured by more recent social changes that were facilitated and communicated through the camera's lens. Like all representation, his reminiscences are a narrative composed in reiteration – heightened by the intervening period of 40 years between event and book.[39]

Like all re-enactments, it is written in the past conditional: it asks, what if? What would they have done? Several scholars have suggested that this mode tends to authenticate popular settler fantasies of the past, and produce an understanding of colonial history as always already settled.[40] Hamilton's embroidery and newly-imagined events and situations after forty years amplify his views, for example regarding class difference. From the start Hamilton's fictionalised reminiscence of overlanding *Experiences of a Colonist Forty Years ago* is structured by the profound difference between the convicts (named 'Slushy', 'Long Bill', 'Little Jack', 'Snob' and 'Uriah', and the ugly overseer North), and the master – obviously representing Hamilton himself – whom he describes as

> a young man, barely twenty years of age, born and bred a gentleman. He had emigrated to Australia for the purpose of working his way in the world, and gaining for himself an independence. He was strong, active, and good tempered; of a mild disposition, but determined character.[41]

This class-consciousness echoes Grey's 1841 description of the overlander, noting that

> The Overlanders are generally descended from good families, have received a liberal education (Etonians and Oxonians are to be found amongst them) and even at their first start in the colonies were possessed of what is considered an independence. Their grandfathers and fathers have been men distinguished in the land and sea service of their country; and these worthy scions of the ancient stock, finding no outlet for their enterprise and love of adventure at home, have sought it in a distant land; amongst them therefore is to be found a degree of polish and frankness rarely to be looked for in such a mode of life, and in the distant desert you unexpectedly stumble on a finished gentleman.[42]

Unlike those travel writers and colonial observers who relished the supposed reversal of the old world social order in Australia, here Hamilton transposed it neatly on to colonial society.

Another effect of this hierarchical distinction is to displace fear of Aboriginal people on to the lower class convicts. The dramatic incident of spying the mussel shells remains, but it is expanded to signify the deep gulf between the convicts and the master. Instead of terming Aboriginal people 'blacks', when the overseer sees remains of fires and mussel shells, he responds, '"Good God, sir", he exclaimed, "here are the niggers"'. When the convict hears 'voices of the natives in the distance calling to each other' he jumps on his horse and gallops away, but the master calmly mounts his horse and joins the overseer at a walking pace.[43] It seems to me that Hamilton asserts his own masculinity by infantilising the convicts and the Aboriginal youths. He satirises the lower-class convicts' fears of the Aboriginal people, contrasted with his own equanimity and detachment: in short, he denies his own fear.

A further key shift in Hamilton's account is from his relatively objective account of the Aboriginal people he encountered to romanticising 'traditional' Aboriginal people. He adds a remarkable passage describing an encounter,

> When the blackfellows had entered the gully they stood eying the intruders on their domain with calm looks and a dignified demeanour – indeed, there

was an unmistakable dignity of bearing about these savages that asserted itself. Naked as they were, one did not detect their nudity; the stately walk required no sartorian help to add to its gracefulness. The erect head, the easy swing of the arms, the firm step, the entire freedom of the limbs gave to these savages a noble presence, which even the soupçon of the flavour of cannibalism could not injure. There they stood eyeing with composure our white friends, who, notwithstanding their dirty garments and civilisation, lacked the dignity of these sable lords of the wilderness.[44]

This view was grounded in an opposition between the noble savage doomed to disappear and inauthentic younger generations, expressed neatly in the frontispiece images produced for Eyre's two volume memoirs. But these relics of tradition are contrasted with the counterfeit younger generation as the basis for attacking Exeter Hall.

In sum, Hamilton's 1880s view of the colony's early days (and his own youth) express a view of a colonial history in which distinctions of race and class are naturalised, defining a hierarchical view of society that places the elite white man at its apex. Hamilton's 'past conditional' temporal framing produces an understanding of the history of Adelaide as always already settled. Anya Schwartz suggests such reenactments entail the narrative closure of troubled pasts in dangerous ways: they produce narratives in which the violence of the past shows up as 'a mere error', a 'lapse that needs to be redressed but does not upset the teleological narrative of history as progress'.[45] In re-imagining relations between Indigenous and settler, between the past and the present, these 'foundational fictions' may sometimes have the troubling effect of severing the past from the present.

By the end of the nineteenth century, the real terror and ambivalence of the 1840s was lost, displaced by the logic of progress and colonial achievement. This process perhaps reached its height in 1932, when the Rufus River Massacre was remembered as 'the historic fight which put an end for all time to the hostile attacks on parties travelling cattle overland from New South Wales by the Murray route'.[46] Hamilton's accounts of South Australia's colonisation were structured by the emotional logic of Hamilton's imperial cultural hierarchy, and his political deployment of compassion sought to define specific objects of empathy. However in this fraught colonial context pity for Indigenous people became limited indeed.

The anger and fear felt by white colonists was politicised and channelled into aggressive responses – that battled with 'Exeter Hall' attempts to arouse pity and promote humanitarianism. Where colonial triumphalism sought to forget or deny the past in reiterative narratives, images help us recover the emotional and moral uncertainties of these early years.

Acknowledgements

This lecture was given on the Country of the traditional owners of Adelaide, the Kaurna people, and I pay my respects to their Elders, past and present. I am grateful to Paul Sendziuk for his invitation to contribute to the 'Foundational Fictions' series, as well as to Robert Foster and Amanda Nettelbeck for their warm hospitality in Adelaide. I am also grateful to Julie Robinson, Maria Zagala and Tracey Lock for their generosity in showing me the George Hamilton work held by the Art Gallery of South Australia, which I hope to explore further.

7

Walking the Line in Historical Fiction

LUCY TRELOAR

Several times a year, when I was a child, my family drove the long inland route from Melbourne to Adelaide – the car stifling, the people somnolent, the dog panting. Each time we passed the inland margins of the Coorong my mother would look out of the window and say, 'That's where your ancestor, John Barton Hack and his family lived'. We would look out at the landscape of rolling saltbush and shimmering sky. 'Imagine', and she would piece out the fragmentary stories about this six-year period that have remained in our family for 160 years. Together, they make up no more than a small paragraph. Had I come across the words in an archive, I doubt they would have given me pause. What the words cannot convey is the tone and manner of her delivery, which seemed wondering, appalled and somehow incantatory, filled with some inherited emotion, as if the family was still wondering where it all went wrong. It seemed a place to be recalled but not returned to, a place that was escaped but remembered as something profound, as if the family had been sideswiped, hard. The stories were just the fragile shapes that held those strange feelings together, and that gave them occasional voice.

The past is impossibly distant in some ways, yet we are all aware of it and wonder about our connection to it. Philosopher Janna Thompson describes society as an 'intergenerational community' of institutions and moral relationships that persist through time and generations.[1] In the intergenerational community of my family, the Coorong still means something, though what I am not entirely sure. The truth of it lies somewhere in the raw feelings of our shared oral history. When I finally visited the Coorong and experienced its resonance and grand melancholy

I began to see why, and immediately started work on my historical fiction *Salt Creek*, building the novel around the things I had been told for so long and my wondering about the silences.² Where were the Ngarrindjeri? I was thinking also of the disjunction between the pride many South Australians, including my parents, feel in their free-settler heritage and the state's founding ideals, and the complicity of South Australian governments through their administration in the frontier massacres, dispossession and clearances of the Gulf Country of the Northern Territory from 1881. Historian Tony Roberts' 2009 *Monthly* essay, 'The Brutal Truth', which revealed that senior colonial politicians and South Australian police condoned or 'turned a blind eye' to frontier massacres in the Gulf Country of the Northern Territory, was a shocking revelation to me.³ Part of me had believed in the dream of South Australia. And there were the earlier massacres in South Australia itself, and the deaths, disease, starvation and theft of country that went with European 'settlement': all that darkness beneath the light. I was interested in that darkness.

I knew at once I would have to make changes to what was known in my fiction. Hack – a man ever hopeful and apparently untormented by his terrible luck and questionable judgement – was no one to build a story around; more problematically, he was revered in the family as a founding father of South Australia. I had to loose the book from him so I could write about someone more compelling – I had a domestic Captain Ahab in mind – and explore themes that I had a personal interest in without offending family sensibilities. I took many of the circumstances of Hack's life until his move to the Coorong and gave them to a man I named Stanton Finch, altering some events in his life for plausibility, to assist plot, and to create a character and a story that interested me and that I hoped would interest readers. To be clear, the changes were made in the service of a work of fiction, not of history, though the Ngarrindjeri, the history of the region (including notable figures such as the missionary George Taplin, and the murderer of Salt Creek, Malachi Martin), South Australia, and Hack's background were crucial to the development of character and plot.

Most people understand the importance of facts, evidence and 'the truth' in the study of history, but these things do not always make a good story. In this chapter I will explore how writers of historical fiction balance what is known against the demand for captivating characters and a compelling narrative arc. In so doing, I will be contributing to the 'conversation' that was sparked by historian Inga Clendinnen following her critique of Kate Grenville's 2005 award-winning historical novel, *The Secret River*. Set in the 19th century, Grenville's story is centred on William Thornhill, an Englishman transported to Australia for theft, and his efforts to settle and farm land already inhabited by Aboriginal people. Much of the criticism of Grenville's work, I will argue, was based on a fundamental misunderstanding of the different roles and processes of novelists and historians. Drawing on my experience writing my own historical novel *Salt Creek*, I hope to dispel some of the foundational fictions surrounding historical writing and show what historians, and students of history, can learn from novelists when it comes to understanding the past.

Invention sometimes feels truer than the truth, and it is often more important to the novelist for the felt truth to be represented than the actual truth. As novelist Jane Rawson says, 'the truth in a story has very little to do with the facts of it'. This is where real meaning lies in fiction, if not always in history. A simple example: one of my family stories tells of my great-great-great grandmother dying in childbirth while being rowed across the Coorong lagoon at dead of night. When I kayaked to the landing stage at Parnka Point and looked across the narrow lagoon to the mainland I could see that it would not do at all. It was too narrow for the epic and perilous journey that had haunted my imagination for so long. It was not a difficult decision to shift the location of their property to dramatise the journey – an enhancement of the literal truth. Another example, less significant to me, is my alteration of the shiploads of sheep Hack/Finch lost at sea, from the unlikely truth (two) to the plausible (one). A person who is unlucky is less interesting than a person whose personal flaws are his downfall. Fiction freed me in many such ways, to wonder and to invent and to explore.

There are no absolutes in historical fiction about the boundaries between fact and fiction, or about process and approach to material. A recent informal survey I conducted among members of the Australian Historical Novelists' Society revealed that for some writers too much research amounts to procrastination and can blur the writer's vision; for others it suggests ways forward, sparks ideas and is done concurrently with the writing. Writers as well as readers of historical fiction believe that too much historical detail bogs down action and distracts rather than informs the reader. As US novelist Anne Lamott says, this breaks the sense of the novel as 'a vivid and continuous ... dream' that the writer of fiction is aiming for.[4] Too little detail can have the same effect. It is as if the novel is a set on a low-budget TV show: slam the door too hard and the set begins to wobble, disturbing the illusion of reality. 'You must be able to justify your decisions to the well-informed', says English novelist Hilary Mantel. 'But you will not satisfy everyone. The historian will always wonder why you left certain things out, while the literary critic will wonder why you put them in'.[5] Yet historical truths about dates, events, culture and actual people were important to me. They made the time and place I was writing about feel real, and existing within that 'reality' helped the writing. As closely as I could, I removed the Hack family from the Coorong and inserted the Finch family, who shared the same background, and allowed events to unfold.

The apparently relaxed attitude that historical novelists have towards the facts is troubling for historians. Tonally, discussions of Australian novelist Kate Grenville's work by historians Inga Clendinnen, Mark McKenna and, later, Sarah Pinto have a quality of personal affront rather than criticism of the perceived encroachment of literature on the discipline of history that has been suggested by others.[6] This is not so different from my response to Clendinnen's 2006 *Quarterly Essay*, 'Who Owns the Past', in which she critiques Grenville's novel, *The Secret River*, as part of a wide-ranging discussion about the role of history and the differences between history and fiction. It had been somewhat amusing me until I came across a passage in which she depicted novel writing, and historical fiction in particular, as a frivolous and pointless enterprise. 'Novelists', she says, 'enjoy their space for invention because their only binding contract is with their readers, and that ultimately is not to instruct or to reform, but to delight'. She concurs with the contrarian novelist Henry James that historical novels are 'condemned ... to a fatal cheapness', as if the whole writing world had reached a consensus that James was the ultimate arbiter of matters of literary taste, style and substance.[7] Respectfully, I disagree. Why not say their purpose was to rivet, challenge, distress, provoke, shatter, enlighten or transport? The disciplines and desired outcomes of a novelist are not those of a historian. The binding contract for writers of literary fiction (a world that crosses genres and can include historical fiction) is with their artistic vision, with the expression of the truth as they see it with relation to their subject and with the creation of a compelling narrative. Whether readers are 'delighted' by the results is up to them.

In much of the criticism directed towards historical fiction and the fallacies that they are riddled with, there appears to be the presumption that non-fiction history, in contrast, is uncorrupted and incorruptible. In his discussion of 'the latest or "cosmopolitan" wave of frontier narratives', however, literary studies academic Chris Conti sees each phase as 'distinguished according to the ideological needs of the period regarding the need to explain, justify or critically reflect on the progress of settler culture since the First Fleet'.[8] The same could be said of histories, he notes. The 'legal fiction of *terra nullius* indicates [historical documents] are, often enough, vehicles of the national myth'.[9] Violence was 'inked out of frontier history' in the past and has been written back into it in fictional as well as non-fictional histories – in each, as Conti says, 'with an eye to the damaging legacy of colonialism on the present'.[10] Earlier histories of Australia that whitewashed the horrors of its colonial past are as guilty, if not guiltier on account of carrying the imprimatur of historical 'truth', of what Mark McKenna describes as 'posing as "a sweet alternative to the real thing"'.[11]

If historians have only a hazy conception of the fiction writing process, this may also be true of novelists. According to Clendinnen, 'making coherent stories out of the fragments we find lying about is a natural human inclination, and socially a necessary one, but when doing history it must be resisted'.[12] Fragments are of many kinds and come from many sources: oral tradition, histories, personal observation, interviews and so on. But a writer's choice of fragments is not arbitrary. In fact, it more closely resembles recognition than selection. 'I know it when I see it', one writer told me. Here, I think of broken crockery, a runaway girl and a greyhound called Skipper – examples of the fragments that emerged from a vast mass of material and appeared in my book. Such fragments are the answer to a question or fill the place that the unconscious creative self recognises. The writer might not understand the connection to the novel's scheme for some time, even until post-publication. To historians, a discipline in which the verifiable is privileged, this might seem strange. Yet connection to the fiction for writer and reader is key to the effectiveness of any novel, and increasingly for historians and their readers too, despite the fundamental differences in the two forms of writing.

Clendinnen also notes that 'in the novelist's "past" everyone behaves delightfully "in character", and everyone submits to the plot'. She concludes: 'The novelist might surprise her readers. She will never surprise herself'.[13] If only this were so. Many writers are in fact confounded, surprised and distressed by their characters' thoughts, actions and choices. While writers use a range of approaches when developing character and plot, the deeply rational and structured novelist of Clendinnen's imagination is a rare being. Characters drive plot as often as the reverse. Some novelists believe the ability to imaginatively enter unknown worlds through research and to empathise can help give insights into characters and historical events. For Australian novelist David Malouf (and for Kate Grenville some time later),

> Our only way of grasping our history – and by history I really mean what has happened to us, and what determines what we are now and where we are now – the only way of really coming to terms with that is by people entering into it in their imagination, not by the world of facts, but by being there.[14]

Crucially, he concludes, 'and the only thing really which puts you there in that kind of way is fiction ... It's when you have actually been there and become a character again in that world'.[15] Historians, like Clendinnen, disagree. Of Grenville's approach to characterisation in *The Secret River*, for example, Clendinnen says: 'So here we have it: Grenville's secret method for penetrating British minds ... is Applied Empathy'.[16] Malouf is the target of even greater sarcasm: 'Some engaged reading, some preliminary flexing of the imagination, a run, a vault, and presto! you are there'.[17]

In other critiques of Grenville's novel, the exploration of what Conti describes as the Thornhills' 'uncommon sensitivity to the significance of their encounters with local Aboriginals' is seen by literary studies academic Sue Kossew as a problematic 'double perspective'.[18] How, Kossew asks, could William Thornhill, 'bound in his own historical time-frame' yet be 'sensitive to many of the repercussions of his actions?'[19] Thornhill, I would argue, could see the effects before him without need to wait for the long arc of repercussions. Acting as some people then did while also being 'sensitive' to, or aware of at least some of their consequences, was possible. I am not sure that inhabitants of the not so distant past are always as inscrutable as Clendinnen suggests. People were as adept at compartmentalising in the past as they are today. It is worth noting, for example, that the first written record of the phrase 'out of sight, out of mind' dates back to the 1500s.

In my thinking about the world of *Salt Creek*, I was curious about people's awareness of the consequences of their actions, in particular the thinking of a person with Hack's background. Hack's maternal grandfather, John Barton, was one of the Quaker founders of the movement to abolish slavery in England. He was one of those who recruited English politician William Wilberforce to their cause, a move that led to its ultimate success. Hack arrived in Australia in the immediate aftermath of the abolition of slavery and had been raised in a politically aware family in an England that was experiencing social upheaval around this issue. What might he have been thinking, I wondered, as he watched the treatment of Aboriginal people? There is scant evidence. Hack's diaries contain few references. He employed Aboriginal people as shepherds on his properties, apparently paid them above the normal wage, and was regarded as a generous employer.[20] A comment and a proposal Hack delivered to a Legislative Council committee on the 'plight of the natives' leave his thoughts and feelings open to interpretation. He told the enquiry that 'No European could ever do them any material good'.[21] He also notes: 'Every tribe that I have had any opportunities of observing, have gradually gone on diminishing, and the children have decreased'. He does not explicitly lay responsibility for this with the Europeans, yet the reason for his support of the 'Kangaroo Island solution' – that Aboriginals be rounded up and removed to Kangaroo Island – is open to interpretation. Might this be a response to personal shame and recognition of guilt, of not wanting to be reminded of the terrible damage he, on the Coorong, and other Europeans elsewhere had caused? Or was it, as is more commonly suggested, a desire for the nuisance of them simply to be removed? Given his comparatively generous treatment of them on his property and his admiration of them as workers, shame or guilt seem the more likely explanation.

There is some similarity between Hack's comment on the plight of the Aboriginal people following European settlement and a passage in Charles Darwin's *Voyage of the Beagle*, a further contemporary example of compartmentalisation: 'The number of aborigines is rapidly decreasing ... Wherever the European has trod, death seems to pursue the aboriginal'.[22]

Here, Darwin is referring to First Nations people generally. His doleful tone is a personal acknowledgement that there was a downside to Empire but later are lines of grandiloquence and patriotic fervour:

> It is impossible for any Englishman to behold these distant colonies without a high pride and satisfaction. To hoist the British flag, seems to draw with it as a certain consequence, wealth, prosperity and civilization.[23]

The shift from the distancing 'Europeans' in the first statement (Everyone's to blame) to 'Englishman' (We're so great) in the second is telling. I see no sign – if we can extrapolate from the remarks of Darwin and Hack – that an ability to hold apparently contradictory positions, and to be aware of the actual and anticipated repercussions of actions did not exist in the colonial period. We can, I believe, see some way into the thinking of the time and ponder what people might also have been feeling. I would not call this 'Applied Empathy', but a close reading of text.

There is a difference for many, perhaps most of us, between what we feel and think and what we do and say. Colonisation is ongoing despite people's awareness of its devastating impacts on Aboriginals and a widespread belief that we are more 'civilised' now. Commercial interests still override the claims of traditional ownership in Australia, as in the not-so-distant case of Hindmarsh Island, and the more recent one of the Butterfly Caves in New South Wales. I imagine that stakeholders justify their actions through ideas such as the greater good, inevitability of outcome, the thought that the actions of someone else might be worse, personal or corporate financial necessity, duty to shareholders, and so on. 'The past is a foreign country. They do things differently there', noted British writer L.P. Hartley in his 1953 novel, *The Go-Between*, but in some ways and in some cases perhaps the ways 'they' thought and the things they felt were not so different. Where self-interest is involved people will do things that they know to be wrong.[24] Why do they do this, and how do they live with themselves? It's a theme of enduring interest to me.

Overall, Clendinnen's reaction to historical fiction is at the very least intemperate, and, I believe, misinformed. As with many other critics of the interviews that Grenville gave around the publication of *The Secret River*, and which continued for so long, Clendinnen's writing somewhat resembles that of a novelist who has discovered the antagonist that will help propel her work. Her material leaps to life, the words almost fly off the page. Her indignation-fuelled thoughts are racing and objectivity recedes. What matters to her about this subject, and the content itself, becomes clearer and more engaging.

To judge an historical novel primarily as an historical project that aims (and fails) to tell a coherent or accurate history, as Clendinnen, Mark McKenna and John Hirst have done, or as an opportunity to do some political work as Sarah Pinto does (see below) is to misunderstand its aims and achievements. Sarah Pinto's focus on 'the workings of emotion within historical representation, and particularly on the historical and political work these emotions have the potential to perform' is thought provoking.[25] But I am troubled by the suggestion that the political work a book can do should be taken into consideration in an author's framing and writing of a fiction as a matter of course. Writers' aims vary: some might be interested in making a particular social, political or environmental point; others will approach their work with a view to exploring character, and any political or historical 'work' will be secondary to that. The central melancholy that Pinto identifies in *The Secret River* is not in my view the flaw or authorial failing that she perceives. It is an expression of the character of William Thornhill, human nature, and perhaps also the stage that public recognition of Australia's colonial past had reached at the time of writing: self-absorbed (or 'narcissistic', as Pinto says) recognition of the horrors of Australia's past. 'As a novelist you must be true to psychology, not ideology', says novelist Michelle de Kretser, as Grenville is, I believe, with Thornhill.[26] In *That Deadman Dance*, fellow Australian novelist Kim Scott is interested in the things that connect Australians now as they did at times in the past, not only the ways colonisation went wrong.[27] However, indigenous academic and writer Larissa Berendht, like Pinto, is impatient with hand-wringing historical fictions: 'We know you did wrong. We've been telling you for hundreds of years. We know you're sorry. Now what? It's time to move on'.[28] I understand the exasperation, and can only say that a novelist is not being wilfully slow to keep up with the times. They are doing what they can, writing where the energy is. They can't 'just move on' until they're ready. For example, I might have liked life to run smoothly for English Addie and Ngarrindjeri Tull in *Salt Creek*, to make a point about what should have been possible. But it would have struck a false note, misrepresenting attitudes and likelihoods. Had I written about the next generation, I might have explored how social, cultural and racial barriers began to break down, including in terms of relationships between European women and Aboriginal men. As evidence for that I have the story of one of Hack's granddaughters who in the 1870s married an Aboriginal man and went to live in the Adelaide Hills, and of another grandson who married a Ngarrindjeri woman. A similar story appears in Australian novelist Shirley Barrett's fine work *Rush Oh!* set on a whaling station in Eden, NSW, in the early 1900s.[29] Quietly, one of the young women in the novel runs away with her Aboriginal lover to Sydney, where they have several children. It is gently and plainly done, a way forward, but in the service of story and character, not politics or ideology.

If the historical novelist is not there to tell history or to make a political point, what is their purpose? 'Their job', says English writer Hilary Mantel, is 'to put the reader in the moment, even if the moment is 500 years ago', and 'to take the past out of the archive and relocate it in a body'.[30] This, historian Jeremy de Groot says, 'allows readers to pitch themself [sic] into a different moment, to think outside themselves'.[31] But such writing is also an expression of the time in which it is written. As Mantel says, 'Historical fictions of all kinds allow us to think about ourselves now. Accuracy is not the point'.[32]

Early examples of South Australian pioneer fiction dwell on the supposed ruthlessness and barbarity of Indigenous people. They are full of fabrications, untruths, and misrepresentations. That is, they are typical of historical fiction in their willingness to manipulate material to satisfy an audience. In these fictions Indigenous people are savage, murderous and attack unprovoked, and the retributive actions of the 'pioneers' are depicted as reasonable. It is almost as if they are absolving themselves of guilt – speaking to South Australia's foundation documents and their promise of a more enlightened approach to Aboriginal people. As the Letters Patent establishing the Province of South Australia (19 February 1836) stated: 'Provided Always that nothing in those our Letters Patent contained shall affect or be construed to affect the rights of any Aboriginal Natives ... to the actual occupation or enjoyment ... of any Lands therein now actually occupied or enjoyed by such Natives'.[33] The separation between these fictions and South Australia's foundation documents is absolute. In the 1854 novel, *Clara Morison*, by South Australian author, teacher, journalist and leading suffragette Catherine Helen Spence, Aboriginal people are hardly mentioned, except as useful employees in rural areas: See this passage, for example: '"In the Tatiara country," said Reginald, "they are very serviceable ... they camp out with [the flocks] all night, and never need to put up the hurdles".'[34]

By the 1880s there has been a shift, according to University of Adelaide historians Amanda Nettelbeck and Robert Foster. Fiction, having thrown a blanket over past horrors now draws back the cover and cautiously begins to peek beneath. For example, in Ellen Liston's 1882 short story 'Doctor', published in the *Observer* of 17 June 1882, which explores the spearing of Annie Easton in 1849, the narrator reaches back 30 years to reflect on 'the culture of settler violence' and the echo of disquiet that lingers.[35] The admissions of the scale of violence and the unease and language used are fascinating. Simpson Newland's 1893 novel *Paving the Way* presents another example.[36]

Newland, a pastoralist, author and politician, depicts frontier life in South Australia as a boy's own adventure, with chapter titles such as 'Bail up!' and 'A Deed of Derring-Do'. *Paving the Way* is divided into two distinct voices: an engaging narrative voice characterised by action and dialogue, and a reflective non-fiction voice in which Newland considers the causes of misunderstandings between Aboriginals and settlers – laying some cautious blame on the latter – in a desire to face unpalatable truths. Here, the writing is choppy and riddled with caveats; he is clearly worried about how his comments will be received. 'Enterprising young men, taking their lives in their hands, drove their flocks before them', he writes, 'no one really understood that the natives were divided into many hostile tribes ... It is not to be wondered at if, under these circumstances, deeds were committed at which humanity shudders'.[37] Nonetheless, it marks the shift in attitude towards Aboriginal people that was then beginning, and which he articulates more clearly in his 1900 novel, *Blood Tracks of the Bush*.[38] His anxiety about how this material will be received is evident. As a member of parliament (1881–1886) during the great pastoral boom of the top half of the Northern Territory, which was then administered by the South Australian government, and as a visitor to the region during that period, he knew well of the massacres taking place through the Gulf region, and of the complete dispossession of Aboriginal land.[39] His retirement from parliament at the height of the horror in 1886, ostensibly because of the strain of his duties on his health, to me suggests, rather, shame at any further complicity with the government sanctioned horror. He was 51 and sufficiently healthy to live another 38 years.

A close reading of the text from a novelist's perspective, with an awareness of writing 'craft' and grammatical convention, reveals other possibilities, as for example in the chapter 'Civilising the Blacks', which depicts a battle between Aboriginal people and armed soldiers. Simpson Newland is not a sophisticated writer, but he is an accurate one in terms of language features and novelistic conventions. He consistently writes in the past tense, except at a key moment in the battle scene depicted, when mid-sentence he shifts to the present tense:

> Had he rushed to close quarters, the charge might have been fatal to the white men but the Australian blacks rarely close in hand-to-hand combat. Still they pressed [past tense] closer and yet closer, the white men *now receiving* [shift to present tense] many wounds. The inspector again *shouts* 'Fire,' and more black forms *are stretched* on the grass, but the old chief still wildly *encourages* his followers and *advances*. A dozen barrels *are levelled* at him and at length *he sinks* to the ground, hurling his last shaft at the foe as *he falls*. The loss of their leader was [return to past tense] decisive and the savage warriors melted away ... [40] (my italics)

The writing in this paragraph lapses into and mimics the oral storytelling mode, which is typically in present tense. An historian, accustomed to the shifts of gears in point of view and tense that are permissible in histories might not notice this, or might think it nothing more than a grammatical error that suggests Newland is just not a very good writer. It is true that he is not a good writer, but his grammar is generally accurate. For a novelist, these wavering tenses are a significant and revealing error. Shifts in tense in a novel, if used, are signposted by a scene break or a change in point of view or through being embedded in dialogue. Here, they represent the author's loss of control of his material. It is as if he is bearing witness to a friend, caught up in the recounting. The writing is not the constructed excitement of fiction, but reveals Newland himself, unconscious, swept up in the story, reliving the horror and perhaps also the excitement of the moment. A better novelist would note this, see what it revealed, and restore his writer's mask by correcting the tense. An historian and an historical novelist see different things in material. If I were an historian, I might search other texts to see what grammatical subtext could reveal. As a novelist I could take that small insight and use it to build a character, perhaps one who shared some of Newland's characteristics.

More recently, Kate Grenville's *The Secret River* rose from a political setting that sought to recognise and apologise for the wrongs of the colonial past. *Salt Creek* was developed in a context that included a heightened awareness of cultural appropriation, the environmental effects of European farming practices on the Australian landscape, a growing awareness of climate degradation and climate change more generally, and new studies that explored the sensitive and sustainable agricultural techniques that Aboriginal people used to such effect. It is, then, partly informed by contemporary concerns. Jane Rawson, a writer interested in climate change and dystopian fiction and prepared to blur genre boundaries, takes historical fiction in a radical direction in her 2017 novel *From the Wreck*, which combines literary, historical and speculative features. It begins with the story of her ancestor George Hills, one of only eight survivors of the wreck of the *Admella* off the South Australian coast in 1859, and then swoops into a speculative world. Rawson's subject, using the medium of historical fiction, is existential loneliness and the beauty and fragility of our planet. *From the Wreck* shows the capacity of historical fiction to contain truths of the period being written from, the period being written, and even those of a projected future.[41]

Historical fictions have a social effect, even if this is not a writer's purpose. They illuminate the past and its connection to the present. Their success at achieving this is related to their mode of delivery: the fact that they are stories. But what does a story provide that traditional non-fiction does not? Writer and historian Cody Delistraty says stories are helpful to our rational selves, allowing us to feel that we 'have control over the world' or helping us to make sense of it. They 'allow people to see patterns where there is chaos', and help us to relate to each other as well as to the world. He cites a 2013 study in which psychology researcher Dan Johnson found that reading fiction also significantly increased empathy, including empathetic behaviour, towards others, particularly those with perceived 'outsider' status ('foreigners, people of a different race, skin color, or religion').[42] Delistraty argues that reading literary fiction, in comparison to non-fiction or commercial fiction, has a unique ability to engage 'the psychological processes needed to gain access to characters' subjective experiences'.[43] This does not mean that historical fiction is better at telling history than historical non-fiction, but it does suggest that it is better at engaging readers' attention and feelings than non-fiction. This is partly the result of the conventions and constraints of the writing forms, as observed above. A novelist does not intend to lead readers astray, but their first loyalty will be to their creative work. It is what the discipline of fiction requires. Strict accuracy might be secondary, and the writer will feel free to make imaginative leaps in the absence of information. Readers understand this about fiction; it is part of the unwritten contract between writer and reader. Historians might have greater trust in readers; they are not fools waiting to be duped by historical novelists. The reader can and does tease out the threads connecting and separating fact and fiction in other contexts such as author interviews, writers' festivals, via endnotes, and social media. They question writers and make judgements, sometimes uncomfortable ones for the writer. There *is* a degree of transparency, but it occurs outside the text rather than within it.

The rise of 'narrative non-fiction' – writing that uses a range of literary styles and techniques, including a story arc, to create factually accurate narratives – appears to be partly the result of the recognition of the techniques novelists use to engage readers. Its increasing prevalence in non-fiction history is fascinating. The great US short story writer Flannery O'Connor once said: 'Fiction begins where human knowledge begins – with the senses – and every fiction writer is bound by this fundamental aspect of his medium'.[44] Hilary Mantel agrees. 'Your real job, as a novelist', she says, 'is not to be an inferior sort of historian, but to recreate the texture of the lived experience: to activate the senses, and deepen the reader's engagement through feeling'.[45] Interestingly, the senses are often mentioned in reader reviews (e.g. 'I felt the wind on my cheek'). Many historians appear to have comprehended the value of 'being there' in the place they are writing about, both as a means of creating immediacy and connection, and to acknowledge their presence in shaping the work. Historians who formerly focused on documenting, summarising and interpreting the past are increasingly willing to evoke it to better communicate their subject and their process. Much historical non-fiction has become richer, more approachable and its subject matter more thought provoking and memorable as a result. Freeing the idea of story from fiction (as Malouf does not) has enabled historians to frame their work within a narrative, and thereby expand the reach and accessibility of their work. That is, histories have become better tools of communication. A brief consideration of three historical non-fiction texts written over recent years suggests increasing recognition of that fact.

The first of these, Clendinnen's *Dancing with Strangers*, claims objectivity. 'The historian's situation is complicated', she says, 'because we have to look through other people's masks if we are to see anything of the world we want to fathom: that is, we have to read their words instead of using our own eyes'.[46] Throughout the text, unacknowledged and unrecognised, though felt, are the author's feelings, not only her thoughts. What we actually get is her view of 'their words'. Her summary of the documents related to the first months of the colony suggests a boys' own adventure rather than an invasion force. Of one young soldier she says, 'he took himself off on an adventure ... Part exploration, part jaunt, and altogether a glorious day'.[47] When she writes, 'Letters are another beguilingly informal source', she means that *she* is beguiled; she cannot conceal her empathy: 'His love for his distant sibling is as palpable as his loneliness'.[48] And there is a sort of collective hagiography: 'These were impressive men ... [with] competence over a wide range of scientific and artistic endeavours ... nearly all of them wrote: fine flowing sentences ... effortlessly expressed'.[49] Even the less educated are said to be 'in love with words and their protean possibilities'.[50] It is a puzzling account despite its engaging emotion and voice. On reading Clendinnen's *Quarterly Essay*, I began to understand why. Clendinnen's recollection of attending a Dawn Service with her father has the wondering tone, sensory detail and emotional resonance of a formative memory that it seems to me is key to understanding the way she views the world. Clendinnen's 'sound of a lone bugle', takes us to the soldiers she stood alongside, her father included. And there is the description of one of her 'few relics': her father's business card with a handwritten reading he was to give at the Dawn Service on the reverse. 'My throat still tightens as I read those words ... that strange blend of emotions – pride, grief, anger', she writes.[51]

For a writer, there is no complete concealment of self behind our words. We are everywhere in our choice of subject, our tone, and in the details and characters and people we choose to dwell on. As Hester Finch, *Salt Creek*'s narrator remarks of a childhood story: 'Of course, to recall some things is to consign others to obscurity'.[52] The *Quarterly Essay* passage is in some ways a declaration of Clendinnen's personal bias – even if she is not aware of it. In *Dancing with Strangers*, it is as if she cannot help but see in the British soldiers of the late 1700s the retired servicemen of the late 1930s, and to express through her lyrical language her affection and empathy. These feelings, I believe, have a direct bearing on her conclusion about the outcomes of the British invasion: 'Tragic it certainly was. But it could so easily have been worse'.[53] It is a curious statement in light of the many horrors to come. Could she be as guilty of 'Applied Empathy' as Grenville? An acknowledgement of her feelings would have been more honest. Still, her empathy provides a way into this material for the reader.

By contrast, in *From the Edge* Mark McKenna immediately locates himself in the text in time and place: 'The view through the departure lounge windows at Sydney Airport looks across the docking bays to runways in the near distance. The flat expanse of the tarmac shimmers in the heat …'[54] He is there, and in a story sense he is acting as a first person narrator in a fiction; he is the reader's eye, the reader's way into this world. There is instant engagement. McKenna goes on to set contrasting scenes of the present (asphalt, runways, dammed water, drained wetlands) and the past: the bay 'illuminated by the "moving lights" of the tiny cooking fires burning on flat stones in the bellies of the Gweagal women's bark canoes'. It is a vivid and compelling device. There is the detailed envisioning of Banks, looking at the shore from the *Endeavour*: 'Banks lifted his telescope to observe the country and its people at closer quarters …' At this I felt my eye involuntarily narrowing. Then, Banks 'spied a group of Gweagal men gathered "on the rocks opposite the ship, threatening and menacing with their pikes and swords"'. It is gripping stuff. But it is partly so gripping because McKenna has stepped through the frame of the text and taken the reader with him. This novelistic device holds the reader's attention, creates emotional engagement, and makes the material more memorable. Imagine with me, Mark McKenna is saying, narrow your eyes and look, and we do.

The point of view McKenna has adopted then shifts. McKenna's and

Banks' points of view blur: 'As Banks looked through his telescope at Botany Bay, the faces and bodies of Aboriginal men and women filled the frame, like museum exhibits in a glass case'. McKenna is imagining that Banks might have seen the Aboriginal people like museum exhibits; he does not know this. It is McKenna's metaphor, not Banks'. McKenna, the first person narrator, then entirely disappears. The voice becomes distant and passive: 'The country was scanned and quickly assessed'. Instantly, the reader is looking in once again from the outside.

Nonetheless, the personal element in this book here and elsewhere does have the effect experienced in fiction, of drawing the reader into the physicality of scene and an imagining of characters' actions, even if it is inconsistent in its application. The reader quickly learns what the rules are for this book (as a reader also does for historical fiction) and is able to shift from first person observation to the historian summarising and interpreting information, and even the occasional choral voice (the first person plural seldom used in fiction): '*Our* colonial perspective is just beginning to recede. *We* have only recently discovered ...'[55] In a novel, the instability of tense and point of view would create confusion, breaking the immersive experience, and the thinly drawn characters would invite brisk notes from editors. But to ascribe what would be serious mistakes in fiction to history makes as little sense as an historian criticising a novelist for their relaxed attitude to the facts. Historians are not claiming to write novels.

The promotional interviews (which form the meta-fiction that surrounds the 'birth' of many books) done by McKenna in the lead-up to publication of *From the Edge* suggested a collection of ripping yarns. The book, in my view, did not deliver that. The chapter 'Walking the Edge: South-East Australia', in particular, to a writer and reader of fiction, felt like a missed opportunity for a thrilling novel in which events are compressed or stretched, episodes are delineated to create tension and engagement, and great voids in the archive are filled with the work of an imagination.[56] This, of course, would be an entirely different kind of work, not a history, but perhaps something with a climax more engaging than 'Clark's moment of salvation had finally arrived'.[57] This is not a criticism of McKenna's approach generally, but an exploration of the reaction of a reader more accustomed to fiction. I imagine that historians are sometimes similarly irritated by the intrusions of the personal and narrative when it is an argument or a subject that is more important.

The final example is Rebe Taylor's essay on the Wedge Collection, which offers another way forward.[58] In a sense it is a development of McKenna's approach. Taylor locates herself as the first person narrator from the opening of her investigation in which she visits the Saffron Walden Museum to view their collection of wooden Indigenous artefacts, collected by John Helder Wedge in Victoria and Tasmania in the 1830s. The reader has immediate access to her personal responses to the artefacts, and to the questions she is seeking answers to: 'As I looked at it [the Wedge Collection] that day I wondered: why is it so little known? Why is it in a little museum in Essex? What is its story?'[59] Taylor frames her search for answers as 'a detective-story account'.[60] This explicitly articulates the structure of the piece, advising the reader of the presence of plot, creating expectation and connection, and establishing narrative drive. It makes the material accessible and keeps the reader turning the page. Taylor chose this framing device 'because it felt honest ... I wanted the reader to get a sense of this kind of starting place'.[61] 'As a historian, walking on Indigenous people's Country, and telling their history, you have to show your presence and involvement – not be omnipresent'. Acknowledging opinions and feelings is important, she says, so 'readers can see the motivation or drive that accompanies the need to tell a story out of the archives, and shape its direction'.[62]

Taylor's emotional connection to her material, and particularly to the plight of the Aboriginal boy known as Wheete Coolera, who Wedge abducted, is felt throughout, no more so than when she tries to imagine his feelings on dying among strangers, or the passage in which she visits the site of his abduction. Her detective story uncovers a great deal about Wedge and communicates it to readers. It also reveals to the author and reader the personal motivation that drove her, albeit unwittingly: 'I took a moment to look out across the surf. I knew why I had come: to try to bear witness to the scene of Wedge's crime; because it felt important to remember. 'I am sorry!' I shouted into the wind ... I turned away, and almost ran back to the warm car, exhausted'.[63] This is the climax of the piece. It is an emotionally and intellectually satisfying essay, which communicates information in a memorable and engaging way through the first person narrative perspective, sensory detail, and the interwoven stories of Taylor's detective work and her subject. The personal in no way detracts from the historical story, but enhances it. Its strength, Taylor says, is that it reveals the architecture of 'HOW history is made'.[64] History cannot always be exciting, and not every subject lends itself to such a narrative arc or the presence of the author. I think it is possible, though, to see other places where this approach works and might work again.

Historical fiction has the further useful effect from an historical perspective of perhaps reviving and certainly validating the importance of the oral tradition among some readers. I am sometimes approached by women (invariably women – the keepers of oral tradition?) after talks. They are self-effacing, not confident of the value or interest of their stories, but emboldened at hearing the scant fragments I used to build a novel to offer their own. These stories are enthralling, and I tell the women so. 'Write them down so they don't get lost,' I say. I feel my inadequacy. The ones they most like to recount – possibly because it is in the context of talking about *Salt Creek* – relate to contact with Indigenous women. They suggest communication that is not dramatic or characterised by tension or conflict, but about connection.

For instance, Aboriginal women were the midwives of choice in at least one part of northern Victoria. In the Wimmera, Aboriginal women took a European woman in to protect her from her violent alcoholic husband, and tend her wounds if they were too late to save her. In South Australia a farming family looked forward to the seasonal arrival of Aboriginal people on their farm and took them fruit pies in welcome, and kept their camping ground in its original condition. In Strathalbyn, an Aboriginal woman told me of growing up on a horse stud with the owners' children 'just like we were brothers and sisters'. Her father managed the stud, as his father and grandfather had before him. It was land her family had been connected to for millennia, a fact acknowledged by the owners.

In 2016, I heard a story of a different sort from the Fleurieu Peninsula. It was a wet winter and a wetland area near Silver Sands Beach had filled and spread through paddocks of grass. Ducks, swans and other waterfowl dotted its surface. A relative mentioned that it had been a traditional winter meeting place for Aboriginals, and said the last 'corroboree' held there was in the 1920s. According to her, someone 'who lived nearby' said he would 'shoot the buggers if they came down from the hills again'. Her tone became harsh; I was sure the words were not hers. 'Who?' I asked. There was a pause, an awkward turning of her head, and she said, 'It might have been – . I don't know'. The hurried quality of shame suggested something close to home. I had the feeling that it was another piece of oral history that had begun with my great grandfather, who built a holiday house there in the 1920s. That story, less palatable these days, would have disappeared in another generation. It was the only time I had heard it.

These stories though small and impossibly fragile are freighted with possibility, as well as significance to those who hold them. Perhaps the women's stories are less benign than they appear. Could they be saying in part: 'See, it cannot have been so bad. These nice things also happened. They cannot have hated us'. Alternatively, is the sense that European women were mystified by antipathy towards Aboriginal people in light of such generous acts? Or were such acts by the Indigenous women in part diplomatic gestures? It is on such fragments that a novelist's attention snags.

Mark McKenna shows an interesting use of such material in *Looking for Blackfellas Point*, using what he terms 'geologies of fable', that is oral histories, to explore gaps and silences in the archive, as Taylor has done more recently. Through this process, novelist and academic Camilla Nelson, notes, he creates 'a dialogue with the archive, and between the present and the past, mediated through the subjectivity of the writer'.[65] McKenna says of these 'geologies of fable',

> It was not history I could document or prove, but the survival and power of these stories was undeniable ... I also realised that the reasons why the stories survived and were constantly retold mattered as much as whether they were true. Instead of dismissing this 'geology of fable' because it could not be substantiated, it enriched the history I was writing.[66]

The 'power' he refers to is about the emotion felt in the telling and the hearing of the story. It was the emotion contained in my family 'fable' that enriched – more than that, which drove – the historical fiction I was writing. It is emotional connection that makes stories matter, that keeps them alive and that makes people care. Historical fiction plays a part in helping them survive, and is perfectly equipped to explore such forgotten corners of our history, many of which might merit no more than a footnote or a passing reference in a work of non-fiction. There is no disrespect to history in such a pursuit that I can discern. McKenna's and others' use of oral history and recognition of its power suggests that this point has been acknowledged.

Historical fiction writers owe an enormous debt of gratitude to historians. Their writing could not proceed without the vast body of historical research that precedes them. Historical fiction does not necessarily develop knowledge, though it certainly disseminates it, but it can, I think, be part of developing understanding and empathy. Fiction knows few boundaries. That is its strength. It allows works such as Jane Rawson's *From the Wreck*, at once a foundation fiction and an elegy to the future's past. That historical fiction is able to encompass that should be cause for celebration rather than despair. Is *Salt Creek* history? Not exactly. As with other historical fictions, it is not intended to replace history, only perhaps to augment it, to make people think and wonder and feel. Author Ursula Le Guin once observed: 'The distinction between fact and fiction is not always easy to make. But it exists. It exists the way red and blue exist'.[67] History is contested and doubtless always will be. It should be. It matters. But writing, like history, is a big room; there is space inside for us all.

8

Legends of the Nineties: Literary Culture in Adelaide at the End of the Nineteenth Century

PHILIP BUTTERSS

South Australia has no place in Australian literature's greatest foundational fiction – the story about the birth of a distinctive national literature in the 1890s. When Arthur Jose was asked why he had neglected Adelaide in his memoir that was later published as *The Romantic Nineties* (1933), he replied: 'what was there to neglect? Adelaide was, from the literary point of view, a dependency of Melbourne, a community of appreciative audiences, not of exhilarated writers'.[1] He had already dismissed Melbourne as irrelevant to the origin story he was recounting: it was 'not romantic' and it was 'obsessed with respectability ... of the ruling English type'.[2] In Jose's memoir, and in others such as George Taylor's *Those Were the Days* (1918), Australian literature was born in the bohemian literary world of Sydney during that golden decade. Later, the highly influential trio of radical nationalist accounts of Australian literature and history – Vance Palmer's *The Legend of the Nineties* (1954), A.A. Phillips's *The Australian Tradition* (1958), and Russel Ward's *The Australian Legend* (1958) – would similarly show no interest in Adelaide's literary culture at the end of the nineteenth century.[3]

Yet the widespread use of the term 'the Athens of the South' for Adelaide had its source in the 1890s, and South Australia's reputation for poetry and Adelaide's reputation as a city particularly interested in literature were significant among the reasons for that title. One observer with relevant expertise was William Mitchell, who took up the chair of English and Philosophy at the University of Adelaide in 1895. He arrived in his new home with high expectations, having been told in London that 'Adelaide, in proportion to its population, might claim to be the most literary city in

Australia'. It is impossible to assess whether that claim was correct, but Mitchell soon confirmed that there was, indeed, a 'widespread interest in literature' among the 130,000 people in the city and its surrounding suburbs.[4] Sydney and Melbourne had many more writers and larger literary cultures, but their populations were three and three-and-a-half times larger, respectively. The long-lasting use of the phrase 'the Athens of the South' had its direct origins in a speech in 1899 by Hallam Tennyson, the new governor of South Australia, though those were not his exact words. This chapter surveys Adelaide's largely ignored literary culture in the 1890s, and examines the source of one of the city's persistent identities.

'A community of appreciative audiences'

Jose did not lay eyes on Adelaide before or during the 1890s, but he was certainly correct that it was 'a community of appreciative audiences'. This is most evident in the city's impressive network of organisations interested in literature. Since the late 1850s, there had been active groups focusing on self-education, known variously as young men's societies, mutual improvement societies, and literary societies. The 1880s saw a substantial increase in their number and, importantly, the formation of a vigorous and well-run umbrella group, the South Australian Literary Societies' Union, which enjoyed strong endorsement from the governor, politicians, and the university. The activities of the Union and its member organisations were broad, and included a mock parliament, debate tournaments, and talks on diverse topics of scientific, cultural and social interest. As well as offering lectures on authors, recitations of poetry, and theatrical performances, the literary societies operated as a training ground for authors by arranging writing competitions, and by publishing creative writing in the Union's year books. Many contributors went on to publish books of verse or prose.[5] When Mitchell arrived in Adelaide, he was immediately struck by what he regarded as the 'very large numbers of literary societies in the town'.[6] At the end of the decade, the Union reflected on its sixteen-year history, concluding that it had made an 'indelible mark' on Adelaide's social and cultural life. With some pride, it noted that it represented 30 societies with a combined membership of 1,300 people.[7] A few years later, the number of member organisations would pass the previous peak of 37, which had been recorded in 1894.

Other literary groups also flourished during the nineties. One commentator has written of 'the spectacular rise' of the South Australian branch of the Australasian Home-Reading Union, an organisation aimed at encouraging recreational and instructive reading. The literary societies were overwhelmingly masculine, although some had a sizeable proportion of 'Lady Associates', notably the Adelaide Young Men's Association.[8] Similarly, at the inaugural public meeting of the Australasian Home-Reading Union in April 1893, it was men who dominated the podium and the speech-making. Women, however, were much more visible in its operation: the first report was by the secretary, Miss Hardy, and each of the eleven 'reading circles' was led by a woman.[9] Most groups were studying English literature, although there was some interest in French and German literature, and one was combining a study of history and Shakespeare. By the end of 1894, the number of active circles had risen to thirty-five; however, that level of commitment would not last for long.[10] Other bodies with literary interests that operated during the 1890s included the Savage Club (founded in 1883), the University Shakespeare Society (founded in 1884), and the Bohemian Club (founded in 1885). The city's oldest literary organisation, the Adelaide Book Society, had been formed in 1844, and it continued to circulate reading material among a handful of the most privileged members of Adelaide society.

The formal education system, too, was fostering an interest in literature, and Mitchell was very pleased by the level of literary schooling he found on his arrival. The Education Act of 1875 had made it compulsory for children up to the age of thirteen to attend elementary school, and by 1892 tuition was free. For older students, there had long been an assortment of private schools, as well as governesses and tutors, and these had now been joined by state-run institutions, such as the Model School in Grote Street, public schools in Tynte Street and Sturt Street, and the Advanced School for Girls in Franklin Street. At the end of 1895, Mitchell assessed the English literature papers of several hundred students sitting public examinations and found the results 'highly gratifying'.[11] A serious commitment to literary education is also evident in the fact that the University of Adelaide was the first Australian university to offer English literature as a course of study – from its foundation in 1874.[12] As well as running daytime and evening lectures for his students, in July and August 1895, Mitchell offered an extension course of six lectures for the general public that was well-attended, in spite of its specialised topic: English Literature and Philosophy from 1700 to 1750.

For a small and still relatively young city, Adelaide was well served by bookshops and libraries. As early as the end of the 1840s, Catherine Helen Spence's sister, Mary, had been irritated by a new arrival's surprise that she was reading books recently published in London.[13] By the 1890s, Adelaide bookselling institutions such as E.S. Wigg & Son (founded in 1849) and W.C. Rigby (founded in 1859) were flourishing in Rundle Street and King William Street, respectively. At the end of 1894, E.W. Cole took over the bookselling business in Rundle Street that had originally been started by another Melbourne firm, George Robertson, in 1875. Books could also be bought from an array of other outlets such Cawthorne and Co. on Gawler Place and Frearson's Printing House on North Terrace. A newspaper article on the reading habits of the general population in 1897 noted that Adelaide had reason to be proud of its Public Library on North Terrace, which held 40,000 volumes.[14] Certainly, the Depression of the 1890s meant the introduction of austerity measures: funds for book purchases were reduced from £500 a year to just £88, and half the library's gaslights were turned off to save money.[15] However, according to the librarian, Joseph Adams, readers continued to make good use of his institution's literary holdings, with Tennyson, Shakespeare, Twain, Dumas, Wilkie Collins, Dickens, Thackeray, and George Eliot among the most widely read. Adams observed that the bush ballads of Adam Lindsay Gordon and Banjo Paterson were the most popular Australian material, and expressed his surprise that Henry Kendall and Brunton Stephens had 'very few admirers'. The Adelaide Circulating Library, in the Institute Building next door, contained more than 20,000 volumes, including a great deal of popular fiction from authors such as George Macdonald, Walter Besant, Marie Corelli, and Conan Doyle. In 1897, its subscribers numbered almost 900. There were also between four and five hundred subscribers to Wigg & Son's circulating library, and the company had a policy of immediately allocating a dozen copies of any popular work for lending.[16] Robert Frearson's circulating library of 500 books was sold at auction in 1891.

The Theatre Royal in Hindley Street might have been the only venue for serious drama during the 1890s, but Adelaide was blessed to have

Wybert Reeve as its manager. In addition to being competent and energetic as an administrator, he saw the theatre as a vocation, and was an actor, playwright, and Shakespearean scholar. Reeve managed to keep the Theatre Royal viable with performances night after night throughout the decade, devoting about one third of each year's program to what he called 'first class pieces'. Reeve delivered lectures to the University Shakespeare Society and wrote articles for its journal. His other contributions to theatre included adapting literary works, such as his friend, Wilkie Collins's *The Woman in White*, and the Australian novelist, Rosa Praed's, *Policy and Passion*.[17] The Theatre Royal was on the regular touring circuit, and Reeve brought the best overseas and Australian performances to Adelaide. Undoubtedly the most memorable event of the decade was Sarah Bernhardt's week-long season in July 1891, when she starred in *Camille, La Tosca, Jeanne d'Arc*, and *Fédora*.[18]

Adelaideans were also appreciative of occasional visits from writers.[19] Sometimes these were tantalisingly brief, such as the few hours when a young, but already famous, Rudyard Kipling passed through on 25 November 1891, arriving on the overnight express from Melbourne and almost immediately boarding the *SS Valetta* in Largs Bay for his voyage back to India. The *Advertiser* was pleased to arrange an exclusive audience, but, at the outset, Kipling stated that he did not like interviews, and his generally terse responses proved this to be true.[20] William Lane, whose labour-movement novel, *The Workingman's Paradise*, had been published in 1892, spoke to a large and enthusiastic audience at Adelaide's Albert Hall the following April, seeking support and funding, a few months before leaving for Paraguay to establish 'New Australia'.[21] The tour by Mark Twain allowed a much more satisfying opportunity for literary Adelaide to savour a celebrity writer's presence than had Kipling's fleeting stopover, as is evident from a report of a lecture he gave in the Theatre Royal on Saturday 12 October 1895:

> The reception given to the world-famed humorist was overwhelming. When the curtain rose ... the whole audience greeted him with waving handkerchiefs, hand-claps, stamping, and lusty cheers, according to the sex, fancy, and fashion of the worshipper, and the ovation was prolonged till Mark Twain was in danger of getting a crick in his carbuncle bowing his acknowledgments.[22]

The response to Twain was not unanimous, however, and Alfred and Margaret Cheadle told their children that they found him 'shaggy' and 'not as good as his books'.[23]

A further indication of Adelaide's general reverence towards writers is the enormous crowd that assembled in May 1894 to witness the unveiling of a statue of Robert Burns, funded by public subscription, and prominently located on the corner of North Terrace and Kintore Avenue, in front of the Institute Building.[24]

'Not of exhilarated writers'

As well as being right about Adelaide's appreciative audiences for literature, Jose was correct to say that the city did not make any significant contribution to the body of bush-focused poetry usually associated with the Sydney *Bulletin* in the 1890s. Certainly, there were Adelaide writers who, like the bohemians at the *Bulletin*, imitated the ballads of Gordon and later Kipling, but none had the ability of Paterson, Lawson, and the most competent of their peers.[25] The chief exception was C.J. Dennis, whose first two poems in the Adelaide *Critic* share the *Bulletin* writers' enjoyment of Australian bush vernacular and their egalitarian worldview,[26] but he was a decade younger than Jose's favourites, and did not begin his publishing career until February 1898. These early efforts anticipate the style and values of *The Songs of a Sentimental Bloke* (1915), which would eclipse the sales of Paterson, Lawson, and anyone else from the 1890s. By then, though, Dennis was living in Victoria.

In spite of not having any claim to long-lasting significance, a number of South Australian poets were known in London during the nineties, and this was important to Adelaide's being named the Athens of the southern hemisphere. Thomas Gill's *Bibliography of South Australia*, compiled in the middle of the 1880s, was far from complete, but it still managed to list books of verse by almost twenty writers.[27] At that point, the only Australian poets with any level of recognition in Britain were Gordon and Kendall, but Douglas Sladen would suddenly turn the English literary world's attention to Australian poetry by publishing three anthologies in London in 1888.[28] *Australian Ballads and Rhymes*, released on 26 January to mark the centenary of colonisation, was an immediate success, and ultimately sold 20,000 copies. It was soon followed by an enlarged version, titled

A Century of Australian Song, and a third anthology, *Australian Poets: 1788–1888*. After gaining some colonial experience in Sydney and Melbourne during the first half of the 1880s, Sladen had returned to England and assembled material for his anthologies, largely through advertisements in Australian newspapers. South Australian poets and their supporters responded willingly with contributions, and the three volumes included pieces from many authors associated with the colony, including Emma Anderson, Arthur Baker, H.H. Blackham, Ettie Bode, Alfred Chandler, 'Lindsay Duncan' (Mrs T.C. Cloud), Isabella Giles, Adam Lindsay Gordon, John Howell, Frances Lewin, George McHenry, 'Agnes Neale' (Caroline Agnes Leane), W.N. Pratt, James Sadler, Percy Sinnett, and Sarah Welch. In his introductions to *Australian Ballads and Rhymes* and *A Century of Australian Song*, Sladen referred to Chandler as one of 'the two young native-born Australians whose poems have attracted the most notice in England', and he named 'Agnes Neale' and 'Lindsay Duncan' in a short list of the female poets 'who enjoy the greatest reputation in Australia'.[29]

Today, the large body of verse in newspapers, or in self-published volumes of poetry during the 1890s, is probably only of historical interest, as is the case with Caroline Leane's 'Adelaide: A Song' from her *Shadows and Sunbeams* (1890). Active in the Adelaide Literary Society as one of its first associate members, Leane was described by Sladen as the 'Australian Adelaide Proctor', in reference to the English poet whose religious beliefs and social themes were echoed in her work. The poem shows that a fascination with Adelaide's dark underbelly could be seen even in the nineteenth century:

> *O Adelaide! we who gaze on thee,*
> *Entranced at thy loveliness stand;*
> *O beautiful, beautiful city!*
> *Fair pearl of our bright southern land.*
>
> *But when night in her dark cloak enfolds thee,*
> *And the stars burn in glory on high,*
> *There cometh a moan from thy bosom*
> *That quivereth up to the sky –*

A moan from the hearts that are breaking
With sin and with sorrow crushed low,
For there's blood on thy white robes, O city!
Foul stains on thy garments of snow.

O Adelaide! we who behold thee,
Aghast at thy guiltiness stand;
O sorrowful, crime-blotted city!
Stained pearl of our bright southern land.[30]

By and large, the city made only a minor contribution to the corpus of Australian novels in the late nineteenth century, although one exception was Catherine Martin's *An Australian Girl*, published anonymously in London in 1890.[31] A few years earlier, Gill's *Bibliography of South Australia* showed that the small colony had already produced a respectable body of novels, listing four by Catherine Helen Spence, fourteen by Matilda Evans ('Maud Jean Franc') and others from William Storrie, 'Iota', Effie Stanley, and George Isaacs. *An Australian Girl* was immediately regarded as significant, with Desmond Byrne stating in *Australian Writers* (1896) that Martin had achieved 'the most perfect description of the peculiar natural features of the country ever written', and adding, 'For the first time the Bush is interpreted as well as described'.[32] Among other supporters was Martin's friend, Catherine Helen Spence, who agreed with the English poet and critic, F.W.H. Myers, that *An Australian Girl* and the subsequent novel, *The Silent Sea* (1892), were 'on the highest level ever reached in Australian fiction'.[33] *An Australian Girl* is also remarkable in addressing spiritual and philosophical questions at considerable depth, although probably at some cost to its popularity. Most of all, Martin's novel is important for its delineation of a proudly Australian version of the new woman, epitomizing strength, independence and self-determination.[34]

In spite of the positive early reactions, *An Australian Girl* was undervalued for a very long period. Paul Eggert has argued that its success was hampered by the excessive cautiousness of its publisher, Richard Bentley, who failed to issue a cheap Australian edition until three or four years after the initial reviews. Eggert suggests that, by then, the canon of Australian nineteenth-century novels had largely been established.[35]

During the last decades of the twentieth century, feminist critics showed conclusively that women novelists of the 1880s and 1890s, such as Martin, were systematically devalued through a masculinist bias against their interest in domestic topics and their use of the romance genre.[36] This reappraisal of Australian literary history resulted in a renaissance for *An Australian Girl*. New editions by Oxford University Press and University of Queensland Press appeared, and so did a substantial body of criticism discussing the book's gender politics.[37]

The other significant novel from the 1890s was Simpson Newland's *Paving the Way* (1893), set in the area around Encounter Bay and later in the Darling district. Paul Depasquale is critical of Newland's skills as an author but unequivocal about the book's importance, asserting that *'Paving the Way* is *the* South Australian novel of pioneering life: its scope is vast, its range of characters wide and representative, its narrative dimensions epic, its basic honesty impressive'.[38] Roland Grantley, the chief protagonist, arrives in South Australia in the late 1830s as a boy, and goes on to become a consummate bushman. He expresses the kind of views underpinning the efforts of the colonists: 'I will mould my own future and carve out my own destiny. In a land like this there are big prizes for the bold, the energetic, the enterprising'.[39] Yet the novel is critical of colonisation in general, and highly disapproving of much of Grantley's own behaviour, particularly his greed, his violence towards Aboriginal people, and his poor decisions in personal relationships. In the preface to the original edition, Newland notes that the time has not yet arrived when the full truth about colonisation can be written, but, in the novel, he is surprisingly explicit about frontier killings, depicting Europeans as the ultimate cause of each instance of violence. Perhaps also surprising is the fact that, in a colony which prided itself on being free of the convict stain, Daniel Cleeve – named as one of the 'oldest pioneers' and portrayed as one of the most important characters – is an ex-convict.[40] *Paving the Way* was widely admired during the 1890s, and there have been at least a dozen editions since, in Britain, America and Australia. In 1943, when Australian literary studies at tertiary level were in their infancy, it was included in the English syllabus at the University of Adelaide as part of a course on Australian historical novels. Today, it deserves to be better-known than it is.

In dismissing Adelaide as an outpost of Melbourne, Jose was implying that it, too, was bound by a 'respectability ... of the ruling English type'. Certainly, literary culture was well-supported by the Adelaide establishment: wealthy individuals, government, churches, and the university all endeavoured to encourage the reading of good literature and to foster creative writing. The prominent lawyer and politician, Josiah Symon, for instance, was heavily involved in the 1897–98 Australasian Federal Convention while he was also president of the South Australian Literary Societies' Union, and a member of both the University Shakespeare Society and the Australasian Home Reading Association.[41] Later, he would be patron of the Poetry Recital Society, founded by his wife, Lady Mary Symon. The Symons might have been politically conservative, but, since the 1830s, literary organisations in Adelaide had also included those with a progressive commitment to workers' education and to breaking down privilege.[42] When the great trade unionist W.G. Spence spoke to a large gathering at the Democratic Club in Flinders Street in February 1891 on the topic of 'The Reconstruction of Society', he urged members of the working class to get themselves onto the committees of circulating libraries to ensure that more radical books were ordered.[43]

Much of the verse written in Adelaide during the nineteenth century could also be classed as bound by respectability – and a good proportion was religious – but there was also a tradition of critical and disruptive poetry, going back to the first piece published in the colony.[44] Alfred Chandler was more radical than many, often using his poetry to support an egalitarian Australia where 'old systems of unhappy serfdom' were defeated, where labourers were valued, and where 'freedom' reigned.[45] In 1899, Herbert Hall published *Lay of the Laborer*, a poem in which he criticised current inequality and called for a fundamental redistribution of wealth and property.[46] Although its sentiments were radical, its form was not, and Hall's verse is sometimes almost unreadable in its attempt to imitate high poetic diction. Similarly – given their critiques either of gender norms or of the pioneering days – it would be impossible to categorise either *An Australian Girl* or *Paving the Way* as a simple embodiment of 'respectability ... of the ruling English type'. During the first decade of the twentieth century, a small coterie of self-styled bohemians would found the *Gadfly*, a satirical weekly in which they would publish radical verse and prose.

The city's size in the 1890s had both advantages and disadvantages for literary Adelaide. A population of 130,000 in a relatively contained area proved perfect for developing a community of audiences for literature, and the Literary Societies' Union was able to encourage fruitful interactions between a wide array of literary organisations. On the other hand, there was not sufficient interest to sustain a good journal of criticism; that was also the case in the much larger capital cities: Sydney's *Centennial Magazine* lasted only from 1888 to 1890 and Melbourne's *Australasian Critic* from 1890 to 1891. The chief drawback was that Adelaide did not have an enormous pool of literary talent; nor was the city large and lively enough to attract or keep all of the most able writers.

The local-born Guy Boothby was one who left, having tried his hand at writing for the theatre in the early 1890s. Audiences for his comic opera, *Sylvia*, were impressed by the music, written by Cecil Sharp, who was resident in Adelaide between 1882 and 1892. The libretto, however, was seen as imitative, though the public, critics, and the theatre manager, Wybert Reeve, tried to be supportive during *Sylvia*'s three performances.[47] Boothby's melodrama about the French revolution, *The Jonquille*, staged at the Theatre Royal in August 1891, was less well received, with the *South Australian Register* noting, dryly, that at least it possessed 'the merit of being short'.[48] Arriving in London in 1894, Boothby was enormously prolific and successful as a novelist, publishing over 50 books before his death in 1905 and earning a considerable income. Among those who left Adelaide in the late nineteenth and early twentieth centuries to pursue careers elsewhere were Alfred Chandler, Charles Rodda ('Gavin Holt') and C.J. Dennis. Others who would follow prior to 1920 included Alice Grant Rosman, Leon Gellert, Doris Egerton Jones, and Vernon Knowles.[49]

'The Athens of the Southern Pole'
Adelaide's pleasure in seeing itself as a literary city was evident in the joy at the appointment of Hallam Tennyson as governor of South Australia in 1899. Since Alfred Tennyson's elevation to the poet laureateship in 1850, he had come to be a great favourite in the colony – read silently or to others, quoted in conversations, letters, sermons and speeches, reprinted in newspapers, and recited at countless literary events, school graduations and other public occasions.[50] Hallam Tennyson might officially have been

the representative of the British crown, but Adelaide saw him equally, or perhaps more, as his father's son, the heir of one of the great literary figures of the age. The *South Australian Register* immediately interpreted the appointment as augmenting the local literary heritage and reputation:

> South Australia has given to the world a master poet of Australian life in Adam Lindsay Gordon, and it may be counted a further honour to be now linked with the family of the greatest English poet of modern times.[51]

Delighted at having a Tennyson as its governor, the colony greeted him very warmly; he was even more generous in return. The governor and his wife, Audrey, arrived at Port Adelaide on 10 April 1899 to be met by a crowd of thousands of people and a triumphal arch bearing the word 'welcome'. After the speeches, a massed choir of 1,500 schoolchildren sang the national anthem and gave a rendition of 'Song of Australia', whose words had been written by the local poet Caroline Carleton and whose music had been written by the local composer Carl Linger.[52] At the civic reception in the Town Hall that same afternoon, Tennyson praised Adelaide's attributes in a speech carefully pitched to endear himself to his audience. He warmed the crowd by mentioning his father, and they responded with loud cheers. He went on:

> For long I have looked upon Adelaide as the young Athens of the Southern Pole. With your keen desire for knowledge, with your keen desire for intellectual culture, with your yearning for artistic perfection, with your Hellenic pride in all manner of athletic prowess; for long I have admired South Australia for your excellent system of education – (cheers) – for your admirable Real Property Act – (cheers) – and for your love of progress. I have an especial interest in South Australia, because you are pre-eminently, it seems to me, the land of Australian poetry – the home of Adam Lindsay Gordon, of Lindsay Duncan, of Agnes Neale, of Alfred Chandler, and many others.[53]

There might have been some reservations about possible slippage between 'Southern Pole' and 'south pole', but many in the audience would have recognised the phrase as a reference to Alfred Tennyson's widely-known poem of empire, 'Hands All Round', which named Australia as 'the strong/ New England of the Southern Pole'.

The governor's use of his father's words to anoint Adelaide as the youthful cultural centre of the southern hemisphere was, of course, very well received locally, and it was to have an enduring effect on the city's image. One of those in the official party at the Town Hall that day was the chief justice, Samuel Way, and he referred warmly to this speech repeatedly in his letters, assessing it as 'much the finest effort of the kind [he] ever heard' and noting, with pleasure, its 'distinct literary flavour'.[54] The Adelaide press, too, was in raptures, though *Quiz and the Lantern* provided a blunter appraisal, reporting that 'gush has been ladled out all round' and that the governor had come 'well prepared to butter us up'. However, even this journal felt gratified, and the article went on to admit that the speech was 'a very good one'.[55] The governor's words received extremely wide coverage, with lengthy excerpts reprinted in metropolitan and regional newspapers throughout Australia.

Not surprisingly, feathers were ruffled in a few of the other colonies. A columnist for the *Sydney Morning Herald* asserted that Tennyson had, indeed, been referring to 'the Antarctic zone', and that Sydney, therefore, continued to be 'the Athens of this continent'. In Hobart, the South Australian governor's words were dismissed as 'scrumptious flapdoodle'. Nowhere was the flattery more blatant than in his description of South Australia as 'the land of Australian poetry', and in his references to local poets, evidently based on the introduction to Sladen's anthologies. A Victorian newspaper observed, with justification, that 'very few indeed' had heard of Duncan, Neale and Chandler, and also pointed out that Adam Lindsay Gordon identified himself with Victoria rather than South Australia.[56]

By the late nineteenth century, the globe was dotted with neo-Athenses. Edinburgh had long been known as 'the modern Athens', and Catherine Helen Spence had referred to it as such in *Clara Morison*, Adelaide's first novel. In the USA, Nashville was frequently called the 'Athens of the South'. Zurich was sometimes termed 'the Swiss Athens'. Even in South Australia, there was a prior claimant: the nearby city of Gawler was popularly known (with a degree of irony) as 'the colonial Athens', in acknowledgment of its surprising contribution to the colony's cultural life.[57]

In fact, Adelaide, itself, had very occasionally been referred to as 'the

Athens of the South' or 'the Athens of the Southern Hemisphere' from as early as the mid-1860s, but it was Tennyson's speech that caused the appellation to spread widely and helped it to stick. Outside South Australia, the phrase has normally been applied with irony. For example, in 1971 an article in the *Canberra Times* began, 'As every right-thinking Australian knows, Adelaide is the City of Culture, the Athens of the South, the Festival City', before providing a lengthy summary of a recent survey which showed that Adelaideans were vastly more interested in popular entertainment than in high culture.[58] For locals, too, if the term has expressed pride, it has usually also contained a note of affectionate self-mockery. Most often, it has been used to draw attention to Adelaide's failure to live up to the ideal. Five years after Tennyson's speech, one Adelaidean called for a statue of Adam Lindsay Gordon, arguing that in a city described by the ex-Governor as 'the Athens of the southern hemisphere', there should be more 'outward and visible signs of culture'.[59] In 1925, at a public meeting in the Town Hall, a similar argument was made in favour of a national band.[60] More recently, Alison Broinowski suggested that Adelaide under Don Dunstan might have been the closest the city ever came to the ideal of Athens under Pericles, and she says that, 'If the claim about the "Athens of the South" is to apply', contemporary Adelaide needs to make an effort, drawing on its considerable strengths in 'art and culture, design and creativity, education and a civilised lifestyle'.[61]

In some periods more than others, Adelaide has been successful in fostering strong democratic institutions, excellent educational establishments, good planning and design, attractive architecture, and a thriving cultural life. Notwithstanding the severe economic depression, the 1890s was in some respects one of those high points; in fact, Tennyson failed to mention the decade's greatest achievement: legislation to allow women's suffrage. Adelaide might not have been a city of 'exhilarated writers' in Jose's sense of the term, but it had many keen authors, a few of whom made lasting contributions to Australian literature. The public library and university provided solid institutional support for lovers of literature. Newspapers contained plenty of local and international verse, as well as regular reviews. Circulating libraries and bookshops offered easy access to the best and worst of British and American fiction and poetry. Even if theatre patrons had few choices of venue, they could enjoy international and national touring companies as well as local actors. Literary societies flourished throughout the city and suburbs. In the 1890s, for its size, Adelaide was a highly literary city.

9

South Australia: The Pivotal State

STUART MACINTYRE

John Hirst was just one of many gifted historians to be raised and trained in South Australia but then pursue careers elsewhere. He also exhibited characteristics that can be traced to his origins. He was a Methodist who abandoned his intention of entering the ministry but retained the calling of a plain-living man of conscience. He was a product of Unley High School with a strong commitment to public education, impatient with inherited privilege, a man who lived out his civic republican values. He trained in the History department of the University of Adelaide directed by Hugh Stretton, and it might have been Hugh's example in standing down from his chair that led John to resist all invitations to become a professor. Like Hugh, he was an accomplished stylist, able to distil a clear meaning from the most complex subject and express it in a supple, lucid prose.

John's doctoral thesis formed the basis of his first book, *Adelaide and the Country* (1973), which explored the structure and operation of an extended city-state. Let me remind you of its argument. John saw South Australia up to the closing decades of the nineteenth century as dominated by its metropolis. Everything, he wrote – agriculture, grazing, mining, social and political life – revolved around Adelaide. Partly for geographical reasons, partly because of its Wakefieldian design, settlement was confined to little more than 100 kilometres from Adelaide, and his book traced the way successful pastoralists gravitated to city residences, where they joined commercial and professional men who themselves had interests in the colony's land and minerals.

Like all good historians, John was interested in change, its causes and consequences. He found that as farmers pushed further north and onto the Yorke Peninsula in the closing years of the century, they expected government to serve their needs. A political system arose in which urban parties, labour, liberal and conservative, appealed to the country, the first two offering new forms of State assistance until a single non-labour party made a long-lasting accommodation with rural interests. Within this new configuration, a strongly centralised form of decision-making and administration persisted: transport and communications, police and courts, schools and hospitals, all were controlled from the city. This was an instance of change that John made his own, not so much a turning point as a reconfiguration in which the deeper continuities persist.[1]

John completed his thesis and revised it for publication after moving to a lectureship at the new La Trobe University. More than this, he switched his research from South Australia to New South Wales. Graeme Davison tells me that John made clear in conversation at the time that this was a conscious decision, for while *Adelaide and the Country* had good reviews, it was received as a contribution to regional rather than national history and John was sufficiently young and ambitious to want to make his mark nationally. This is the conundrum that Robert Dare identified in a contribution to *The Wakefield Companion to South Australian History*: if South Australia was different, as its historians so long affirmed, then it seemed to have very little to do with the larger contours of Australian history and could accordingly be disregarded.[2]

An early product of John's ambition was an irreverent essay disputing Geoffrey Blainey's contention that *The Tyranny of Distance* was a dominant theme of Australian history. Not so, he argued; Australia was characterised by an unusual mobility.[3] That was followed by his upsetting Russel Ward's radical nationalist *Australian Legend* of the nomad bushman with the consensual nostalgia of the pioneer legend, and then came even more iconoclastic reinterpretations of the convict system as well as the advent of democracy.[4] John's instinct was always to challenge the accepted wisdom and this came to extend beyond historiographical publications to essays and op-ed commentaries tilting at such progressive orthodoxies as feminism, multiculturalism, egalitarianism, nationalism, conscription and the Family Court.[5]

In a lecture to the History Council of South Australia that was published in *Turning Points: Chapters in South Australian History*, John returned to his place of origin.⁶ His avowed purpose was to reconsider the distinctiveness of South Australian history and in doing so he took a typically contrarian approach of playing down the local characteristics and suggesting how so much that happened here was determined by its position within a larger whole. Hence it was a free colony with no established church, few Irish and greater restraint on squatters, but some of these features merely anticipated what would happen elsewhere. That the paradise of dissent became a city of churches, their number swollen by the number of denominations, simply demonstrated the early triumph of the voluntarist principle in religion; in any case, sectarianism was never a serious threat in eastern Australia since Protestants and Catholics learned how to accommodate their differences. Conversely, the curbs on large landholdings here were imposed by the need to keep smallholders from moving there.

Midway through his lecture, John threw out one of his provocations: 'There has been a tendency to ascribe anything distinctive or unusual in South Australia's history to its distinctive origins'.⁷ The dangers of such originalism are undeniable. The formation of history as a distinct branch of knowledge in nineteenth-century Europe was closely linked to new understandings of nationhood as deeply rooted in the past, understandings that were served by tracing a distinctive path through which the nation acquired its unique identity. A settler society, with its uprooting of both the settler and Indigenous peoples, not to mention the throwing together of previously separate nationalities (Hirst observes that the colonists used the term British far more often than the inhabitants of England, Scotland and Wales, let alone Ireland), who were then overlaid by successive waves of new settlers, seems singularly unlikely to possess such a formative past.

Yet I am not so sure that it is possible to dismiss South Australians' distinctiveness so readily. Some of you might be familiar with a book by the American historian David Hackett Fischer, a scholar even more vigilant than John in correcting other historians' fallacies.⁸ In a vast cultural history of the United States, *Albion's Seed*, Hackett Fischer discerned four British folkways that transmitted distinctive regional cultures to the new nation, that of the Puritans in New England with their concern for education and enterprise, the Anglican gentry of Virginia who established the plantations, the Quakers who settled the midlands and Delaware valley and founded the industries, and the settlers from Ulster and the Scottish border who influenced the Western ranches and Southern agrarian ways.[9] Fischer illustrated his folkways by reference to peculiarities of speech and dress, patterns of work and worship, architecture and cuisine, moral norms and social structures – a rich range of evidence that is underutilised in regional studies here.

A society's distinctiveness comes not simply from its legacy of institutions and arrangements, for it encompasses the way its members understand their past. The practical import of South Australia styling itself a Province rather than a colony might be insubstantial, but it mattered to South Australians, as did their marking of Proclamation Day and failure to observe Australia Day. The fact that former convicts made their way here and, according to Paul Sendziuk as well as John Hirst, brought practical skills that helped establish the new settlement did not detract from the popular belief that South Australia enjoyed a unique measure of liberty because it was free of the convict taint.[10]

In recasting South Australian history as a product of its circumstances, Hirst places it back within Australian history. He plays down the widely shared narrative of a self-sufficient, organic community in favour of a people who occupied just one part of the continent and made a series of creative responses to national events that threatened their fortunes. Hence South Australia was situated at a safe distance from the convict east but used the Murray River to open up trade with the country's farming heartland. It faced what he calls 'an existential crisis' in the 1850s when the gold rush drained its labour force but established an assay office to lure back business by offering a higher price for Victoria's gold.[11] We may think of other difficulties: the declining production of copper, the absence of other mineral deposits, the low rainfall in most of the colony and the limits on land suitable for agriculture. South Australia went into recession in the 1880s ahead of the eastern colonies and was burdened by a much larger public debt.

Thus Hirst sees the impulse for Federation in South Australia at the close of the nineteenth century as yet another endeavour to repair its fortunes. The colony enjoyed the benefit of proximity to the new mines at Broken Hill, so that ores were transported for smelting at Port Pirie and supplies sent from Adelaide. Similarly, it was the chief supplier of the even newer gold fields in Western Australia. Both these outlets were at risk if the governments of New South Wales and Western Australia closed them off by levying duties on inter-colonial trade, so South Australia had every incentive to join a customs union. Moreover, the new Commonwealth was likely to build a railway across the Nullarbor, relieve South Australia from the burden of administering the Northern Territory and even complete the line running north. South Australia would thus become the terminus of a national transport system, fulfilling the promise of its location at the centre of the continent.[12]

It is striking that Hirst's pragmatic explanation of the federal movement in South Australia makes no allowance for the case he had propounded so forcefully in his book on Federation. There he was scornful of the proposition that this was merely a practical business arrangement, insistent that the Commonwealth was brought about by an intense national sentiment and pursued by its creators as a sacred duty. South Australians play a lesser role in Hirst's *The Sentimental Nation*, the most passionate and affirmative of all his books, for they are subsidiary to the principal actors from the two larger colonies. Charles Kingston's determination that the Constitution be democratic is acknowledged, along with his fiery obduracy, but it is those who had to unite the disparate elements that he credits with making the real sacrifices.[13]

A note of condescension is also noticeable in Alfred Deakin's influential account of *The Federal Story*. 'Measured by all-round ability', Deakin judged the South Australian delegation elected to the opening session of the Federal Convention in Adelaide as 'undoubtedly the strongest', but thought its members lost both cohesion and momentum when the Convention moved to Sydney and Melbourne. He also dwelt on their supplicant position: 'it was recognised that theirs was a poor colony seeking what it could gain'.[14]

I think Deakin and Hirst do less than justice to South Australia's part in the Federal movement, and I shall briefly suggest why since the reasons seem to me to go beyond the creation of the Commonwealth to this state's subsequent fortunes.

The Pivotal State

Hirst's explanation of South Australia's commitment to Federation stresses its centrality. Lying between the eastern and western colonies, and with an indented coast that gave ready access to farmland, this late addition to the British settlement of Australia enjoyed early success – and then saw the others outstrip it. The Province made up 15 per cent of the non-Aboriginal population in 1851 but just 11 per cent by 1871 and during the 1880s it fell behind Queensland to become the fourth most populous of the competing polities. Lacking the natural resources of its rivals, it aspired to serve as a hub for transport and communications (so that the construction of the Overland Telegraph preceded the interest in a transcontinental railway) and share the benefits of industries beyond its boundaries.

But this is to ignore the crucial role that South Australia played in the design of the new Commonwealth. In the absence of Queensland from the 1897–98 Convention, South Australia stood between the two major colonies, New South Wales and Victoria, and two with tiny populations, Tasmania and Western Australia. Much of the drafting of the Constitution was taken up with balancing the majoritarian expectations of the larger colonies with the safeguards the smaller ones sought, and here the South Australians were uniquely placed to strike a balance. Their colony was not just central, but in deliberations conducted among an equal number of delegates from each of the five colonies it was pivotal – a description that I chose for this essay before I recalled that John Bannon had anticipated me by describing South Australia as the fulcrum of Federation.[15]

After John Bannon turned from leading his state to exploring its political history, he became the most ardent champion of its contribution to the Federal movement, and here I can only summarise some of the evidence cited in his extensive studies. First, South Australia was closely involved from the outset through Richard Baker's production of a *Manual of Reference* for the first, 1891 Convention, Tom Playford's advocacy that the new entity should be nothing less than a Commonwealth, and Kingston's draft Constitution, with its explicit provision for responsible government and restrictions on the Senate amending money bills. Second, after the failure of the colonial parliaments to ratify the work of that 1891 Convention, Kingston took up John Quick's suggestion of a new one that would be directly elected and submit its proposals to the people through referenda; he chivvied Reid and the other premiers to adopt that scheme and drafted the necessary enabling legislation for passage through their parliaments. Third, he secured the support of the two smaller colonies for the second Convention to begin its work in Adelaide, with him as the president, Baker as the chair of committees and Edwin Gordon Blackmore, the clerk of South Australia's Legislative Council, guiding its procedures.

Then there were the particular contributions made by South Australian delegates to the second Convention. Kingston promoted industrial arbitration as a federal power, James Howe invalid and old-age pensions. Josiah Symon, who chaired the judicial committee, championed the High Court as well as a federal power over the Murray waters. John Cockburn argued for the widest possible franchise. Above all, Kingston and Patrick Glynn joined with three Tasmanians to secure a compromise on the question that threatened to bring the Convention to a standstill: the Senate's power to amend money bills.[16]

Bannon argues persuasively that the South Australian delegates mediated between the larger and smaller colonies and quotes John Cockburn's lofty description of his own colony 'standing ... in the centre of all the colonies, holding out a hand to each of them' – though we need to remember that Cockburn was a consistent supporter of states' rights.[17] Hence the South Australians were adamant that the colonies retain their sovereign status, and while they eventually accepted the deadlock provision for a double dissolution followed by a joint sitting of both houses – as Glynn put it, 'out of deference to the prejudices of the larger colonies' – they insisted that the referendum needed to amend the Constitution must be a dual referendum, requiring approval by a majority of the states as well as a majority of voters.[18]

What then of Hirst's contention that South Australia was actuated by economic self-interest? There was no lack of appeal to such considerations in the public debate that preceded the referendum on the Federal Bill in 1898. As Ronald Norris showed, when the South Australian delegates put their work before the voters they laid heavy emphasis on the material consequences. Working through a Commonwealth Bill League, they dwelt on the perilous position that would follow if small, sparsely populated South Australia, 'now stationary and depressed', voted to stay out of the Commonwealth. Conversely, they made extravagant claims for the rich benefits that would flow from Federation: the stimulus it would give to local industry, the increased railway revenue and even the 'federalising of the South Australian debt'.[19]

The voters of the colony responded by endorsing the Bill by 35,800 votes to 17,320, albeit on a relatively low turnout of 40 per cent. The margin increased markedly a year later, when the revised Constitution was put for ratification in a second referendum: this time the 'yes' vote was 65,990 against 17,053.[20] Yet those revisions, necessary to satisfy New South Wales, worked against South Australian interests. They placed the future capital within New South Wales – 'why not Port Augusta?' a member demanded when Kingston reported the decision to the House of Assembly.[21] The provision that the Commonwealth would remit three-quarters of all customs and excise revenue to the states, an arrangement that Frederick Holder had pursued so vigorously, was now to operate for only ten years. South Australian efforts to have a clause in the Constitution forbidding New South Wales from diverting the waters of the Murray-Darling river system were unsuccessful; indeed Richard Baker gave a casting vote at the Convention to abandon this provision in what he called 'the interests of federation'.[22]

Other South Australian expectations would prove illusory. The Commonwealth did not take over state debts. The provision for an Inter-State Commission to adjudicate on disputes over trade, river commerce and railways, matters dear to South Australia, proved nugatory: the Commission was not established until 1912 and was ineffective. Similarly, the railway to Western Australia was not commenced for more than a decade, by which time the goldfields were attached firmly to Perth. There was no northern railway and South Australia had to wait a decade to be quit of the Northern Territory.

South Australia therefore remained heavily dependent on primary production and was hard hit when overseas demand fell away in the 1920s. Like Tasmania and Western Australia, it felt disadvantaged by the tariff protection of local manufacturers that raised the cost of materials and wages but provided very little benefit to the state's restricted manufacturing sector. Its share of the national population had already fallen by 1921 to 9 per cent and continued to dwindle. In 1927, the South Australian government appointed a royal commission to investigate the effects of Federation on the state's finances and make a case for federal assistance. Soon South Australia was receiving assistance, like the two other mendicant states, but even so it was hit particularly hard by the Depression.[23]

Revival

Then came what was indisputably a turning point: a State-directed strategy of industrialisation. South Australia's manufacturing industries were handicapped by distance from the principal markets and the state's lack of its own energy supply. These disadvantages were overcome by reducing the costs of production with cheaper labour (which was assisted by the State provision of low-cost housing), attractive pricing of utilities and other government concessions to lure domestic and foreign companies to set up operations here. The story of this transformation has been well told,[24] and here I want to emphasise that South Australia benefitted from the ingenuity of those who directed the state, not just in the formulation of a coherent plan and the design of efficient public enterprises but in their skills of advocacy in Canberra.

Initiated in the 1930s, the strategy yielded benefits that lasted 50 years. The turning point, in my view, came during the Second World War when the Commonwealth government acquired unprecedented control over national life. Unlike the previous war, when Australia contributed soldiers but little else to a distant conflict, this one required the country to mobilise all available resources for a war in the Pacific. South Australia became a major site of munitions production with plants at Finsbury, Hendon and Penfield, the General Motors-Holden factories and railway workshops given over to war work and six other government factories built in regional centres. With the exception of Finsbury, these Commonwealth establishments, many with advanced equipment, were sold or leased after the war to private firms and dramatically boosted the state's manufacturing capacity.[25]

At their height, the country's munitions factories alone employed more than 130,000 workers and other war production a further 430,000.[26] Most of this activity occurred in New South Wales and Victoria, but South Australia contributed a disproportionate share. Why? The conventional view is that any serious threat at the outbreak of war was expected to be directed at Sydney or Perth, and that South Australia's location afforded greater safety. More tellingly, almost no war industries were established in Queensland because that state was fully stretched meeting the needs of the air bases and military camps created there after Japan entered the war. As important, in my view, was the supply of under-employed labour in South Australia when the war began. So rapid was the transformation to full employment that when the federal government prohibited the production of a long list of civilian goods in 1942 in order to divert labour to the war economy, it applied the restrictions initially to just Victoria and South Australia where the shortage was most acute.[27]

The appointment of Essington Lewis, a South Australian, as Director-General of Munitions, was propitious, as was the role of another South Australian, Norman Makin, Minister for Munitions in the Curtin government. I would place greater emphasis on the effectiveness of the premier, Tom Playford, in pressing the interests of his state. With the possible exception of New South Wales, it could not be said of the state premiers during the Second World War that this was their finest hour. They were grudging in their acceptance of controls, bitterly resentful of the Commonwealth's usurpation of income tax, and instinctively uncooperative with the national scheme for post-war reconstruction. When the states were first asked to establish liaison arrangements for planning reconstruction, Playford insisted that it remain in his hands – though J.W. Wainwright, his most valuable public servant, proved very effective in working with the Commonwealth Department of the War Organisation of Industry. Playford continued to resist national plans for housing, soldier settlement and much else. Even so, he struck up a productive relationship with Ben Chifley, first as wartime Treasurer and then as post-war Prime Minister, who afforded vital assistance with Commonwealth funds, property and equipment.

At the end of 1942, amid much fanfare, the six premiers and leaders of the opposition met their counterparts in Canberra to discuss transferring a long list of powers to the Commonwealth for the purposes of post-war reconstruction. These were needed because the activities it was currently directing through the defence power would no longer be available after the war, when they would be crucial for the tasks of demobilisation. The meeting was called a Constitutional Convention, in reality an attempt to get the states to transfer the powers in order to avoid a referendum. The chances of them doing so seemed low; even before it met, several of the Labor premiers made known their reluctance. So Lloyd Dumas, editor of the *Advertiser*, was astonished to learn that Playford had joined with the other five premiers in agreeing to refer powers over employment, prices, trade, transport, health and other matters to the federal government for five years after the end of the war – though Playford subsequently told him that some of the states were unlikely to pass the legislation needed to give effect to this agreement.[28] He predicted accurately: four of the states, failed to abide by it, including his own.

The premiers had good reason to give that undertaking at the end of 1942. There was widespread criticism of their obstructionism in the national emergency after the fall of Singapore when the country fought desperately to throw back Japanese troops advancing on Port Moresby. If the premiers needed any reminder of the public mood, a Gallup Poll conducted on the eve of the Constitutional Convention found that 60 per cent of those surveyed believed the states should be abolished.[29]

Curtin's failure to proceed to a referendum when it became clear the premiers could not or would not fulfil their undertaking is perplexing.[30] He was facing an election in 1943 and chose to stand on his war record and avoid a divisive debate on the Constitution. But Curtin procrastinated after his landslide victory in August of that year, and then used a trip to Washington and London in the first part of 1944 to put off the plebiscite until August 1944. With each passing month, the war threat receded and with it the popular acceptance of Canberra's wide-ranging controls. A public opinion poll in October 1943 found 50 per cent intended to vote yes, 25 per cent no, the remainder either undecided or offering no opinion. By February 1944, support had fallen to 42 per cent and opposition had risen to 30 per cent; in April that lead had evaporated.[31]

It did not help that Curtin entrusted the referendum campaign to his thrusting Attorney General, Bert Evatt, who persuaded the Cabinet that all 14 of the powers sought should stand or fall together. This was widely perceived as overreach, an impression Evatt did not dispel on his national campaign tour, with Fin Crisp (the former South Australian Rhodes scholar and a future professor of political science so critical of the work of the Federal Fathers) in tow to draft his speeches.[32]

The polls also indicated that criticism of the state governments was lowest in South Australia, Tasmania and Western Australia, and support for enlarging the authority of the Commonwealth referendum highest in New South Wales and Victoria. The South Australian Establishment vehemently opposed any transfer of powers, and leading businesses conducted a campaign through the newly formed Institute of Public Affairs, which spent freely on alarmist advertisements in newspapers and on commercial radio. Both the Adelaide dailies, the morning *Advertiser* and evening *News*, argued strongly for a 'no' vote, even though Keith Murdoch, who controlled both papers, supported the referendum proposal in his Melbourne *Herald*. Murdoch had long pressed the case for a stronger national government in correspondence with Lloyd Dumas, the chairman of Advertiser Newspapers, but failed to shift him. In the immediate aftermath of the Constitutional Convention, Dumas had conceded that 'a referendum to transfer these powers to the Commonwealth would be carried in South Australia', but hoped Murdoch would 'never underestimate the suspicion and distrust of Canberra and Sydney which exists in this community'. Murdoch accordingly allowed Dumas to determine his own editorial policy in 1944.[33]

Dumas confessed that the result of the referendum came as a great shock. The transfer of powers was decisively rejected in New South Wales, Queensland and Tasmania, lost narrowly in Victoria but was supported in South Australia and Western Australia. Nationally it attracted 46.5 per cent 'yes' votes to 53.5 per cent 'no' votes. The outcome in Tasmania and Queensland was unsurprising, and Jack Lang's opposition reduced Labor support in New South Wales. Western Australia's 51.4 per cent 'yes' vote was perhaps indicative of a feeling of vulnerability induced by the war, but that factor did not operate as strongly in South Australia, where 51.5 per cent supported the proposals. Against expectations, it had acted once more as the pivotal state – except that the Federation did not turn with it. But something was happening in South Australia at this time that inclined it towards a national outlook, and in the remainder of this chapter I want to suggest why.

Common Cause

In 1942, as the prime minister warned Australians of 'the enemy that now thunders at our gates', he implored them to set aside their pleasures and devote every waking minute to the war effort. 'Your time, your energy, your thinking capacity, the whole concentration of your nature', he insisted, 'must be devoted to the service of the nation'.[34] Curtin chided the employers who resisted economic controls as well as the industrial conflict and absenteeism that hindered essential industries. Answering his appeal, a South Australian trade union leader published an article in the

Sunday *Mail* in August 1942 that regretted the disunity. 'If we are to win the war', he said, 'a common denominator of patriotism and self-sacrifice must be found', and that required providing 'tangible evidence of a far better deal for the great masses of the people in post-war days'. A prominent clergyman welcomed the message of this notorious industrial militant and agreed that 'If we are to win the war, most of us have to change our old habit of thinking of, and working for, self'. 'Some idea big enough to join us together' was needed, and it would be found 'with a vision and a plan of working together in common purpose'.[35]

The trade unionist was Tom Garland, secretary of the Gasworkers Union and soon to be president of the Trades and Labour Council. The clergyman was the Reverend Guy Pentreath, headmaster of St Peter's College. A more unlikely combination could scarcely be found. Garland, a Glaswegian who had served in the Royal Navy during the First World War, was a diminutive, self-educated communist, convicted in 1940 for a breach of the National Security Regulations when the Communist Party was campaigning against the imperialist war. Speaking at the Prospect Town Hall a few weeks after the fall of France, he had described the prime minister as a 'fifth columnist' and predicted 'Menzies and his government are going pull the Weygand and Petain trick here in Australia'.[36] Pentreath, an Englishman educated at Haileybury who had graduated from Cambridge with first-class honours in classics, championed the war effort from its outset. But after Pentreath proclaimed that Mr Garland had hit the nail on the head, the two men came together and drew others into their circle.

These included three more union secretaries. One was a communist, W.A. Sams of the Shop Assistants, but the other two, A.B. Thompson of the Engineers and Andy Angrave of the Plasterers, were not: Thompson would be a leading anti-communist by 1945. There were two university professors, the economist Keith Isles and historian G.V. Portus, along with A.R. Callaghan, the principal of Roseworthy Agricultural College. Charles Duguid, a doctor prominent for his involvement in the Aborigines Protection League and the first lay moderator of the Presbyterian Church, participated, as did an under-recognised progressive businessman, Sidney Crawford. Notable additions were J.W. Wainwright, the Auditor General and guiding intelligence of the state's industrialisation strategy, and Alex Ramsay, an economist on secondment to the Department of Post-War

Reconstruction who was about to join the South Australian Housing Trust and lead it with distinction.[37]

The participants spent several months working out the nature and form of their campaign. It would be called the Common Cause, indicating the goal was to bring people together in common purpose. Common Cause was a voluntary association that linked the immediate purpose of defeating the enemy to the promise of a better future. Hence the prospectus described it as a 'movement which aims to forge from all our disunited wills a single sword for victory and a new world of free and happy peoples' – and this was accompanied by a biblical passage taken from the Gospel of St Matthew: 'whatsoever ye would do that men should do to you, do ye even so to them'.[38]

The movement was launched in March 1943 at an overflow meeting in the Adelaide Town Hall. That was followed by a series of further public meetings, at weekly intervals, in suburban town halls – first Unley, then St Peters, Glenelg, Prospect, Norwood, Marryatville, Woodville and Burnside – and subsequently in country centres. These were the catalyst for the formation of local branches, while special-interest groups catered for members involved in the organisation's educational, clerical, library, broadcasting, speaking and financial work.

The founders were all men, though Roma Williams (who taught at Adelaide High School and was the wife of the economics lecturer Bruce Williams) spoke at the initial public meetings. A reporter at the Adelaide Town Hall described the audience as 'predominantly middle class', with substantial numbers of school teachers, civil servants, businessmen, clergymen, 'a few doctors, girls in voluntary services uniforms and a sprinkling of society women'. He also judged there more women than men, and the subsequent formation of a women's group led to the establishment of premises in Waymouth Street with a restroom, library and meeting space.[39]

The public meetings dwelt on the evils that divided the community – poverty, unemployment, bad housing, malnutrition, the falling birth rate, a lack of educational opportunity and rampant individualism – as well as the need for a new international order that would bring a lasting peace. There was much discussion of the proposals of the Department of Post-War Reconstruction, with a particular emphasis on town planning, public housing, public health and community development. But Common Cause went beyond merely discussing the new order to establish a nursery at Brighton and kindergartens in Brighton, Nuriootpa, Stirling and Keith.[40]

The Common Cause Community Kindergarten at Nuriootpa was only part of its extensive involvement in that town's experiment in community development. The townspeople had purchased a hotel and a general store before the war and ran them as co-operative ventures to raise money for a sports oval. This and a swimming pool were built by local endeavour. A Common Cause member, the architect Louis Laybourne Smith, now assisted the preparation of a comprehensive plan that incorporated an assembly hall, clinic, gymnasium, library, open-air theatre, cultural and craft centres, boy scout and girl guide quarters, a camping ground and youth hostel. The publication by Common Cause of an account of this transformation, *A Township Starts to Live*, brought a stream of post-war reconstructionists as pilgrims to the Barossa. When the president of the Nuriootpa community centre thanked Ben Chifley for his visit in September 1944, he asked if the Treasurer could possibly provide him with a secretary to help with the volume of inquiries.[41]

'Some disquiet is being occasioned by the activities of Common Cause', the acting editor of the *Advertiser* warned Keith Murdoch two months after it was inaugurated. 'Meetings would typically begin', he explained, 'with a communist who delivers anti-imperial and class-conscious propaganda, then an idealist will follow with a speech that seems to imply agreement'.[42] Much was made of the communist involvement, which included leading activists as well as two of the founding trade union officials. On behalf of Common Cause, Isles and Ramsay insisted that treating communists as outcasts was both stupid and dangerous, while Tom Garland said he was incurring criticism for associating with company directors.[43] That was an exaggeration, for initially the State secretary of the Communist Party welcomed Common Cause as evidence of the 'heightened social consciousness of the middle class', but the enthusiasm cooled as the Party reverted to a more oppositional stance and Garland would leave the Communist Party in 1945.[44]

Guy Pentreath was one of many ordained Christians active in Common Cause. Most were drawn from the Methodist and Congregationalist churches, and the Protestant Federation defended them against the accusation of associating with known atheists. Their chief critic was A.J. Hannan, the Crown Solicitor for South Australia and most active opponent of transferring its powers to the Commonwealth, who condemned these clerics for their materialist appeal to the social gospel. 'Bad housing, malnutrition and kindred evils were less serious in South Australia', he insisted, than immorality. 'The spectacle of a soldier returning after a couple of years' service abroad to find his wife and been seduced in his absence was worse than unemployment'.[45]

The hostility to Common Cause was greatest in its first few months. It appeared between the formation of the Department of Post-War Reconstruction in December 1942 and the August 1943 federal election, when Curtin would appeal for a new mandate to win the war and redeem the people's sacrifice with a new order. Despite Guy Pentreath's insistence that Common Cause 'was a movement of all parties and no parties, of all creeds and no parties', its activity was a clear riposte to the anti-Labor campaign of the Institute of Public Affairs. (Some thought that a reduction in his salary as headmaster of St Peter's was a rebuke, though the governors did not know of his participation when they made this economy measure.)[46] The repeated emphasis on political neutrality did not shield Common Cause from charges of partiality: its statement in June 1944 that the organisation took no position on the referendum to extend Commonwealth powers was belied by its extensive educational campaign on the use to which those powers could be put.[47]

With only 3000 members at its peak, Common Cause was never a mass movement and it fell away after 1944. Pentreath resigned at the end of 1943 to take up a headmastership in England; Ramsay gave up the position of honorary secretary when he took up his Housing Trust post, and Isles was overseas in 1945. It continued with an attenuated membership until 1949, more a pressure group than a catalyst of common endeavour; under Duguid's presidency, it would protest against weapons testing and injustice to Indigenous Australians in the post-war years. But it in its heyday it attracted national interest. There were efforts elsewhere to ground reconstruction in civic endeavour and create community centres as living expressions of that spirit. South Australia went furthest and it is not fanciful to see these activities contributing to the referendum result. When

Keith Murdoch visited Adelaide in early 1945, he told Dumas he would like to see some men, but doubted the Adelaide Club would be a suitable venue.[48] The three he singled out for discussion were J.W. Wainwright, Keith Isles and Tom Garland. Only in South Australia was such a creative combination possible.

10

The Great Man of History: Industrialisation and the Playford Legend

PAUL SENDZIUK

South Australia underwent profound industrial and urban transformation during Thomas Playford's period as premier, spanning from 1938 until 1965. The state's reliance on primary industries for employment and income gave way to rapid growth in the manufacturing sector that was based mainly in Adelaide and newly emerging industrial towns such as Whyalla. Factory employment grew by 168%, an increase greater than that achieved in any other state over the same period.[1] Coal mines and power stations were developed in the north of the state, providing for the first time a secure and cost-efficient source of energy, and the ready availability of funds for building construction and public housing enabled migrant workers and South Australians to move into new rental properties or take up home ownership like never before. In the process, the suburbs and smokestacks of Adelaide multiplied, and new industrial centres were forged.

This story has taken on a mythical quality, with Tom Playford viewed as the catalyst of industrialisation. That the Premier should be lauded for realising this transformation is not surprising. Playford's longevity in office certainly gave him the platform and opportunity to initiate and effect change. He garnered a reputation for acting unilaterally and being a charming and effective negotiator, which allowed him to 'get things done'. One of Playford's biographers labelled him a 'benevolent despot' – a description that seems to have been suggested by Playford himself – while the historian Nic Klaassen notes, with admiration, that the Premier was 'shrewd, persistent and persuasive … ruthless and cunning'.[2] All three of Playford's biographers, whose book-length volumes range in tone from appreciative to hagiography, place him front and centre of developments that occurred in the state.³ But while Playford's resolve and canny political skills were crucial in some respects, the roots of South Australia's transformation lie elsewhere.

Chiefly, they lie with the true architects of the industrial development of the state, particularly Auditor-General J.W. Wainwright, whose influence on Playford's predecessor, Richard Butler, and Playford himself far exceeded the remit of his position. Wainwright sat on royal commissions on the railways (1930), dairy produce industries (1933), transport (1937) and electricity supply (1931, 1945), and on boards and committees concerned with secondary industries, public transport, regional development, forestry, dairying, abattoirs, building materials, taxation, public service efficiency, and financial relations with the Commonwealth. His understanding of the structural impediments in the economy and of the hardships endured during the Great Depression by business, workers, and the unemployed alike, derived from this service and forged his resolve for change. Remembered for his hard-working, self-effacing but rather humourless manner, Wainwright prepared a series of meticulous and convincing arguments for state intervention in the economy that promoted the manufacturing sector. Other chief advocates of industrialisation and the mechanisms for its achievement, such as the provision of low-cost housing for workers and the granting of concessions to industrial firms, included Keith Wilson, Horace Hogben, Edward Holden, and Frank Perry, all of whom enjoyed unfettered access to Premiers Butler and Playford and sometimes sat alongside Wainwright on government advisory committees and commissions of inquiry. Tens of thousands of workers who took jobs in factories and literally stoked the fires and oiled the cogs of industry also deserve greater credit than they have generally been given in this story. Playford played his part by recognising when others had good ideas and by trusting them, even if this placed him at odds with his previously held views and the *laissez faire* liberals in his own party.

State intervention

When Butler assumed office for a second time after the defeat of the Labor government in 1933, he initially felt that salvation from the Depression lay in further stimulating agricultural production, the state's traditional source of wealth.⁴ However, the volatility of commodity markets and the wider scope for growth in the industrial sector of the economy convinced his key advisor, Wainwright, otherwise. Manufacturing in South Australia was stymied by high energy prices due to the necessity of transporting coal from New South Wales, and its distance from the primary markets in the eastern states. Wainwright believed that both industrial firms and migrant workers could be attracted if wages – the primary expense of manufacturing – and the cost of living in South Australia could be kept lower than in the other states. Government provision of infrastructure and concessions would also be required to entice industrial development. The threat by General Motors-Holden in 1935 to relocate its manufacturing plant from Woodville in Adelaide to Fishermans Bend in Victoria due to South Australia's higher rate of taxation and wharfage charges brought this last issue into sharp focus. It spurred the government to lower these rates and charges and to provide inducements for other industries. These included the construction of the Birkenhead Bridge at Port Adelaide,[5] assistance to build a wharf to serve the Imperial Chemical Industries Ltd's salt and alkali plant at Osborne, and proclamation of the Lefevre Peninsula as a 'protected' industrial area.[6]

In a number of cases the government enacted legislation that guaranteed assistance to companies subject to them establishing specific manufacturing facilities. Butler, for example, gave BHP secure mineral rights and committed his government to building a water pipeline from the River Murray to Whyalla in exchange for the company agreeing to build a blast furnace in that city.[7] (As a backbencher, Playford was a stern critic of the scheme, arguing that the provision of Murray water was a pipedream that should be totally ruled out.[8] He changed his mind upon becoming Premier and politically benefited a great deal.) Twenty years later, in 1958, BHP agreed to build a £30 million steel works in Whyalla in return for exclusive rights to prospect for iron ore in the Middleback Ranges and long-term mineral leases.[9] In the same year, Standard-Vacuum Refining Company (Australia) Pty. Ltd. also agreed to construct an oil refinery south of Adelaide in return for the state government undertaking to build houses for workers near the refinery site, to link the site by rail and road, and to supply fresh water and electricity.[10]

Wainwright understood that more sustainable means of attracting and retaining industry in South Australia rest with keeping wages and the cost of living below those of the cities of Melbourne and Sydney. The basic wage was set by the Arbitration Court, which received submissions from employers and unions, but its determination was partly tied to the cost of living, over which government could assert some influence by applying price controls and intervening in the housing market to lower the cost of accommodation. The former was facilitated by the onset of the Second World War, during which the Commonwealth government capped the price of many goods in order to prevent profiteering. The South Australian government assumed this responsibility in 1948 and retained price controls on hundreds of products long after most other Australian state governments had removed them.[11]

Providing cheap public housing was an even more effective strategy, as it lowered the cost of living, stimulated the building industry, and attracted migrant workers to the state after the Second World War when housing shortages were experienced across the country. Wainwright, again, was at the forefront of the housing proposal, arguing that low-rent houses would save industry and state and local government hundreds of thousands of pounds per year directly in wages because of reduced cost of living increases.[12] He worked in concert with Keith Wilson, co-founder of the Political Reform League, and Horace Hogben, an accountant and Liberal and Country League (LCL) member in Butler's government after 1933, who were additionally concerned about the sub-standard and relatively short-supply of accommodation that resulted from the building industry coming to a standstill during the Depression.

Following intense lobbying of the LCL government, a Housing Trust was established in 1936 with the remit to build low-cost homes for rent by South Australian workers. Playford, then still a backbencher, opposed the proposal on the grounds that it would be a burden on taxpayers that benefited relatively few people.[13] Subsequent Acts of parliament gave government authorities the power to order the improvement or demolition of sub-standard dwellings and enabled easier terms of finance for prospective home buyers who wished to free themselves from landlords.[14] Working-class families benefited from these reforms, but their plight was not the primary motivation for the establishment of the Housing Trust and the building of new homes. If it was, poor people would not have been excluded from renting them. The Housing Trust meticulously scrutinised applicants and only those with unblemished records as tenants, with excellent references and a demonstrable ability to meet fortnightly payments, were chosen. Those who had irregular work and income or who were deemed unlikely to maintain the cleanliness and appearance of a dwelling were turned away.

While relatively few houses were built before and during the Second World War due to scarcity of materials and labour, under the direction of Chairman Jack Cartledge and General Manager Alex Ramsay the Housing Trust became the state's *de facto* economic and metropolitan development authority after 1945.[15] Building was initially restricted to Adelaide, but was extended to Whyalla in 1940 as BHP's blast furnace and ship-building facilities became operational, and to Port Pirie and Port Augusta in 1941, Millicent in 1942 and Mount Gambier in 1945, following industrial and infrastructure developments in those country centres.[16] In 1946 the Trust also began to build homes for sale, targeting middle-class home-buyers and enabling the Trust to invest the profits in further construction. On average it built over 3,250 houses and flats each year between 1950/51 and 1966/67,[17] peaking in 1954 when Trust homes accounted for 47% of all residential dwellings built in South Australia that year.[18] Over the period 1945–70, the Trust provided a remarkable 31% of house and flat completions in South Australia. The comparable percentages for state housing authorities in other states in the same period were: 21% in Western Australia, 18% in Tasmania, 15% in Queensland, 14% in New South Wales, and 11% in Victoria.[19] The Trust was able to build the homes cheaply and quickly by utilising bulk-purchased materials and in some cases pre-fabricated structures, and by employing only a limited number of architectural designs that minimised space and adornments. This resulted in some rather austere and repetitive streetscapes, especially before gardens began to grow and the dirt roads were paved.

Given the extent of its building program, the Trust's choice of location and mix of housing type had a profound impact on the social-demographic characteristics of the city of Adelaide, which remains to this day. As Susan Marsden, historian of the Housing Trust, has noted, during the Playford era the Trust concentrated its construction of rental housing in the belt of suburbs running from the southwest through to the northwest and north of Adelaide's centre, wherever large areas of cheap land were available. The

Census of 1966 revealed these suburbs to be of the lowest socio-economic status. Housing areas outside this sector, which were developed for private purchase partly by the Trust, were of much higher socio-economic status. They included coastal suburbs near Glenelg and in former market garden districts such as Lockleys. The Trust was very reluctant to build rental estates in high-status suburbs in the east and the inner south, which helped preserve their prestige.[20]

Beginning in 1954, the Housing Trust began developing industrial estates, acquiring land for industrial firms and in some cases building factories, thus determining where they too would be situated. It was the only state housing authority to become involved in such activity. It coordinated the provision of water, sewerage, electricity and other services on industrial estates, and facilitated the extension of roads or rail lines to them if need be. It then concentrated the construction of rental accommodation adjacent to these areas.

The planning and building of the satellite town of Elizabeth, located 27 kilometres north of the Adelaide CBD, epitomised this activity. Established in 1955 and originally intended to house those working at Salisbury's Weapons Research Establishment and other northern suburb industries, Elizabeth soon became a self-sustaining industrial town and merged into the outskirts of Adelaide. International manufacturing firms such as Pinnock, Kenwood, and General Motors-Holden (GMH), the state's largest private employer, took up residence, attracted by the Housing Trust's generous provisions. In developing Elizabeth, the Trust was granted greater powers to oversee the complete planning and provision of the town. This included setting aside land for schools; planting public gardens; and establishing sporting facilities, a shopping centre and a town square – public amenities that were generally lacking in other residential areas developed by the Trust, much to their detriment.

Elizabeth absorbed much of Adelaide's population growth when the city as a whole was experiencing its most rapid growth and highest rates of immigration since the nineteenth century. Between 1954 and 1966 the population of the northern Adelaide Plains, incorporating the Elizabeth and Salisbury areas, increased almost ten-fold to 68,711.[21] In a setting of post-war housing shortages, during which housing authorities in other states discriminated against migrants by stipulating qualifying periods of residence before they were placed on housing waiting lists, migrants were attracted to Elizabeth by the prospect of securing private accommodation and a decent job. British migrants arriving in the late 1950s could secure a home in Elizabeth within a week or two of arrival, which many preferred over being accommodated in a hostel for months at a time, even if the hostel was located much closer to the city centre and in more salubrious surroundings. The Housing Trust was active in recruiting such migrants and, through an office it established in London, ran a Migrant House Purchase Scheme that attracted many British couples and families.[22] Sales staff joined the migrant ships at Fremantle, WA, the first point of arrival for many migrant ships, to ensure those who had committed to Adelaide continued their journey, and to entice others.[23] By 1966, British-born residents constituted 44.5% of Elizabeth's population, making it one of the most 'British' residential areas in Australia.[24]

The South Australian Housing Trust assisted in accommodating tens of thousands of migrants who came from elsewhere as well. They included Germans and Dutch who also settled in Elizabeth in high numbers, Italians and Greeks, and Central and Eastern Europeans such as Poles, Latvians, Lithuanians, and Czechs, who arrived as Displaced Persons soon after World War Two and were initially accommodated in outlying migrant hostels in Smithfield, Mallala and Willaston before being distributed throughout country areas and Adelaide. These migrants arrived through Commonwealth government schemes, and not at the behest of the Playford government. They became both essential workers in the now-thriving manufacturing and construction industries, and a key new market for the products that were being manufactured, grown, and built.

Industrial development during and after World War II
The Second World War provided another means of stimulating the industrial sector of the economy. Essington Lewis, the Managing Director of BHP, who was South Australian born and educated, exploited the opportunities that the onset of war provided. He cannily predicted an increased demand for iron and steel products and ship-building as war in Europe and Asia loomed, and negotiated with the Butler and then Playford governments to establish such facilities in Whyalla, then just a tiny country town.[25] Whyalla's population grew from about 1,100 in 1939 to nearly 8,000

by the end of the war.[26] By the end of the Playford era it had become South Australia's second biggest city, with a population exceeding 21,000 people.

During the war, Wainwright, who served the Commonwealth as South Australia's Deputy Director of War Organization of Industry, and Premier Playford actively lobbied Lewis (who became Director-General of Munitions from June 1940) and Norman Makin (Minister of Munitions) for government war contracts.[27] They argued that Fremantle and Sydney were unsuitable locations for war-related industries because they were most likely to be attacked, whereas South Australia's southern-most position kept it relatively safe from enemy action (although a German raider laid mines off the southeast coast near Beachport in 1941 and a German submarine fired at local shipping near Kingston SE in 1944[28]). They also noted that Adelaide's advanced motor vehicle industry and the facilities of the South Australian railway workshops could manufacture munitions equipment. Finally, they pointed to South Australia's largely under-employed, regionally distributed population, which was available to work in war-related industries.[29] The Commonwealth government was convinced, and three major munitions plants were built in Adelaide's west and north at Finsbury, Hendon and Penfield (in the district of Salisbury) in 1940 and 1941. The Penfield works consisted of 1,405 buildings covering an area of 3,672 acres and employed approximately 6,400 people.[30] Along with the Islington railway workshops, which produced shells and components for Beaufort bombers, they formed the backbone of the state's industrial contribution to the war. By 1942 at least 87 metropolitan manufacturers were also under contract to the Ministry of Munitions. General Motors-Holden became engaged entirely on defence projects, manufacturing aircraft components, armoured vehicles, marine craft, torpedoes and weapons, and its workers – some 5,000 at its Woodville plant – became government employees for most of the war's duration.[31] Factories in regional centres such as Peterborough, Port Pirie, Murray Bridge and Whyalla also manufactured products for the war and soaked up the state's surplus labour.[32]

The large munitions factories were refitted after the war and became the focus for further industrial development. By August 1946 every available building except two at the Finsbury works had been acquired or leased by private industry, these being mainly devoted to engineering, automotive, and whitegoods production.[33] In 1947 the entire plant at

Hendon was purchased by Philips Electrical Industries, which moved its production headquarters from Sydney and was soon employing nearly 3,500 workers.[34] Philips was the country's largest producer of electronic components and its Hendon plant became a major centre of technological skill development and research. The enormous Penfield complex was occupied by the Commonwealth's Department of Defence after the war for the development and testing of weapons, particularly rockets.

The Second World War thus provided a context for Playford to present the advantages of locating factories in South Australia, and he negotiated successfully for the state to receive war production contracts. But he and his party did not create the conditions that enabled the establishment of war industries and their transfer to private enterprise after 1945. Nor was Playford the only premier to persuade the Commonwealth government to direct its capital towards a particular place. Large munition works were established in most of the Australian states, some of which enjoyed the additional economic benefits of large numbers of American service personnel being stationed there. The South Australian premier was opportunistic, but he was not the catalyst for the industrial development that occurred during and immediately after the war.

Coal, electricity, and industrial relations

Playford's role in securing energy resources – a vital component in attracting and maintaining industrial enterprise in the state – is more unique and has been rightly praised by historians. When Playford took office, the Adelaide Electric Supply Company (AESC) had a virtual monopoly on power supply in Adelaide and some rural areas. It largely relied on the importation of black coal from New South Wales as its source material, the cost for which was transferred to private consumers and manufacturers. This monopoly, as well as the disruption to coal supplies due to striking coal miners in New South Wales that caused 'black outs' and the cessation of work in SA during and after the war,[35] compelled Playford to seek control of energy production. He wanted AESC to generate power from the lower-grade sub-bituminous black coal (often erroneously called 'brown' coal) reserves at Leigh Creek in the Mid North. Claiming it was unsuitable for use in its boilers, the company refused to comply. Following Wainwright's advice, the government proposed limiting the price that could be charged for electricity and capping dividends paid to AESC shareholders, measures that were also firmly resisted by the company.[36] Tensions between both parties led to a Royal Commission (Wainwright served as one of the three commissioners), which recommended the acquisition of AESC by the state.

Playford's decision to pursue this course of action divided parliament and the broader community and threatened to split his own party, which was founded on the principles of private enterprise and limited government interference. Of the 17 witnesses who gave evidence to the Royal Commission only two (a representative from the Communist Party and Australian Labor Party leader R.S. Richards) pushed for acquisition. Edward Holden, who served as a Liberal in the Legislative Council during 1935–47 and was one of Playford's key allies and chief beneficiaries of the industrialisation plan, refused to vote for the government takeover, as did leader of the LCL in the Legislative Council, Collier Cudmore, who famously labelled Playford a 'Bolshevik'.[37] Naturally AESC also rejected the proposal, with director Stanley Murray buying advertising space in country newspapers to make the company's case to shareholders living in the LCL's heartland.[38] The Bill to absorb AESC and establish a Trust to take over its assets and operations, although supported by the ALP in the House of Assembly, was defeated in the Legislative Council by LCL member Sir Walter Duncan's casting vote in December 1945, after much debate.[39] However, with minor amendments and some political wrangling, the Bill was passed in 1946. Over the next seven years AESC was entirely absorbed into the new Electricity Trust of South Australia (ETSA), which also took over operation of the Leigh Creek mine in 1948. Within a decade it became the state's primary source of coal.[40] By the late 1950s South Australian consumers were enjoying some of the lowest-priced electricity in the Commonwealth.[41] During this period ETSA also undertook a vigorous program of power transmission line construction in rural areas, replacing many small schemes based on diesel plants in country towns. By 1956 five times as many country consumers had access to ETSA electricity than was the case in 1946.[42]

Playford could now promise interstate and overseas industrial firms secure access to reasonably priced power. He could also entice them by pointing to South Australia's reputation for industrial peace. This was not an idle boast. For all but one decade between 1913 and 1997 South Australia recorded the lowest number of working days lost to strikes in the country.[43] The number of days lost in South Australia fluctuated between one-third and one-half of the national average, reaching the lowest point in the 1930s when an annual average of only 19 working days per 1,000 workers were lost (compared to 852 days in NSW, 155 days in Victoria and 244 days in Queensland – South Australia's main competitors in attracting industrial development).[44] The insecurity fostered by the Depression, and the failure of union action to alleviate the plight of workers and those who lost their jobs at the end of the 1920s and early 1930s, certainly contributed to this. But the early and later trends point to further deep-rooted reasons for the moderation of the labour movement. These include the state's effective system of compulsory arbitration and the corporate sector's encouragement of labour compliance by making strategic concessions regarding wages and conditions at key times.[45] The religious and ideological orientation of the South Australian workforce – composed of a higher proportion of moderate-minded Methodists and nonconformist Protestants and a relatively smaller number of traditionally more militant Irish Catholics compared to other states – also cannot be overlooked.[46] The key point is that industrial compliance in South Australia both pre-dated Playford's premiership and endured long after his term in office ended.

Playford did his bit to maintain harmony, however. Regular meetings at Trades Hall were arranged for Wainwright to brief union organisers on how their members could assist the government achieve its goals in exchange for improved conditions,[47] and in the 1940s a representative of the Australian Workers' Union was secretly authorised to certify who was suitable to be employed at Leigh Creek (thus securing work for members of his union) in exchange for ensuring that no member of the militant Miners' Federation of Australia obtained a job there.[48] Trade union leaders were also taken into the government's confidence in 1938 during its negotiations with British firm British Tube Mills Ltd., which was considering the construction of a tubular steel factory in Kilburn in Adelaide's north. In return for a 'closed shop' (i.e. the employment of only union members), the unions promised to keep the factory free from strikes unless a majority of unionists working at the factory demanded otherwise in a secret ballot.[49] Similarly, union representatives were consulted following Holden's threat to move interstate, and were supportive of the government decision to cut company tax and other charges in order to keep the motor body manufacturers in Adelaide.[50] Trade union officials and employers were invited to lunch together, and union officials attended the annual dinner of the Chamber of Manufactures. Both parties participated in occasional cricket matches, including one in January 1949 that was umpired by the leader of the ALP Opposition, Mick O'Halloran, and Premier Playford himself, with Sir Donald Bradman relieving.[51] The Plasterers' Society of South Australia led by the uncompromising James Cavanagh (later a Labor Senator for SA and Minister in Gough Whitlam's government) was a notable exception to this rule, antagonising the Playford government and occasionally other factions of the labour movement by its determinedness to strike, pursue recalcitrant employers in court, and blacklist particular businesses and enterprises – including the Housing Trust and ETSA for periods of time – on both industrial and ideological grounds.[52]

Assessing the Playford 'legend'

It was Playford's determination to seek accommodation between workers and their bosses, to 'nationalise' the electricity company, retain price controls long after the war had ended, and intervene in the housing market, that led the ALP Opposition leader of the 1940s and 1950s, Mick O'Halloran, to ruefully quip that Playford was 'the best Labor Premier South Australia ever had',[53] and suggest that 'Playford can often do more for my voters than I could if I were in his shoes'.[54] O'Halloran never had the chance to test his assertion. A 1936 reform to the *Constitution Act* abolished multi-member electorates and redistributed electorates in the state so that country seats outnumbered the more populated city seats by a ratio of 2 to 1.[55] The 'Playmander', as this electoral malapportionment became known, effectively consigned the ALP to opposition for more than thirty 30 years. The ALP attracted more votes than the LCL after preferences were distributed in the 1953 and 1962 elections, and consistently won the majority of metropolitan seats and those centred on industrial towns, but could not break the LCL's stranglehold in the more socially conservative country areas. The 'Playmander', above any of the particular achievements of the government, kept Playford and the LCL in power. Ironically, the LCL's hold on 'country' seats came to an end partly as a result of the government's success in establishing Elizabeth and other industrial areas on the urban-rural fringe, bringing their traditionally Labor-voting blue-collar populations within the boundary of rural electorates.

Like O'Halloran, some historians and certainly popular memory have been kind to Tom Playford, to the extent that all the achievements of his period in office have been largely credited to him.[56] Yet, as has been shown, the plans and implementation of the mechanisms for industrialisation and urbanisation predated his premiership and were designed and executed by others, chiefly a remarkable cohort of clever public servants such as J.W. Wainwright and the Housing Trust's Jack Cartledge and Alex Ramsay.[57] The Second World War also made possible a scale of industrial development and income generation that would have been otherwise impossible, regardless of the determination and energy of a Premier. Moreover, while the South Australian economy and population – not to mention the city of Adelaide and towns such as Whyalla and Port Pirie – were utterly transformed in this period, this transformation largely mirrored what was happening in other states (although South Australia still led, marginally, in several important categories such as population growth and manufacturing job creation). It has thus been suggested that, rather than charting distinctive development, the main achievement of the Playford governments was to ensure that South Australia matched the rising standard of living, industrialisation and modernisation that was occurring elsewhere in Australia, at a time when high Commonwealth-set tariffs protected industries and jobs, Commonwealth-provided welfare initiatives rewarded war service and enhanced the purchasing power of the poor, and conspicuous consumption became a way of life.[58]

A focus on the achievements of the Playford era also risks overlooking the social and environmental costs of the pursuit of industrial and urban development. Statistics testifying to the tremendous growth of Adelaide's suburbs only obliquely reveal the geographical class divide promoted by uneven Housing Trust activity, and obscure entirely the dull and repetitive streetscapes and uninspiring architecture that resulted and which now blights parts of the city. Nor do they illustrate the many suburbs that, unlike Elizabeth, failed to be provided with parks, social amenities, libraries, and even electricity and sewers for a time.[59] Indeed, as Jenny Stock notes, while 'development' was given top priority, areas of lesser concern to the

Premier, such as education, health, social welfare, and the arts, atrophied or got by with less than optimal funding.[60] (Until support was given to the establishment of a Festival of Arts in 1960, which only eventuated due to generous donations from private citizens, the government did not fund any theatre or musical productions, and apart from the ABC-funded orchestra all locally produced artistic activity was necessarily amateur.[61]) Playford maintained that once people had money in their pockets they could choose whether or not to support the arts or acquire health insurance, and that the provision of welfare to the poor was the matter for private charity not the public purse.[62] He could hardly be accused of Bolshevism on these fronts. Equally, while tens of thousands of migrant workers settled in South Australia, insufficient attention was paid to their needs and desire to maintain their own cultural and language traditions, which might have prevented them from leaving, as many did. The Premier famously rejected a proposal to introduce foreign language training into schools because, in his words, 'English is good enough'.[63] Playford's attitude towards the natural environment as a place to knock down, pave over, fence in and pollute if a buck could be made, was equally renowned.[64]

Nor should the much-lauded growth in South Australia's manufacturing sector escape critique. Manufacturing certainly grew but generally remained confined to particular industries that were already prevalent before the Playford period, such as metal industries (including motor body manufacturing) and whitegoods production, with a corresponding lack of non-durable goods industries such as textiles, clothing and paper. As Dean Jaensch has observed, the industrial development strategy originally intended to reduce dependence on rural industries thus created a 'new overdependence' on a narrow manufacturing sector that was vulnerable to shifts in consumer demand and, because it relied on foreign capital, the whims of corporate bosses based in the United States, Europe and Japan, who cared little about the local social consequences of their decisions.[65] When consumer credit and foreign capital dried up in the 1970s, and especially at the turn of the century when car manufacturers began to replace their Adelaide plants with those in countries where labour costs were cheaper, which then affected 'feeder' industries and businesses that made car components or catered for the car-making workforce, Adelaide's northern and western industrial suburbs were devastated. The very success of the Housing Trust in situating workers close to industrial areas in the 1950s and 1960s came to constitute a grave problem, as these suburbs became characterised by endemic unemployment and the associated social problems, while housing and rental prices fell and residents who had the means – often those with the most talent and potential to become community leaders – left.

The Scottish essayist and historian Thomas Carlyle once opined that 'the history of the world is but the biography of great men', and, indeed, historians are often seduced to explain the genesis and achievement of particular movements, ideas and events according to the will, energy and intellect of individual 'great' men or women.[66] To do so in the case of Tom Playford and the industrialisation of South Australia would be to ignore the complexity of the situation. It would require overlooking Playford's hesitancy at key junctures, disregarding context (social, political and economic) and comparison with other places and eras, and minimising the contributions of 'little men', such as J.W. Wainwright, to the cause. Carlyle's other famed dictum, that he would rather die of exhaustion than boredom, might well have applied to Tom Playford, but less so his assertion about history's propulsive force.

* This essay is a modified version of a chapter that appears in Paul Sendziuk and Robert Foster, *A History of South Australia*, Melbourne: Cambridge University Press, 2018.

11

Nineteenth Century Dreams, Twentieth Century Realities: Reframing the Abolishment of Capital Punishment in South Australia

STEVEN ANDERSON

These days the 'Dunstan Decade' is fondly remembered by most as a time when South Australians blew the dust off their statute books and embarked upon a series of radical social, cultural and legal transformations. Couched among other prominent legislative reforms, the Dunstan government abolished capital punishment on 23 December 1976.[1] It followed three previous failed abolition Bills initiated by Dunstan himself: first, in 1959 during the furore over the case of Rupert Max Stuart; second, in 1965, a year following the execution of Glen Sabre Valance (the state's last); and third, very soon after he became Premier a second time in 1970.[2] Dunstan's advocacy was carried out during the 1960s and 1970s – a unique time in history. A youthful baby-boomer generation was challenging accepted norms, Australian and international governments were abandoning the death penalty *en masse*, and the television and print media were keener than ever before to sensationalise the drama intrinsic to all capital cases. Given these facts it is very tempting to frame the abolition of capital punishment in South Australia as a post-World War II invention, energised by the charisma and advocacy of the long-time Member for Norwood. Yet historians of the Australian gallows ought to resist this temptation. As this chapter will demonstrate, the push to abolish capital punishment needs to register nineteenth century debates, not just ones from the twentieth century. It is high time the triumphant men and women of December 1976 were re-cast – not as figures on the cutting edge of criminal law reform – but merely as agents of change, finally implementing an idea that was as old as the settlement itself.

It is not enough to list abolitionists from nineteenth century South

Australia like a butterfly collector, noting them by shape, size, origin, and number to confirm that they merely existed. Any analysis must go deeper than this to uncover the justification behind a position that was, to be sure, a minority one throughout the colonial period. This chapter will closely examine two published lectures, delivered by David McLaren (1785–1850) and William H. Burford (1807–1895), to better understand the abolitionist case during the colonial period. McLaren delivered his lecture on 10 December 1840 to the Literary and Scientific Association and Mechanics' Institute at a Baptist Chapel on Hindley Street.[3] Burford, on the other hand, spoke at White's Rooms on King William Street in July 1874.[4] Outside of local newspaper and parliamentary records, these two lectures are extremely rare examples of nineteenth century abolitionist publications (with a close relationship to Adelaide) remaining in the safekeeping of either the State Library of South Australia or the National Library of Australia.[5] To round out the discussion a brief snapshot of abolitionist activities in colonial South Australia will be provided to better understand the exact form that opposition took prior to Federation. This investigation is limited to the pre-Federation period of 1836 to 1901. The post-Federation decades are worth examining too but my timeframe ensures that there is appropriate space devoted to proving that the abolitionist voice in South Australia could be heard further back in time than is usually acknowledged.

The scholarship on capital punishment in South Australia is limited but has been steadily growing in recent years. Mark Finnane, R.M. Hague, Alex C. Castles and Michael C. Harris all give brief but helpful mentions to capital punishment in South Australia in an historical context.[6] In the 1970s A.R.G. Griffiths offered a qualitative analysis of the available capital punishment data in South Australia while David Towler and Trevor Porter's *The Hempen Collar* (1990) is still the most useful compendium of primary sources relating to the issue.[7] Alan Pope in *One Law for All?* (2011) provides a detailed, book-length analysis of the interaction between Indigenous people and the criminal law in the earliest period of settlement, including for capital cases.[8] Case studies of particular executions tend to cluster around the infamous 'Maria Massacre' of 1840, the Rainberd murders of 1861, and the troubled life and death of Elizabeth Woolcock.[9] In my doctoral thesis I examined the transition from public to private executions in colonial Australia, an often overlooked aspect of the nation's penal history, which frequently referenced the South Australian experience.[10] In other forums I have explored the patterns of execution in the first twenty-five years of European settlement in South Australia as they applied to Indigenous offenders and one-time convicts.[11] James Gregory's *Victorians Against the Gallows* (2012) offers tantalizing details about abolitionist activities in colonial South Australia that provided me with many fruitful leads.[12] Most recently, Andrew Russ and Bianca Zanatta from the South Australian Parliamentary Research Library have provided a welcome overview of the application and eventual removal of capital punishment in the state.[13] Taken together, these sources were invaluable in understanding what was already known about capital punishment in South Australia and how they might be expanded upon to better understand the push to abolish capital punishment in greater death.

Since an extended analysis of their thoughts on capital punishment is to follow, it is worthwhile providing a brief biographical sketch of both McLaren and Burford. The Scottish-born David McLaren was an astute (if not sometimes unlucky) businessman most remembered for his involvement with the South Australian Colonization Commission and later with the South Australian Company from 1835 to his death in 1850.[14] He only resided in the colony itself from 1837 to 1841, acting as Manager of the South Australian Company. McLaren was a passionate evangelical and lay preacher who, according to one account of his life, through both 'business and belief' tried his upmost to 'make Adelaide a strictly Protestant Evangelical preserve'.[15] The mix of business acumen and evangelical verve was something McLaren shared with Burford. Burford was also a hard worker whose candle and soap manufacturing business allowed the family to accrue relative affluence after moving to Adelaide from his birthplace of England in 1838.[16] He felt a deep calling to God, which was displayed throughout his life, especially in his support (both financial and through active service) of the fledgling Churches of Christ movement that took root in South Australia.[17] Burford also had a brief, two-year involvement in public life as a Member of the colony's first House of Assembly in 1857.[18] The lives of both men differed in important respects but, across time and place, they held at least one core belief in common – a desire to see the colony of South Australia abolish capital punishment forever.

Douglas Pike's contention that South Australia was a 'paradise' for religious dissent is certainly borne out in the debate over capital punishment in the young colony.[19] Both McLaren and Burford's lectures were, at heart, complex examinations of whether or not the punishment of death was sanctioned by divine authority. The key passages cited in favour of retaining capital punishment were found then, as they are today, in the first five books of the Jewish and Christian Scriptures. It is in these books – Genesis, Exodus, Leviticus, Numbers, and Deuteronomy – that Mosaic Law was laid out and that an account favourable to the use of capital punishment can be easily constructed. McLaren and Burford recounted key Old Testament passages that favour the use of death for the benefit of their audience (Genesis 9:6 and Leviticus 24:17, for example) and noted how difficult it was to argue against these passages.[20] McLaren noted the difficulty in overcoming these assumptions when speaking contrary to Old Testament regulations. He said that 'however plausibly or powerfully supported by learning and eloquence', the abolitionist position was viewed as something that 'must be wrong', or worse still, as nothing less than a 'rebellion against the authority of Heaven'.[21] Burford saw that biblical arguments around the legitimacy of capital punishments were always reduced to a discussion about what part of the Christian Bible (the Old or the New Testament) the interlocutor choose to emphasise: 'The issue is just here – wholly here ... They must choose between the two covenants'.[22]

Nineteenth century abolitionists, almost always, emphasised New Testament teachings when it came to constructing a position favourable to the abolition of capital punishment. McLaren remarked that: 'I think it must be admitted, that the general tendency of the Scriptures of the New Testament are adverse to the taking away of life.'[23] He navigated away from the regulations of Mosaic Law by suggesting that these were 'temporary' and 'local' to the Israelites of biblical times, not something to be viewed as 'permanent' and 'universal' to be upheld for all time.[24] Burford – somewhat more dogmatically it must be said – suggested that for a Christian to prioritise the Old Testament was to 'sin against Christ' and that it was Jesus who was 'our divinely-appointed Lawgiver' who favoured 'mercy and love' above all else.[25] Burford went even further by labelling Christian ministers who were 'content to jog along, clinging to the Old Covenant instead of the New' as nothing less than 'the chief hindrance to the abolition of capital punishment'.[26] By establishing the primacy of New

Testament teachings both speakers were keen to support their claims with quotes from the gospels. For instance, both drew upon the same verse in Luke ('For the Son of man is not come to destroy men's lives, but to save them'– Luke 9:56), among others, to convince the audience that the scriptures were in opposition to the death penalty.

A series of secondary arguments, again theological in nature, were then proffered by both men. Both McLaren and Burford shared the view that executions by man encroached upon God's divine authority to take away life. McLaren stated simply that: 'He imparted life, and He alone is entitled to determine its continuance.'[27] Burford was more direct: 'When Governments or Magistrates abuse or go beyond the power with which God has invested them, they are no longer God's minsters but perverters of His laws.'[28] Widespread nineteenth century views on suicide being a 'sin' pursued a similar logic whereby man was usurping God's role as life-giver and life-taker. Another secondary argument for both McLaren and Burford was to suppose that, in accounting for a murder, vengeance itself was the province of God rather than the victim. It is rather ironic, given their outwardly stated preference for New Testament teachings, that both men cited Deuteronomy 32:35 to support their position ('To me belongeth vengeance, and recompense').[29]

Given the nature of these arguments it is worth speculating as to whether there was a correlation between particular denominations and the desire to see the end of capital punishment in the Australian colonies. Prior to his attachment to the Churches of Christ movement Burford worshipped with the Independents and Scottish Baptists while McLaren was, at different turns in his life, associated with the Baptists, Calvinists, Congregationalists, and Presbyterians.[30] There are other prominent figures in the colonial Australian abolitionist movement worth mentioning, such as the well-known politician Henry Parkes in New South Wales (a Congregationalist) or the prominent public librarian Alfred J. Taylor in Tasmania (a Unitarian), who offer further clues on this subject.[31] Indeed, there appears to be a perceptible connection between nonconformist Protestantism and the abolition movement in the Australian context. More traditional forms of Christianity well supported in the colonies, such as Catholicism or Anglicanism, are by comparison not as strongly represented in the abolitionist debate. A colonial pamphlet authored by the Rev. John

J. Ford and issued by the Catholic Truth Society in Melbourne lends its support for the retention of capital punishment (albeit with qualifications) and further strengthens the idea of a doctrinal divide on this particular issue in the period under investigation.[32]

Turning now from theological arguments to more secular ones, it is interesting to note how both men shared the same belief that punishment – as a general rule – ought to reform the criminal rather than merely avenge a past wrongdoing. McLaren declared that the 'object' of any penal code was not just to 'punish' and 'protect society from the occurrence of crime' but also to 'reform the criminal'.[33] On a number of occasions Burford references a similar idea, stating at one point that no punishment can be 'just' unless it has as its 'object' the 'reformation of the offender'.[34] In addition to stressing that punishment ought to reform the criminal, McLaren hinted at another major current of nineteenth century thinking – the importance of certainty in the administration of justice. McLaren wrote that: 'it ought never be forgotten, what centuries have proved, namely that the efficacy of judicial punishments in preventing crime, arises much more from their *certainty* than from the *severity* of the punishment'.[35] Any modern reader familiar with the literature on crime and punishment will immediately recognise the influence of the Italian Enlightenment thinker, Cesare Beccaria, upon this pronouncement. Beccaria's belief that certainty, rather than severity, is what mattered in administering punishment was widely deployed with an almost axiomatic confidence by McLaren and many of his contemporaries residing in the Australian colonies.[36]

What followed from the belief that punishment ought to be both certain and reformative in nature was a litany of complaints that the death penalty, by its very nature, defeated the ends of justice. Burford was keen to point out how troublesome it was that juries, instead of fearlessly sending the guilty to the gallows, were frequently liable to 'pause and hesitate'.[37] Such juries, continued Burford, were bound by a sense of 'tenderness' toward the plight of the offender and would eventually 'acquit prisoners, whom but for the circumstance of their life being endangered would certainly be convicted'.[38] To support his position he then offered a lengthy quote from book four of William Blackstone's widely circulated *Commentaries on the Laws of England* (1765–1769) mirroring this theme that jurors 'through compassion' will often 'forget their oaths' and set the guilty man free.[39]

Burford concluded: 'Thus, the chance of total freedom from punishment is the greatest where it ought to be the least, and the very fact of the severity of the law causes the extremist violation of it'.[40] McLaren also drew upon Blackstone in his speech, referring (in all but name) to the idea of 'pious perjury' first articulated by him in the *Commentaries*. McLaren provided a number of examples where juries in England valued stolen goods just below the threshold that would make it a capital offence.[41] He added to Blackstone by citing a number of occasions when, if two charges were formulated against a prisoner, invariably the non-capital charge was the only one proved by jurors reluctant to have the death of a criminal on their conscience.[42] McLaren summed up his discussion on the behaviour of juries by stating that the 'extreme severity' of the capital code rendered punishment 'not only uncertain, capricious, and momentary, but actually improbable, and thus [something that] encourages crime'.[43]

Miscarriages of justice, and the irreversibility of executions, were also at the forefront of their thinking. In Burford's eyes the nineteenth century courtroom was an imperfect institution and he was keen to chronicle some of its shortcomings. He thought that juries were 'plain, half-educated men, but little accustomed to weigh evidence' while judges were prone to summarise evidence in problematic ways for them.[44] Witnesses, he continued, were 'sometimes in error' and 'sometimes fraudulent' depending on the circumstances of the case.[45] Burford chose to support his claims by providing no less than six examples, all English, of cases where innocent persons had suffered wrongfully at the gallows. The examples included an excerpt from a recent speech to Exeter Hall in London (a nucleus of nineteenth century British evangelism) and another drawn from the work of Frederick Pollock who would become a very accomplished legal scholar at Oxford by the end of the nineteenth century.[46] McLaren, too, lamented that 'many, very many' innocent people had been 'sacrificed to false evidence or erroneous verdicts'.[47] Like Burford, he pointed to the 'fallibility of human tribunals' as the key reason behind the 'ignominious destruction of *innocent* life'.[48]

The lectures also register the concern that the spectacle of death challenged the very legitimacy of punishment itself and produced conflicted feelings within the onlooker. At length McLaren complained that the very violence of executions, then conducted in public, had a number of unhelpful consequences:

> The penalty of death ... familiarises the public with a spectacle, the tendency of which is to harden the feelings, to disgust the good, and brutalise the bad, to diminish the regard due to the sanctity of life, to render even murder itself less revolting to the ignorant mind, and it frequently excites the sympathetic and benevolent feelings of the spectators in favour of the criminal, rather than their more powerful feelings in detestation of the crime.[49]

McLaren, in espousing this idea, anticipated a central concern of the debate around public executions (as distinct from the debate around capital punishment) that occurred in the colony a decade later. For instance, in September 1858 when the Chief Secretary of South Australia, William Younghusband, took leave to introduce a Bill that would abolish public executions, he remarked how the 'effect of public executions tended to demoralise and had no beneficial result as an example'.[50] Despite the success of Younghusband's Bill (it was assented in December 1858) the belief in the corrupting nature of the execution spectacle appeared to persist. Burford (speaking in 1874) still believed that executions – 'whether by hanging, beheading, burning, or drowning' – diminished the 'value' that people placed upon their own lives and that of others.[51] Like McLaren, Burford thought that they had a 'debasing influence' upon 'public morals' and that capital punishment had 'the worst possible influence on society'.[52]

The ideas of McLaren and Burford on the abolition of capital punishment were far from original and a close examination of their text offers many clues for where they found inspiration. McLaren favourably records some of the key parliamentary reformers who are, to this day, regarded in traditional historical accounts as tempering England's capital code. In McLaren's account Samuel Romilly was lauded as a reformer 'far in advance of his age', Robert Peel had 'great talents as a legislator and an orator', William Ewart was a 'most active and persevering' advocate of abolition, while Thomas Foxwell Buxton was nothing less than an 'able advocate' in the 'cause of humanity'.[53] Moreover, McLaren and Burford favourably cite the exact same example of the Scotsman James Mackintosh who, while holding the position of Recorder (Chief Judge) of Bombay from 1804 to 1811, refused to execute criminals and (at least in his opinion) was still able to secure the peace and property of everyone in his jurisdiction.[54]

When Burford sought to undermine the credibility of capital punishment as an effective deterrent to crime he used statistical information from 'our history', by which he meant the recent criminal statistics of England and Wales, to make his case.[55] Outside of British examples, the United States, France, Prussia, Holland, Austria, and Belgium are afforded brief mentions as places that had successfully experimented with a less sanguinary penal code.[56]

The desire for both men to reference international examples, as opposed to domestic (i.e. colonial Australian) ones, is noticeable since a nascent capital punishment abolition movement was certainly perceptible in Australia by the mid-nineteenth century. At the time Burford was speaking in 1874 there were clear developments in the colonies to the east worthy of mention. For example, the successive attempts of Henry Parkes in 1860 and 1861 to abolish capital punishment on the floor of the New South Wales Legislative Council were well covered by the Adelaide press.[57] Or, perhaps, an attempt in 1872 by Edward Greville in the New South Wales Legislative Assembly to do the same may have been a more recent example to draw upon in his lecture.[58] Abolitionist literature was also available in the colony. For instance, a lecture-cum-pamphlet by Fredrick Lee, a prominent abolitionist in New South Wales, was very heavily advertised by South Australian periodicals in July and August of 1864.[59] Considering the cross-over between the arguments of McLaren and Burford, one can only speculate (since there is no direct reference) whether Burford had read the earlier lecture. It certainly is possible since the published work by Nathaniel Kentish that carried a full reprint of McLaren's lecture was on sale in Adelaide during the early 1840s.[60]

The eschewing of domestic matters in favour of predominantly British examples could be as simple as the availability (or lack thereof) of information to both lecturers in researching their topic. McLaren states at one point that he was 'indebted' to the British Society for the Diffusion of Information on the Subject of Capital Punishment 'for the information given this evening'.[61] The reason being that he was able to utilise material from that Society which had been reprinted in the columns of the *Morning Herald*, a London-based newspaper that presumably made its way to the young colony. More complex examinations could venture into the identity of Adelaide colonists being more closely tied to that of London than, say,

Melbourne or Sydney. The historian Penny Russell, for one, raises the possibility that colonists viewed themselves as simply 'English people living in another place'; members of a 'fragmented metropolis' rather than exiles living on a 'colonial periphery'.[62] Even in faraway South Australia McLaren was keen to express his solidarity with likeminded people back 'home' and ended his talk with a call to arms for colonists to do all they could to help the British movement: 'we ought to strengthen their hands, encourage their hearts, and aid their efforts'.[63] In fact, only a veiled reference to the Maria Massacre at the start of McLaren's lecture would have prevented it (or Burford's talk, for that matter) from being presented in an unaltered form to a London audience as opposed to the Adelaide one who actually heard it.[64]

McLaren and Burford's published lectures have been examined at length because they are among the few artefacts of abolitionist thought and rhetoric of substantial length generated by members of the general public that remain accessible to the modern historian. To round out the discussion a brief snapshot of the wider abolitionist activities in colonial South Australia will be provided to better understand the contours of the abolitionist 'movement' prior to Federation. In places like England various 'societies' were formed in support of abolition, and South Australia experimented with an abolitionist society at least twice during the nineteenth century. In 1844 the Society for the Abolition of Capital Punishment was established in Adelaide but it soon faded away, the last trace of it in the colonial newspapers being in March 1847.[65] Surviving Minutes from their meetings reveal that members were engaged in lobbying the government for mercy on behalf of at least two criminals, preparing articles on various topics, and inquiring into the local newspaper editors' position on the death penalty.[66] A second incarnation of an abolitionist organisation in South Australia came in 1874 when a Committee was formed 'for the purpose of bringing this matter of capital punishment prominently before the public'.[67] Less active and even more short-lived than the organisation of the 1840s, they did sponsor at least two public lectures on the topic, one of which being the talk given by Burford examined above.

Further fragments of evidence indicate that ordinary colonists were keen to discuss the issue of capital punishment at the community level. Whether capital punishment should be retained or abolished was a favourite topic for debate among the mosaic of young men's societies, amateur debating clubs and literary societies that dotted both city and country.[68] Churches hosted a number of talks about capital punishment. For instance, the Port Adelaide Congregational Church, the North Adelaide Primitive Methodist Church and the Wallaroo Presbyterian Church all, at some point during the latter half of the nineteenth century, had talks given by clergy or laity on the issue.[69] The fledgling South Australian Criminological Society that emerged in the late 1890s even had a local Rabbi address their members so that they could better understand capital punishment from a Jewish perspective.[70] A steady stream of activity in the South Australian newspapers, in the form of Letters to the Editor about capital punishment, allowed yet more voices to enter the discussion.[71] Not all of these forums found a welcome audience for abolitionist views but the very existence of debate and discussion on the death penalty certainly indicates public opinion was not totally settled in the affirmative.

The South Australian Parliament had moments when capital punishment was thrust into the consideration of legislators of all political persuasions. In 1858 South Australian parliamentarians, in line with developments in colonies to the east, abolished public executions for all criminals.[72] However, this reform was offset to some extent in 1861 when an amendment was passed allowing for Indigenous offenders to be executed, as they had been before, in public and at the scene of the crime.[73] Petitions advocating total abolition were occasionally presented to Parliament for consideration. In 1875 two such petitions were received from residents of Adelaide and Mount Barker while in the 1890s a small number of local Quakers petitioned Parliament to the same end.[74] It was also not uncommon for particular cases to energise groups or individuals to action by petitioning the governor for mercy.[75] In 1891, 1894 and 1895 there was a series of unsuccessful motions in the House of Assembly that advocated an end to the use of the death penalty as a whole.[76] The outcome of these votes suggest repeatedly that a majority of nineteenth century legislators were never quite ready to countenance total abolition.

If men like McLaren and Burford can be contextualised as being part of a wider South Australian movement against capital punishment, that movement – in the nineteenth century at least – cannot be characterised as a continual and unremitting assault on the gallows by a particular set of organised and committed colonists over the long term. Colonial advocacy lurched forward in fits and spurts, marked in many ways by discontinuity and disjointedness as opposed to continuity and uninterrupted progress. Still, the South Australian Parliament did provide abolitionists with some cause for joy. This was particularly the case in the reduction of the colony's capital code. As Jo Lennan and George Williams point out, the violent British penal code first adopted by South Australian colonists in 1836 was, at the time of Federation in 1901, whittled down to just two capital offences.[77] These were murder (including petit treason) and piracy with attempted murder. This fact alone indicates a slow but steady ascendency of one attitude over another in regard to the use of the death penalty in the jurisdiction of South Australia. These legislative developments did not equate to total abolition but they still would have encouraged the small but growing minority of colonists who came to share the view of McLaren and Burford.

I have neglected to mention until this point that it was none other than William H. Burford who was the first South Australian MP to float the idea of abolishing capital punishment on the floor of parliament.[78] In August 1857, during a brief two-year foray as a member of the House of Assembly, he moved a motion to present Governor Richard McDonnell with an address 'praying that a Bill be prepared for dispensing with capital punishment in all cases, and substituting secondary punishment in its stead'.[79] Although nothing came of this motion, the fact remains that no less than 119 years had passed between the first attempt in 1857 and the last in 1976. Taken alone, this is powerful evidence that the foundations of the abolitionist movement in South Australia ought to be situated in the decades following European settlement in 1836, rather than in the decades following the Second World War. Don Dunstan's individual advocacy, and the specific cases that animated him to action (such as the cases of Stuart and Valance), need to be factored into any discussion around the end of the death penalty in South Australia. However, those actions should not overshadow the pioneers of South Australian advocacy who had their own set of personal beliefs, controversial cases, and lines of argument that were unique to the milieu of a nineteenth century British colony.

12

Sending Out an SOS: South Australia's Forgotten Anti-conscription Crusaders

CAROLYN COLLINS

On a bitterly cold morning in July 1965, five women gathered outside Adelaide Airport and stood in silent protest as the first contingent of South Australian conscripts bound for the Vietnam War boarded planes for training camps in Victoria. Conservatively dressed, some in hats, all in sensible shoes, they made unlikely radicals. Only their aprons, emblazoned with handwritten anti-conscription slogans – 'kindness not killing', 'youth raw deal', 'no fighting career for our sons' – set them apart from family members there to farewell their loved ones. The women expected to be arrested but for the most part they were ignored. Indeed, had it not been for a photographer covering the conscripts' departure for the *News*, the state's first anti-conscription demonstration in the Vietnam era might have passed unnoticed.[1] Instead, for a short time, the women became celebrities, thrilled to be invited to present their case on Channel Nine's *A Current Affair*. It was just the start. As one of the women later recalled: 'Hectic days followed as we humble housewives were caught up in a huge groundswell of opposition that gradually developed against the Vietnam War'.[2]

The photograph of these five 'humble housewives' is in stark contrast to the more familiar ones of young men with long hair and radical politics who came to personify the anti-war movement, not just in South Australia but nationwide. These images have been reinforced over time by written accounts of this period, many of them composed by participants themselves.[3] In South Australia, narratives of the anti-conscription and anti-Vietnam War movement have traditionally been viewed through the prism of student and Labor party politics, not least because the period helped launch the careers of several future politicians, including two Labor premiers, John Bannon and Lynn Arnold. South Australia also had the distinction for the greater part of this period of having the nation's only state Labor Government, and a premier in Don Dunstan, who opposed the war (although whether he supported the anti-war movement was less clear to some of his supporters).[4] The ALP's involvement, radical student politics and the tumultuous history of the state's largest – and noisiest – protest groups, Campaign for Peace in Vietnam (CPV) and the Vietnam Moratorium Campaign (VMC), have been well documented in the existing literature of this state's anti-war movement, most notably by historian Malcolm Saunders.[5] They are front and centre of the mythology surrounding the foundations of the anti-Vietnam War protest movement.

But beyond the noise of the state's campuses and intrigue of political backrooms there was an array of other groups that also took to the streets to protest against conscription and/or the Vietnam War. Many of these were campaigning in Adelaide long before the formation of the CPV (in July 1967) and the VMC (1969). These included long time peace advocates like the Women's International League for Peace and Freedom (WILPF); the Union of Australian Women (UAW); the South Australian Committee for International Co-operation and Disarmament; the Peace Pledge Union; and the Society of Friends (Quakers). Several left-wing trade unions were also active in the anti-war movement prior to 1967.[6] New groups included the SA Advisory Committee for Conscientious Objectors, formed in 1966 to give advice about the National Service Act to potential conscripts, and the Committee for Vietnam Protest (CVP), founded in the same year by a group of History and Politics students at the University of Adelaide. While I would argue that all these groups deserve more credit for their efforts in launching – and sustaining – the protest against conscription and the Vietnam War in South Australia, the focus of this chapter is the Save Our Sons movement, which was formed by the women who staged that first lonely protest at Adelaide Airport.

The South Australian 'branch' of SOS was part of a loose coalition of groups that emerged across the nation, inspired by a group of Sydney women who came together in May 1965. SOS groups were among the first to protest publicly against conscription at a time when the vast majority of Australians supported their government's stand (and still viewed the peace movement with Cold War hostility and suspicion). And they were among the last to roll up their banners when the incoming Whitlam Government finally called time on conscription in 1973. In the intervening eight years they were a highly visible part of the anti-war movement, demonstrating on the streets of the nation's cities, lobbying politicians, producing and distributing anti-conscription literature, raising money for the broader anti-war movement, and actively supporting conscientious objectors and draft resisters. They also provided valuable practical support to the moratorium movement, in leadership as well as backroom positions. More radical members staged sit-ins at Commonwealth offices, chained themselves to Parliament House, picketed train stations, and set up an underground movement in the eastern states to hide young men who disobeyed the call-up. They were not treated kindly. Labeled as traitors and communists, they were ridiculed and faced hostility not only at demonstrations but sometimes even within their own families. But while many other small protest groups came and went during this period, the SOS endured.

The individuals who joined the SOS did not expect nor seek wider recognition. Perhaps as a result, the SOS's contribution in SA remains largely unrecorded.[7] This seems a shame, for just as the story of the women who opposed conscription during World War One has been preserved as part of the broader history of that period, SOS deserves to be part of the overall narrative of South Australia's response to the Vietnam War. They may have seen themselves as 'small chips in the huge mosaic of the anti-Vietnam War movement in Australia' but without those pieces, the overall picture of this period remains incomplete, even distorted.[8]

In considering SOS's activities and contribution, and in the light of this volume's theme, this chapter challenges two additional foundational myths about this movement and its members, both in SA and elsewhere. First, it tests the 'foundations' of the group, focussing on assumptions about gender, class and political backgrounds of those involved and their degree of experience in activism. How accurate, for example, was the 'humble housewives' tag in relation to the Adelaide group? Second, it examines the movement's effectiveness and significance within the wider anti-war movement; the 'myth' that perceived 'ladies' groups', such as the SOS, were largely decorative and their value marginal at best. The overall aim is to provide a new, more nuanced, layer of understanding about one of the many groups who came together during this period to form a mass protest movement against the Vietnam War.

Keeping up appearances

In November 1964, the Federal Parliament passed the *National Services Act* requiring 20-year-old males to serve for two years full-time in the army followed by three years part-time in the reserves. Conscription already had a controversial history in Australia dating back to World War One when Australians rejected it in two plebiscites, with women at the fore on both sides of the debate. But when the Prime Minister Robert Menzies argued its reintroduction was necessary in light of recent 'aggressive Communism' in Asia, few protested (though it is worth noting that women's groups were among those who did).[9] In March the following year, when the government announced that the conscripts would be sent with regular troops to fight in the Vietnam War, more Australians took notice. Among them was suburban Sydney housewife Joyce Golgerth whose son was among the first batch of conscripts chosen from a birthday ballot in which numbered marbles were pulled from a Tattersalls' lottery barrel. The Leader of the Opposition, Arthur Calwell, quickly dubbed this tacky exercise 'the lottery of death'.[10] Horrified, Golgerth contacted other like-minded women and Save Our Sons was born.

The movement first came to the nation's attention on 19 May 1965 when the *Australian* newspaper reported that a group of Sydney mothers with sons eligible for conscription had banded together to oppose the government's policy.[11] The women argued that it was 'morally wrong' to conscript young men to fight overseas when they were still too young to vote and said they had come together to issue 'a distress call – SOS – to mothers everywhere'.[12] This call galvanised others across the nation. Within a few months SOS groups had formed in Melbourne, Brisbane, Newcastle, Townsville, Wollongong, Perth and Adelaide. While they remained autonomous, all the groups adopted Sydney's statement of aims, vowing to campaign until the *National Services Act* was repealed.[13] In 1965, nobody envisaged this would take almost eight years, or that some of their members would be jailed in the process.

In Adelaide, Hazel Hoare, mother of four boys, read the article and decided to take action. The airport protest was organised and although the turnout was disappointing, the resulting publicity led to a better attended public meeting on 12 July 1965 where the South Australian SOS group was officially formed. The group elected a committee and a president, Unley 'housewife' May Wharton, described in a 1966 newspaper article as 'a 57-year-old grandmother who had been a Liberal supporter all her life'.[14] Like Golgerth, Wharton appeared to personify the group's public image as ordinary suburban middle-class housewives whose personal (if selfish) concerns for the lives of their sons had jolted them out of their kitchens and into the public sphere for the first time.[15] But public appearances could be deceptive – and manipulated.

The founding mothers in Sydney were careful to manage the public image of the movement in order to create an acceptable face of dissent. In the early years, the group was known for its silent vigils, where participants were encouraged to dress conservatively ('hats and gloves, ladies') and behave in a dignified manner, not responding even when they were being publicly abused and threatened.[16] Viewing images from the era it is not hard to see why reporters then, and historians since, have perpetuated the humble housewife image. To this end, Joyce Golgerth, housewife and mother of three, who had no prior political involvement, was the perfect figure head. But SOS documents reveal that Golgerth was a reluctant leader to say the least, nominated by women who knew their own high-profile involvement would immediately tar the new organisation as 'a Communist front'. Indeed, with the exception of Golgerth, the other eight women who founded the Sydney SOS group all had direct links or loose affiliations with left-wing groups in the Communist Party of Australia (CPA), the ALP, trade unions or the UAW, long mislabelled by ASIO as a 'communist front' organisation.[17] Contrary to that first press release, they did not all have sons eligible for conscription. Nor were they all Australians; the group included an American peace activist and an English communist party member, who had been allowed to immigrate against the advice of Australia's diplomatic staff in London.[18] The woman most likely to have been behind the initial idea, Noreen Hewett, was a long-term member of the CPA, an inaugural member of the UAW (who had represented the group on trips to China, Warsaw and Moscow), a trade unionist and a seasoned political campaigner for various causes. Perhaps the only thing she had in common with Golgerth was a son in the first batch of conscripts. Years later, she admitted that she 'knew that if I were the public face of this new organisation, the media would discount it on the basis of my links with the Communist Party, so I asked Joyce [Golgerth] if she would be willing to be the convenor'.[19]

The decision proved important. ASIO could find nothing with which to publicly discredit Golgerth and, as Hewett hoped, her role as the early figurehead helped to negate claims of communist influence. The media, in the main, tended to accept Golgerth's leadership and the SOS on face value without delving into the backgrounds of the other members and this made it difficult for the group to be categorised or dismissed by its opponents. This was also important in the recruitment of new members. Golgerth – like Wharton in Adelaide – represented exactly the constituency that the SOS was seeking to mobilise: middle class, non-political women who would have been reluctant to associate themselves with a UAW-led group, let alone one allegedly under the influence of the CPA. There is every indication that the tactic was successful. As the group grew, Hewett noted that most of the women who joined 'were new to political action' and from a wide variety of backgrounds. They included 'Quakers, Catholics, Methodists, agnostics, atheists, Labor, communist, even Liberal and non-party women who worked closely together'.[20] One ASIO agent who attended an early meeting with the express intention of exposing it as a communist front expressed frustration that the women themselves appeared to have no idea of the political or religious views of their fellow members.[21]

The South Australian group was in a similar situation with UAW women playing a key role in its formation. ASIO agents, always on alert for dire new threats to the nation's security, quickly made the link, noting a letter advertising the airport protest had been signed by a known UAW member and a member of the South Australian Peace Committee, who had once 'addressed a UAW luncheon on the subject of peace'.[22] Two agents sent to the airport reported that four of the self-proclaimed 'humble housewives' (Maureen Cook, Doris 'Dot' Edwards, Hazel Hoare and Audrey Potticary) had existing ASIO files due to their links with the UAW. The fifth woman was, at that time, unknown to the intelligence organisation. The women's 'protest aprons' were another clue. UAW women had cleverly adopted this attire in the 1950s to circumvent anti-demonstration by-laws that prohibited the carrying of placards.[23] As an advocate for women, the UAW had wider concerns about the war in Asia beyond conscription.[24] SOS, however, initially focused solely on repealing the *National Service Act* fearing that opposing the war itself would be perceived as 'too political', a step too far for some of its 'newer' members. In 1965, the Adelaide UAW reported to its national body that the airport protest had been 'initiated by individual UAW members', not the UAW itself. This was reiterated in a 2014 interview with the UAW's former secretary, Beryl Miller, who said while four of the women at the airport protest had been UAW members, their decision to set up SOS had been motivated primarily by the threat to their own sons.

> They were a mixture of women whose husbands worked in blue and white-collar jobs but did not work themselves at the time. They were very much opposed to the war on the basis that their sons looked like being conscripted. Of course, that made them very angry. They wouldn't just sit back and take it.[25]

Miller said while she and other UAW members regularly supported SOS actions, and vice versa, there were no formal connections between the two groups. ASIO agents, however, tried to prove otherwise, keeping track of SOS members who attended meetings of the UAW, CPA and other suspect groups. If nothing else their efforts showed just how busy the members were, attending multiple meetings for different groups each week.

But as SOS president, and later secretary, Mrs Wharton's reputation was above reproach. 'A Christian woman', she was a member of the Woman's Christian Temperance Union and had been, until conscription, a strong supporter of Menzies. Her reason for joining SOS was deeply personal. She had three sons; the eldest missed the call-up, the second was conscripted and the third would be eligible within the next two years.[26] But while her leadership may have helped distance the Adelaide SOS from the UAW, the group was still accused of having 'communist links'. Wharton found this personally galling. 'I have carried placards in some marches and I have been called a malicious communist', she complained to the *News* ahead of the 1966 election.[27] Earlier that same year, she assured those attending a public meeting that despite claims to the contrary, she was not a communist. Her passionate address made an impression on the ASIO agent present who, in an unusually expansive summary, recorded:

> She said she believes herself to be as good a Christian as the next one, as she believes in God, and as a mother she believes God is guiding her to raise her voice in protest to our boys going overseas, including her own son. She said our boys are taught hatred and bitterness in the army – how to bayonet, kill, shoot and maim human beings – and she called on every fair-minded person, mother, father, sister, brother or friend to rise up in protest against it all.[28]

Membership lists show that SOS members hailed from a mix of typically working class and middle-class postcodes across Adelaide, similar to the mix in Sydney and contrary to the 'myth' that SOS was drawn from 'a small constituency of middle-class mothers'.[29] Another 'myth' was that the SOS was an all-female group. Men were never specifically excluded from any group. Daytime meetings, however, did tend to rule out their involvement (along with that of many working women). Adelaide and Perth were unusual in that they not only had male members but also men in executive positions.[30] In Adelaide, women formed the majority and made up the original executive committee but in later years men also became office bearers, including president. Husbands joined the group with their wives, as was the case for government architect (and CPA member) Hal Pritchard and his wife Sadie, who had a son eligible for conscription. Thus, while it employed maternal peace rhetoric, SA SOS was, in fact, a parent group. This was reflected in the slogan on the group's stationery: 'Parents of the World Unite'.[31] Nevertheless, the image of the SOS as a group of 'humble housewives' became an enduring image that has outlasted the Vietnam War.

On the march
The founding mothers established SOS as a peaceful, law-abiding protest movement, believing sincerely, if naively, that once the wider public was educated about the reality of conscription, commonsense would prevail and the government would be forced to scrap it. They relied on traditional protest methods, long employed by the peace movement; the silent vigil was their signature event. In Adelaide, SOS held monthly meetings at Willard Hall in Wakefield Street. Buoyed by the response to its first television interview, members vowed to go 'all out on publicity

campaigns'.³² As a report to the national body of the UAW observed at the time:

> The girls shaped up really well, particularly as most of them had never done anything like this before and despite opposition from their families they are determined to go ahead ... all in all it has been a wonderful experience for these women and they are bubbling over with joy at the results so far achieved.³³

But it was not long before the group's novelty – and newsworthiness – wore off and the hard work began to recruit new members. Education was a cornerstone of SOS's campaign; it organised public meetings where guest speakers lectured on the legal and religious aspects of conscientious objection. It also conducted extensive letter-writing campaigns, targetting politicians, trade unions, service clubs, mothers' groups, church groups, local newspapers and popular women's magazines.³⁴ When US boxer Cassius Clay (Muhammad Ali) spoke out against the Vietnam War, SOS wrote commending him on his stand.³⁵

In November 1965, SOS supported the first joint protest of Adelaide anti-war and conscription groups, contributing to a large advertisement in the *News* calling on the Menzies Government to do all in its power to end the fighting in Vietnam. Authorised by Edna Hutchesson, secretary of the SA Committee for International Cooperation and Disarmament, the diverse group of sponsors included 15 members of the History and Politics Department of the University of Adelaide, the SA Advisory Committee for Conscientious Objectors, Women's International League for Peace and Freedom (WILPF), the Peace Pledge Union, the UAW, several trade unions, the Society of Friends, the Woman's Christian Temperance Union, and the Greek Workers' Educational Association.³⁶

Adelaide SOS members saw themselves very much as being part of a national movement and communicated frequently with Sydney leaders, exchanging ideas, tactics, literature, and contributing to national efforts. As such, their contribution needs to be assessed not only in terms of what they achieved in their own state but within the context of the broader movement. In the early days, this included collecting signatures for two national SOS petitions. The second, comprising 17,000 signatures, created a tower 'more than a foot high' when it was presented to federal parliament by Labor MP Dr Jim Cairns.[37] In October 1966, SOS groups joined noisy protests in capital cities against US President Lyndon Johnson's visit to Australia. While Adelaide was left off the official itinerary, SOS still protested outside Parliament House.[38] But lack of finances and distance prevented Adelaide members from joining their east coast colleagues on two deputations to Canberra in 1965 and 1966,[39] or their Caravan Against Conscription in 1968.[40] However, Adelaide members did support a proposed High Court challenge to conscription initiated by the Sydney group. The group successfully advertised for parents to take part in the test case, promising to pay legal costs. In the end it did not proceed on legal advice that it might do more harm than good.[41]

In the wake of the abandoned High Court challenge, each SOS group set up its own legal aid fund that was used to support young men in their legal fight against conscription. The Adelaide members held fundraising events, sold pamphlets and badges, hosted trading tables and collected donations at meetings. Members also worked in conjunction with other groups, counselling young men and distributing information packages about the *National Service Act*. This included options for those who did not want to fight and a list of lawyers prepared to assist. When conscientious objectors and draft resisters started to appear in Adelaide courts, SOS members were there too, providing financial and moral support to young men whose own families did not always support their stand.

SOS groups produced several anti-conscription leaflets and booklets during their campaign, thousands of which were distributed nationally. These included 60,000 copies of a leaflet 'Conscription is Wrong' that was widely distributed in Adelaide in 1967.[42] They also delivered anti-war literature on behalf of other groups. SOS leaflets were designed to be informative but also to elicit an emotive response. A 1965 Christmas leaflet, for example, demanded: 'Will you think of the thousands of young men being brutalised in Vietnam? Will you think of the Vietnamese families being slaughtered for no fault of their own?'[43]

SA SOS also supported a nationwide campaign initiated by the UAW opposing the production, sale and promotion of war toys for children, such as toy tanks, guns and GI Joe dolls. In a letter directed to local retailers, Mrs Wharton protested:

We say that war toys condition a child's mind to the acceptance of war and hate as an inevitable way of life. We urge you to stock more constructive toys which besides giving our children pleasure will help to train them as useful, well-balanced citizens of the future.[44]

A letter was also sent demanding John Martin's department store refrain from including war related themes or toys in their annual Christmas pageant.[45] The campaign proved effective. By early 1968, war toys were rarely displayed in store windows and retailers across Australia were reporting a dramatic decline in their sale. A spokesman for the Foys department store blamed the decline on a sustained 'campaign waged by the Save Our Sons organisation'.[46] Getting rid of war toys, however, proved easier than ending conscription.

The 1966 election was seen as a de facto referendum on conscription, however, most SOS groups, with the exception of Melbourne, stopped short of endorsing ALP candidates, a reserve they abandoned at future elections. The lead-up was dominated by the high-profile case of Bill White, a young Sydney school teacher who was jailed for defying the call-up. SOS groups across Australia, including Adelaide, closely followed the case and campaigned on White's behalf. Melbourne SOS supporter, Glen Tomasetti, a popular folk singer, composed and recorded *The Ballad of Bill White*, and the EP was sold by SOS groups nationally. White was eventually granted conscientious objector status (but not until after the 1966 election) and thanked SOS for its support.[47] His grateful mother joined the movement.

Buoyed by growing membership numbers, interstate expansion, and apparent public support, SOS was convinced its work would soon be over. The re-election of the Holt Government in 1966 was a crushing blow. In their newsletters and correspondence, SOS members despaired, although Sydney women noted the campaign had brought in many more members and generous donations.[48] In South Australia, Labor suffered an 11.9 per cent swing against it, double the national average. The gloom was exacerbated by Dunstan's defeat at the state election a year earlier. Morale was low but members remained defiant. 'Naturally we are very disappointed at the outcome of the recent elections and feel like sitting down and "licking our wounds"', Mrs Wharton told her Sydney colleagues. 'However, we realise we must redouble our efforts.'[49]

Changing tactics

In the following years, SOS tactics changed. Some groups became more radical in response to crack downs on civil liberties in their cities. They also worked more closely with other anti-war groups, while careful to maintain their own separate identity. In the immediate aftermath of the 1966 election, the protest movement was 'recharged' by the visit of South Vietnam's controversial premier, Air Vice Marshall Ky. SOS members took part in often violent protests as he travelled to Canberra, Sydney, Brisbane and Melbourne. Adelaide was again left off the itinerary but members produced a leaflet highlighting Ky's claim that his only hero was Hitler, pointing out that 'many fathers of today's conscripts fought against Hitler and what he stood for'.[50] The Brisbane protest resulted in particularly nasty scenes with one woman left on the sidewalk nursing a broken foot. SOS secretary Vilma Ward, who spent hours at the city watch house helping 'bail out' demonstrators, called for a public inquiry, alleging 'police brutality and breaches of civil liberties'.[51] Outraged, SA SOS sent letters of complaint to the Bjelke-Petersen Government. Until then Ward had been one of the movement's most conservative leaders, opposing the High Court challenge and strictly monitoring the dress code and behaviour of fellow members at SOS vigils, but the Queensland Government's crackdown on demonstrators radicalised her. She was arrested and faced jail after refusing to comply with by-laws during a subsequent demonstration. Adelaide SOS wrote supporting her 'courageous actions'.[52] A similar crackdown on protests in Melbourne also saw SOS women there launch a campaign of civil disobedience, resulting in multiple arrests. 'We feel that the situation is so desperate that civil disobedience is our only course,' the group's newsletter reported in March 1968. The women were later credited along with university students for the repeal of a controversial Melbourne City Council by-law. Wollongong women also adopted more radical tactics, resulting in the arrest of two members in 1968.

While Adelaide members never radicalised to the same extent, they did reassess their tactics and broaden their aims 'to oppose the war in general'. They also became more overtly political.[53] Perplexed by the new Opposition Leader's 'attitude to troops in Vietnam', for example, they wrote to Gough Whitlam urging him make his position clear.[54] And they supported a push to establish a Civil Liberties Council in the state.[55]

In 1968, they sent a strongly worded letter to Prime Minister Gorton, describing the suppression of alternative views on Vietnam as 'an affront to our democratic rights'.

> [We] feel Australia's military role in Vietnam is wrong – wrong for this country, wrong for Vietnam and for the future peace of the area and the moral wellbeing of our youth.[56]

They may have stopped short of civil disobedience campaigns of their own, but the Adelaide group sometimes walked a fine legal line when it came to supporting the increasing number of young men electing to break the law. Behind the scenes members were kept busy 'counselling' and raising money to support individual cases. When invited, they also spoke on behalf of young men in court. They contributed to efforts to free Adelaide carpenter Chas Martin, who was jailed for two years after refusing to obey his call-up notice, and they also publicised and supported cases interstate including journalist Simon Townsend in Sydney and John Zarb in Melbourne, among others.[57] Privately, they were not always happy with the results. When Elizabeth conscientious objector Robert Bright was 'suddenly declared medically unfit' after three court hearings, SOS members 'deplored' the decision because 'if all [conscientious objectors] are dealt in this way, the effect of their objections become nullified and may never be known to the public'.[58] At a subsequent meeting it was noted that another member's son seeking conscientious objector's status had also been mysteriously declared medically unfit. A similar trend among interstate members' sons had some wondering whether their parents' association with SOS was part of the reason.[59]

Adelaide members sought new ways to spread their message but even relatively simple actions proved difficult. In 1967, for example, the group tried to rent an advertising board at the Adelaide Railway Station but after long drawn out negotiations with hostile railway officials, even the mildest poster was rejected as unsuitable.[60] Sometimes just keeping in touch could be problematic. A telephone chain was established so members could efficiently relay information to each other and respond quickly when impromptu protests were called. But not everyone had telephones, including the group's secretary. She offered to resign but was convinced to stay on after it was pointed out that members could call her next-door neighbor if the matter was urgent.⁶¹ Practical obstacles such as these are easy to forget in today's modern world of instant communication. Old tactics were not abandoned; the airport vigils continued. When members questioned the merit of these 'depressing' events, they were reassured by three young men attending one of their meetings that they had 'good effects in the long run'.⁶²

During the same period, the anti-war movement in SA was gathering momentum. In 1967, SOS members were among concerned citizens who attended a series of meetings seeking the best way to coordinate the activities of anti-war groups in Adelaide. In the end, a brand-new group was formed, the Campaign for Peace in Vietnam (CPV). SOS was represented at meetings of CPV, and later the Vietnam Moratorium Campaign (VMC). Members raised money for these groups and took part in their demonstrations, as well as providing practical assistance, such as secretarial work. They also held joint functions with them, including the screening of an anti-war film.⁶³ SOS members, like Janet Darling and the Pritchards, found themselves increasingly busy with commitments in the new groups. Despite this, SA SOS determinedly maintained its own separate presence. At protests, its striking blue and white banner always attracted a large number of 'new' marchers, mainly women. Unfortunately, most never took the extra step of joining the organisation, much to frustration of SOS leaders. 'We always have a great following at moratorium marches,' one member noted. 'SOS is very well-known and popular'.⁶⁴

The late sixties also witnessed increasing confrontations between police and the anti-war movement in Adelaide as more radical student groups emerged. While SOS was always a strong supporter of other anti-war groups, some members struggled to accept their tactics. After Vietcong flags were flown during one march, a delegation met with the CPV's Brian Medlin to convey SOS's concerns that this was having a negative effect on the anti-war movement's efforts to appeal to the broader public.⁶⁵ On another occasion concern was raised about the 'offensive language' being used by some students. But in an effort to breach the generation divide, SOS members also reached out to younger protesters, inviting them to address their meetings and explain their politics and tactics. Robert Pritchard, a member of the Society for Democratic Action (SDA) and representatives of Provo, Lynn Arnold and Keith Oehne, addressed one meeting. The minutes noted that 'the young people are determined not to compromise their ideas in order to persuade the powers that be'. At the same time, members were apparently reassured; 'though they think of themselves as "anarchists" in the sense of no central government, they appear the gentlest of revolutionaries'.[66]

Despite misgivings about tactics, SOS members did not hesitate to render support to younger protesters when they were arrested by police. On 11 April 1969, 53 protesters, mainly students, were arrested during a protest and sit in at the Adelaide offices of the Department of Labour and National Service. The *Advertiser* reported that about 200 students carrying anti-Vietnam banners and 'red flags' and singing protest songs had demonstrated outside the building. When a group of forty of them ventured inside, police moved in.[67] Robert Pritchard, son of SOS members Hal and Sadie Pritchard, was among those arrested. A month later, thirteen protesters appeared in the Adelaide Magistrates court charged with a range of offences including assaulting police, resisting arrest and behaving in a disorderly manner at another demonstration.[68] This time, the Pritchards' daughter Ann, was among them. Sadie Pritchard subsequently became treasurer of the CPV's legal aid committee.[69] Another member's son, student teacher John Tapp, sustained a broken nose and was charged with two counts of assaulting police and one of resisting arrest. His conviction on all three charges was later quashed in the Supreme Court after news footage 'showed quite clearly that it was the policeman who had moved into and hit Tapp on the bridge of the nose with his fist'.[70] Another SOS member provided a statement that she had witnessed 'men in plain clothes and looking like spectators suddenly spring on University students'.[71] To Tapp's mother, Eulalie, it was 'obvious' that South Australian courts were 'now being used to suppress political dissent':

> From that day on, I was a regular visitor at court where I witnessed the presiding magistrate automatically accept the evidence of the police where such evidence conflicted with that of the defendants and their witnesses.[72]

At the SOS's annual general meeting in July 1969, the secretary reported a busy year in which it was 'quite surprising what we had achieved'. Monthly meetings had been well attended, active membership was up, albeit slightly, with more parents asking to be added to the group's mailing list. Members had 'contributed a great deal of support' to other organisations in the support of conscientious objectors and opposing the war, and the group had been represented at the Left Action Conference in Sydney – where Hal and Sadie Pritchard met members of the Sydney SOS – as well as a conference held by the CPV at the University of Adelaide. They had also 'morally and financially' assisted objector Keith Ohne, who had successfully gained total exemption from National Service. Overall, it was felt that SOS's activities had contributed to 'a stepping up of the campaign against conscription and what is more important, more and more 20-year-olds resisting the draft'.[73] The report concluded with an upbeat prognosis: 'All in all I think our organisation stacks up well both here and in the other states but of course we will, I am sure, do bigger and better things in the coming year.'

However, there was more bad news at the 1969 election which saw the incumbent Gorton Government retain power. Some headway had been made. In South Australia, all five seats targeted by the anti-war movement had changed hands to Labor. The new decade brought more hope. Dunstan was reelected in May, easily taking 27 seats, and the national moratorium movement was gaining momentum. Nationally, SOS was also making headlines. In June 1970, a group of neatly dressed Wollongong women descended on Canberra and chained themselves to railings inside Parliament House.[74] The following year there were nationwide protests after five Melbourne SOS mothers were jailed at Easter after a sit-in at a Commonwealth office.[75] SA SOS responded by holding a protest at the Adelaide Railway Station and sending telegrams to the Victorian Premier Henry Bolte. Police were called after one protester was involved in a 'scuffle' with a railway constable.[76] According to Jim Cairns, national publicity over the women's jailing marked a turning point in the anti-war campaign.[77] In 1971, SOS Victorian leader Jean McLean, one of the so-called Fairlea Five, and a deputy chairman of the VMC in Melbourne, was a special guest speaker at Adelaide's July 31 March Against the War rally.[78]

The lead-up to the first moratorium in Adelaide was hectic. Local SOS members worked tirelessly helping organisers prepare for the week-long event that included a meeting at the University of Adelaide addressed by Jim Cairns, a motorcade around Adelaide Oval on Anzac Day, a week-long vigil on the steps of Parliament House, and various arts events, including concerts, films, poetry reading and folk singing. The conclusion of the program on Mother's Day made SOS's involvement particularly potent. Sydney SOS produced a special leaflet, titled 'Mothers in Mourning' using two black and white drawings donated by political cartoonist Bruce Petty, which was distributed nationally. In South Australia, Petty's illustrations were also used in a powerful newspaper advertisement jointly sponsored by the WILPF and SOS, which was credited for a large turnout of women taking part in the moratorium.[79] While there was much enthusiasm for the moratorium, SOS correspondence also hinted at the underlying tensions and 'difficulties' between the various representatives in the VMC, including in Adelaide where some of the behaviour of more radical students was viewed as 'worrying'.[80] Of bigger concern was a government fear campaign, warning the moratoriums would result in violence in a bid to discourage 'ordinary' Australians from taking part.[81]

In the end, moratorium marches across the country were peaceful, attracting thousands of marchers. The *Sunday Mail* estimated about 6000 marched in Adelaide, 'including a group of mothers marching under the banner "Save Our Sons"'.[82] The only violence nationally occurred in Adelaide on the eve of the main march when protesters attending a Radical Alliance rally were 'attacked' by a small group of soldiers on leave from Woodside Barracks.[83] The local VMC committee believed the attack was premeditated.[84] Nevertheless, the Adelaide SOS group reported that the moratorium had, overall, gone 'extremely well', attracting a lot of new interest.[85]

The second moratorium in September 1970 was also marred by violence in Adelaide with 130 protesters subsequently arrested.[86] The Dunstan Government responded by ordering a Royal Commission, a culmination of months of tensions and political jousting between the ALP, the CPV and VMC.[87] The Adelaide SOS group kept out of the politics but provided 'loyal support' to those arrested, with Sadie Pritchard providing a statement to the Royal Commission.[88] Some believed, however, that the political turmoil surrounding the September moratorium left the local anti-war movement weaker.[89] SOS secretary Audrey Potticary remained upbeat:

> The SOS, in general, has remained actively involved with the VMC and is proud of the fact that in doing so it is supporting the vanguard of the peace movement and supporting young people who are directly affected by conscription and the war in Vietnam.[90]

But SOS members' increasing workload with other groups took its toll. While most were used to juggling multiple responsibilities, the commitment to the moratorium movement was all consuming. Having always struggled to increase its core membership, leaders now found that new protesters were more interested in joining larger, more publicly visible groups. Hampering recruitment was the fact that SOS was still seen by many as a mother's group. Despite the success of the May moratorium and hope that it would inject 'new blood' into the group, so few attended the annual general meeting in June 1970 that it could not proceed. Janet Darling, who found her time increasingly taken up with the CPV and another group she had founded, Children of Vietnam, responded with her 'recipe for stimulation', which advocated SOS becoming either an auxiliary or sub-committee of the CPV.

> As a person I can achieve whatever I now do for SOS within my personal CPV membership, and also with my connections with the various youth peace movements, with far less demand on my much divided time and energies. Thus the disbandment of SOS would leave me personally better off both time and energy-wise, and yet mean me doing not one bit less for the general peace movement.[91]

In the short term, members decided to continue as a separate group but by early 1972, the writing was on the wall. A letter was duly distributed asking members to vote on whether to continue, disband, or place the group into 'caretaker mode'. In March 1972, after a close vote, SOS went into 'indefinite recess'.[92] Like Janet Darling, however, other SOS members did not 'give up' their fight, they just continued to campaign as part of other groups.[93] Eight months later, Gough Whitlam's election heralded the end of conscription. Satisfaction at seeing conscription scrapped was tempered by the knowledge of the scores of lives lost and scarred. The last remaining SOS groups in Sydney and Melbourne disbanded in 1973.

Legacy
There is no doubt that SOS kept up a busy schedule of activities but assessing its effectiveness and legacy is difficult. On the one hand, unlike most protest movements, it achieved its aim: conscription was abolished in 1973. By this measure it was a success. On the other hand, the extent

to which the anti-war movement helped bring this about is contested. Opinion polls from this period show the majority of Australians continued to be hostile towards the protest movement, even after the moratorium campaigns.[94] They might have changed their mind about Australian troops being in Vietnam, but that did not translate to broad support for the anti-war movement itself. Furthermore, some like historian Peter Edwards maintain that the Coalition's decision to withdraw troops ahead of the 1972 election was in response to policy changes in the United States, not to domestic dissent.[95] Hence, it is difficult to draw any conclusion that SOS – as 'one small chip' in the anti-war mosaic – had any significant degree of direct influence on federal government policy. Nor, is it possible to quantify whether the movement actually 'saved' any sons, although anecdotal evidence does suggest that some young men did change their mind about obeying the call-up after contact with SOS groups.[96]

Still, there can be no doubt that members in Adelaide and elsewhere provided valuable practical and moral assistance to many young men faced with the prospect of conscription. As well as counselling, they helped publicise and draw attention to individual cases before the courts, putting pressure on those prosecuting. In some cases, they went further, helping to prepare individuals for their court appearances and organising legal representation. The importance of moral support should also not be overlooked. SOS members in Adelaide spent many hours inside and outside courtrooms supporting young men in their legal battles, some of whom were not supported by their own families. Moral support extended to checking up on family members, comforting mothers and, where necessary, mediating between young objectors and their families. To this end they acted as cheerleaders, family counsellors, and in some cases, substitute parents.

SOS was important in other ways. The presence of older 'respectable' women, and in Adelaide's case, men, served to broaden the appeal of the antiwar movement and reach segments of society that the peace movement had previously been unable to penetrate. One student protester believed SOS lent demonstrations 'a sense of gravity and solidity ... you always felt their presence was a validation that you were on the side of decency'.[97] In his later years, Jim Cairns also noted SOS's significance in bringing the middle class into the broader anti-war movement: 'I don't say that middle class people didn't feel for peace but they had their own way of giving expression to those feelings and it didn't involve getting out on to the streets and fronting a peace walk.'[98] He neglected to note that SOS had been there from the beginning. It had been part of the foundation of the anti-conscription and anti-Vietnam War movement; it did not need to be 'brought in'. The SOS banner in Adelaide acted as a vanguard for women at marches and rallies while the group itself provided those new to the political sphere with a safe space in which to express their dissent. On the whole, SOS women had more positive experiences than younger women involved in male-dominated anti-war groups, who often complained of being treated as second class citizens.[99]

What is rarely recognised is the valuable assistance that groups like SOS, and indeed the UAW and WILPF among others, provided to new groups like CPV and VMC, which never lacked for leaders but often struggled to find those willing to do the 'menial' behind-the-scenes work. In this respect, more experienced SOS volunteers brought valuable organisational and practical skills, which, though often undervalued, formed the backbone of many of these groups. It is noteworthy that when SOS went into recess in Adelaide, it sent a letter to 'assure all the peace and anti-draft organisations that they will still receive full support from SOS members both morally and financially'.[100]

Importantly, the legacy of SOS lived on in the lives of its members, many of whom transferred their skills and experience gained during the anti-conscription campaign to other causes. While some members returned to their domestic spheres, satisfied that they had achieved their aim, others found their experiences had changed them, and there was no going back. Interstate, three SOS women went on to serve in federal and state parliaments. Margaret Reynolds, who founded Townsville SOS, became an ALP Senator; Melbourne SOS committee members Joan Coxsedge and, later, Jean McLean were elected to the Victorian Legislative Council. In Adelaide and elsewhere, SOS members, like the Pritchards, turned their attention to other peace causes, protecting the environment, women's rights, or new political parties like the Australian Democrats. For them, the fight went on. Four decades later, Audrey Potticary, who had attended the first protest at Adelaide Airport, reflected on the SOS's contribution in a history of the UAW:

I found it hard going at times as I had no experience being a South Australian secretary of an Australia-wide movement that was SOS. But with the help and support of the wonderful women of the UAW and other organisations, we felt we made a difference in the successful opposition to the war.[101]

Conclusion

Accounts of the foundation of the anti-war movement in South Australia have tended to focus on efforts by university students and aspiring Labor politicians but it is a fiction to suggest they took to the streets alone. In South Australia, as elsewhere, SOS was one of the earliest opposition voices to conscription, helping to lay the foundation for the broader movement. Yes, it was a product of its time, a movement that relied on traditional maternal peace rhetoric and protest methods that were considered old-fashioned even then but its presence helped bridge the generation divide, contributing to the diversity of the moratorium movement. It provided a 'safe' place for those who had not previously ventured into the public sphere, and who would not have been comfortable being part of more radical groups. Importantly, the movement stayed true to its cause, never diverted by private ambitions or political ideologies. In Adelaide, its membership may have been smaller and less radical than its interstate counterparts but its supporters were just as tireless, protesting alongside the would-be politicians, students, academics and other concerned individuals as well as working behind the scenes. They were ordinary citizens, sincere in their beliefs, who bravely opposed the policies of a popular and long-standing government. In their own way, they made a valuable contribution. In the broader arc of South Australia's history of dissent, it is worth remembering that.

Notes

Chapter 1 | Beautiful Lies?: Foundational Fictions in South Australian History

1. Mark Twain, *Following the Equator* [1897], Auckland: The Floating Press, 2009 [e-book], p. 152.
2. *Ibid.*, p. 161.
3. *Ibid.*, pp. 165–6.
4. *Ibid.*, p. 172.
5. *Ibid.*, p. 152.
6. *Ibid.*, p. 161.
7. *Ibid.*, p. 174.
8. *Ibid.*, p. 175.
9. John Tosh, *The Pursuit of History: Aims, Methods and New Directions in the Study of Modern History*, 4th ed., London: Pearson Longman, 2006, p. 5.
10. *Ibid.*
11. *Ibid.*, p. 2.
12. *Ibid.*, p. xvii.
13. Anna Clark and Paul Ashton, *Australian History Now*, Sydney: NewSouth Publishing, 2013, p. 14.
14. Stuart Macintyre and Anna Clark, *The History Wars*, Melbourne: Melbourne University Press, 2004, p. 1.
15. David Stephens and Alison Broinowski, *The Honest History Book*, Sydney: NewSouth Publishing, 2017, pp. 1–10.
16. Ann Curthoys and John Docker, *Is History Fiction*, Sydney: UNSW Press, 2010, p. 11.
17. *Ibid.*, pp. 5–6.
18. Tosh, *Pursuit of History*, p. xii.
19. Kate Grenville, *The Secret River*, Melbourne: Text Publishing, 2005; Inga Clendinnen, 'The History Question', *Quarterly Essay*, Melbourne: Black Inc., 2006.
20. Tom Griffiths, 'The Intriguing Dance of History and Fiction', *TEXT Special Edition: Fictional Histories and Historical Fictions: Writing History in the Twenty-first Century*, eds. Camilla Nelson and Christine de Matos, April 2015, p. 3.
21. *Ibid.*
22. *Ibid.*
23. *Ibid.*
24. For elaboration, see Paul Sendziuk and Robert Foster, *A History of South Australia*, Melbourne: Cambridge University Press, 2018.

25 Paul Sendziuk, 'No Convicts Here: Reconsidering South Australia's Foundation Myth', in Robert Foster and Paul Sendziuk (eds), *Turning Points: Chapters in South Australian History*, Adelaide: Wakefield Press, 2012, pp. 33–47.
26 Arthur Jose, 'The Romantic 'Nineties. IX', *Brisbane Courier*, 23 July 1932, p. 19.
27 Vance Palmer, *The Legend of the Nineties*, Melbourne: Melbourne University Press, 1954; A.A. Phillips, *The Australian Tradition: Studies in a Colonial Culture*, Melbourne: Cheshire, 1958; Russel Ward, *The Australian Legend*, Melbourne: Oxford University Press, 1958.
28 Nic Klaassen, 'The Battle for Leigh Creek', in Bernard O'Neil, Judith Raftery and Kerrie Round (eds), *Playford's South Australia: Essays on the History of South Australia 1933–1968*, Adelaide: Association of Professional Historians Inc., 1996, p. 138.
29 This is certainly true of biographies that have been written about him, and of the way in which Playford's legacy is evoked in popular memory. See, for example, David Nicholas, *The Pacemaker: The Playford Story*, Adelaide: Brolga Books, 1969; Walter Crocker, *Sir Thomas Playford: A Portrait*, Melbourne: Melbourne University Press, 1983; Stewart Cockburn assisted by John Playford, *Playford: Benevolent Despot*, Adelaide: Axiom Publishing, 1991; and Bob Byrne, 'Adelaide, Remember When ... Tom Playford Ruled South Australia?', *Advertiser*, 14 March 2014; accessible at http://www.adelaidenow.com.au/news/south-australia/adelaide-remember-when-tom-playford-ruled-south-australia/story-fni6uo1m-1226855067404.

Chapter 2 | A Contested Coast? Revisiting the Baudin-Flinders Encounter of April 1802

1 The journals kept by those who accompanied Baudin on his expedition still have many secrets to yield. These are held in the French National Archives, Paris, in the 5JJ series. In addition to this under-exploited resource, the principal new source we have identified is a set of notes by French zoologist François Péron taken contemporaneously to the encounter and containing his unrevised impressions of Matthew Flinders. These are held in the Lesueur Collection of the Natural History Museum, Le Havre, mss 09 015 and 09 016. For a discussion of Péron's notes, see Jean Fornasiero and John West-Sooby, 'Matthew Flinders through French Eyes: Nicolas Baudin's Lessons from Encounter Bay', *Journal of Pacific History*, vol. 52, no. 1, 2017, pp. 1–14.
2 This term recalls a work on Flinders devoted precisely to his own missed opportunities. See Roger W. Russell (ed.), *Matthew Flinders: The Ifs of History*, Adelaide: University Relations Unit, Flinders University, 1979.
3 Baudin left the Normandy port of Le Havre on 19 October 1800; Flinders sailed from Spithead on 18 July 1801.
4 As seen, for example, on Robert Laurie and James Whittle's map: 'A New Map of the World, with Captain Cook's Tracks, His Discoveries and Those of the Other Circumnavigators', London: Laurie & Whittle.
5 'Plan of Itinerary for Citizen Baudin' by French navigator and former Minister of Marine Count Charles-Pierre Claret de Fleurieu. English translation in N. Baudin, *The Journal of Post-Captain Nicolas Baudin* (trans. Christine Cornell), Adelaide: Friends of the State Library of South Australia, 2004, p. 3. The notion that lands inhabited by indigenous peoples could still be 'discovered' was obviously of its time.
6 'Instructions for the *Investigator*s voyage' dated 22 June 1801, signed by the Lords of the Admiralty and counter-signed by Evan Nepean. Reproduced in Kenneth Morgan (ed.), *Australia Circumnavigated: The Voyage of Matthew Flinders in HMS Investigator, 1801–1803*, 2 vols, London: Ashgate (The Hakluyt Society), 2015, vol. 1, p. 128.
7 The race paradigm has certainly entered the popular imagination, as exemplified by Klaus Toft's book *The Navigators: Flinders vs Baudin: The Race Between Matthew Flinders and Nicolas Baudin to Discover the Fabled Passage Through the Middle of*

Australia, Sydney: Duffy & Snellgrove, 2002; and a similarly themed book by David Hill, *The Great Race: The Race Between the English and the French to Complete the Map of Australia*, Sydney: William Heinemann Australia, 2012. The two expeditions are similarly portrayed as being engaged in the 'Race for *Terra Australis*' on the National Gallery of Victoria's web site for its 2012 exhibition 'Napoleon: Revolution to Empire', https://www.ngv.vic.gov.au/napoleon/exploration-and-discovery/flinders-and-baudin-race-for-the-southern-lands.html; accessed 10 January 2018.

8   Letter from Banks to Earl Spencer in Neil Chambers (ed.), *The Letters of Sir Joseph Banks: A Selection, 1768–1820*, London: Imperial College Press, 2000, pp. 219–21. Political preoccupations were not his only motivation: as Harold B. Carter has noted, Banks the scientist was also concerned that the French could make 'new gains in natural history beyond his reach, of new species found for other herbaria than his own'. H.B. Carter, *Sir Joseph Banks, 1743–1820*, London: British Museum, 1988, p. 366.

9   Morgan, *Australia Circumnavigated*, vol. 1, p. 364.

10 Matthew Flinders, *A Voyage to Terra Australis; Undertaken for the Purpose of Completing the Discovery of that Vast Country, and Prosecuted in the Years 1801, 1802 and 1803, in His Majesty's Ship, the Investigator*, 2 vols and Atlas, London: G. & W. Nicol, 1814, vol. 1, p. 188. The captain's fair log on the *Investigator* suggests that it was after the *Géographe* showed French colours that Flinders hove to. (See Morgan, *Australia Circumnavigated*, vol. 1, p. 362.) However, the log also indicates that they had already 'cleared at quarter'.

11 Both ships were around 350 tons, but the *Géographe*, at 124 feet (37.8 metres), was longer than the *Investigator*, measuring 100 feet (30.5 metres). The *Géographe* was also more streamlined than the *Investigator*, despite Flinders' assessment of it as being a 'heavy-looking ship' (*A Voyage to Terra Australis*, vol. 1, p. 188). It is true that the *Investigator*'s fire power compared favourably: two long guns and eight carronades (six 12-pounder and two 18-pounder) as opposed to the *Géographe*'s six guns (reduced from its original 20 when refitted for the voyage).

12 Flinders, *A Voyage to Terra Australis*, vol. 1, p. 188.

13 As an interesting aside, this gesture of courtesy appears only recently to have become part of the folklore surrounding the encounter. It is not mentioned in the major biographies of Flinders, from Ernest Scott's *The Life of Matthew Flinders, R.N.*, Sydney: Angus & Robertson, 1914, to Miriam Estensen's *The Life of Matthew Flinders*, Sydney: Allen & Unwin, 2002. The likely reason is that this salute was not noted in the official accounts of the two expeditions, nor was it recorded in the journals of either captain or of their companions. The one exception is Hyacinthe de Bougainville, a midshipman on the *Géographe*, who noted simply that, having received confirmation of Baudin's identity, Flinders 'removed his hat and his officers did likewise'. Journal of Hyacinthe de Bougainville, Archives Nationales de France (ANF), 155AP6, dossier 2, pièce 5, p. 1 (translations of French manuscript sources are our own). If the source of this information is indeed to be found in what was a family archive and not easily accessible, that would provide further explanation. The gesture is, however, reported by Frank Horner, in his history of the Baudin expedition: *The French Reconnaissance: Baudin in Australia 1801–1803*, Melbourne: Melbourne University Press, 1987, p. 217.

14 Flinders, *A Voyage to Terra Australis*, vol. 1, p. 190.

15 See T.G. Vallance, D.T. Moore and E.W. Groves (eds), *Nature's Investigator: The Diary of Robert Brown in Australia, 1801–1805*, Canberra: Australian Biological Resources Study, 2001, p. 178.

16 The log book of the *Géographe* recorded that Flinders arrived on board at 6.10 pm and departed at 7 (ANF, série Marine, 5JJ 25B, entry dated 18–19 Germinal Year 10 [8–9 April 1802]). According to Brown, this first meeting lasted 'about three-quarters of an hour' (Vallance, Moore and Groves, *Nature's Investigator*, p. 177).

17 Bougainville, Journal, dossier 2, pièce 5, p. 1.
18 Flinders, *A Voyage to Terra Australis*, vol. 1, pp. 189–90.
19 Bougainville, Journal, dossier 2, pièce 5, p. 1. It should be remembered that Bougainville was not present at the meeting. We have questioned elsewhere the plausibility of the accusation that Baudin did not identify his interlocutor. See Jean Fornasiero and John West-Sooby, 'A Cordial Encounter? The Meeting of Matthew Flinders and Nicolas Baudin (8–9 April 1802)', in Ian Coller, Helen Davies and Julie Kalman (eds), *French History and Civilization: Papers from the George Rudé Seminar*, vol. 1, Melbourne: George Rudé Society, 2005, pp. 53–61. Ernest Scott likewise thought it unlikely that Baudin was unaware of Flinders' name until the end of the second meeting, attributing any uncertainty to communication difficulties (Scott, *The Life of Matthew Flinders*, p. 164). Baudin's journal entry for 8 April 1802 certainly names Flinders, though this may have been compiled after he had confirmed the fact. The notes and journals kept by Baudin's companions suggest very strongly that no-one on the *Géographe* was aware of Flinders' name until their first meeting. Their journal entries for 8 April simply refer to their visitor as 'le commandant anglais' or 'le capitaine anglais'. See the journal of midshipman Joseph Brue, ANF, série Marine 5JJ 57, entry dated 18–19 Germinal [8–9 April 1802]. In contrast to the impression he gives in his official account of the French expedition, Péron, in his manuscript notes compiled 'in the moment', likewise does not name Flinders until the following day. See François Péron, *Voyage de découvertes aux Terres Australes*, vol. 1, Paris: Imprimerie Impériale, 1807, p. 324; and Péron, Notes, ms 09 015. It is interesting to note that Péron, who later became one of Baudin's most virulent critics, has nothing negative to say about his captain's comportment towards Flinders in these notes.
20 Morgan, *Australia Circumnavigated*, vol. 1, p. 365.
21 Péron, Notes, ms 09 016. Péron's admission in his notes that the French were painfully aware of Flinders' rights contrasts strongly with his own part in downplaying Flinders' discoveries in the first edition of the official account and the maps of the Baudin expedition.
22 Flinders, *A Voyage to Terra Australis*, vol. 1, p. 190.
23 Morgan, *Australia Circumnavigated*, vol. 1, p. 365.
24 Péron, Notes, ms 09 016. When they later learned that Flinders had left Sydney with the intention of exploring the Gulf of Carpentaria, which was likewise one of their objectives, a similar feeling of despair came over them, as expressed by Jacques de Saint-Cricq, a sub-lieutenant on Baudin's consort ship the *Naturaliste*: 'It is therefore written that we will be headed off everywhere! Discoveries and settlements! The English did the south-west coast before us, they will do the Gulf, and will settle with impunity in the places we have discovered! And yet the *Investigator* left Europe a long time after us'. Saint-Cricq, Journal, ANF série Marine 5JJ 57, entry dated Frimaire Year 11 (Nov.-Dec. 1802). For a detailed study of French reactions to Flinders, see Fornasiero and West-Sooby, 'Matthew Flinders through French Eyes'.
25 This lack of a genuine bond between the two men helps to explain why Flinders was to play a role in propagating the poor reputation of Baudin as a navigator. See Jean Fornasiero and John West-Sooby, 'Doing it by the Book: Breaking the Reputation of Nicolas Baudin', in J. Fornasiero and C. Mrowa-Hopkins (eds), *Explorations and Encounters in French Culture*, Adelaide: University of Adelaide Press, 2010, pp. 135–64.
26 Flinders, *A Voyage to Terra Australis*, vol. 1, p. 193. For more on the Terre Napoléon controversy, see Horner, *The French Reconnaissance*, pp. 8–16, and Jean Fornasiero and John West-Sooby, 'Naming and Shaming: The Baudin Expedition and the Politics of Nomenclature in the *Terres Australes*', in Anne M. Scott, Alfred Hiatt, Claire McIlroy and Christopher Wortham (eds), *European Perceptions of 'Terra Australis'*, Farnham: Ashgate, 2011, pp. 165–84.
27 Reported by Flinders in *A Voyage to Terra Australis*, vol. 1, p. 193.

28 Horner, *The French Reconnaissance*, pp. 220, 250.
29 The Lords of the Admiralty specified in their instructions: 'you are to make the best of your way to the coast of New Holland, running down the said coast from 130 degrees of east longitude to Bass' Strait (putting if you shall find it necessary into King George the thirds Harbour for refreshments and water, previous to your commencing the survey)'. Morgan, *Australia Circumnavigated*, vol. 1, p. 127. Flinders' survey was thus meant to begin a little to the west of Ceduna, which lies at approximately 133° east of Greenwich.
30 Among Alan Frost's numerous books on the subject, see *Botany Bay: The Real Story*, Melbourne: Black Inc., 2011, and *The Global Reach of Empire: Britain's Maritime Expansion in the Indian and Pacific Oceans 1764–1815*, Melbourne: Miegunyah Press, 2003.
31 In addition to Frost's work, see, for the Spanish perspective, Robert J. King, *The Secret History of the Convict Colony: Alexandro Malaspina's Report on the British Settlement of New South Wales*, Sydney: Allen and Unwin, 1990, and for the French perspective, Jean Fornasiero and John West-Sooby, *French Designs on Colonial New South Wales*, Adelaide: Friends of the State Library of South Australia, 2014.
32 Letter from Lord Hobart to Governor King, 14 February 1803, in F.M. Bladen (ed.), *Historical Records of New South Wales*, 7 vols, Sydney: Government Printer, 1892–1901, vol. 5, p. 833.
33 Even then, the interest in forming a settlement on this coast was sparked by a coalition of private groups and individuals, rather than by the government. Interestingly, when spruiking the attractions of the new settlement, the South Australian Company elected to use the works of William Westall, the artist of the Flinders expedition, despite his landscapes bearing little resemblance to what he had observed. His Arcadian views were an attempt to 'airbrush' the arid landscape to meet prevailing aesthetic conventions.
34 Flinders, *A Voyage to Terra Australis*, vol. 1, p. 148.
35 *Ibid.*, p. 158.
36 *Ibid.*, p. 159.
37 H.M. Cooper, *The Unknown Coast: Being the Explorations of Captain Matthew Flinders, R.N. Along the Shores of South Australia 1802*, Adelaide: n.p., 1953, p. 76.
38 Geoffrey C. Ingleton, *Matthew Flinders: Navigator and Chartmaker*, Melbourne: Hedley Australia, 1986, p. 155.
39 Baudin, *Journal*, p. 379.
40 Péron, *Voyage*, vol. 1, p. 323.
41 Baudin, *Journal*, p. 381.
42 *Ibid.*, p. 382.
43 *Ibid.*, pp. 385 and 386.
44 Paul Carter, *The Road to Botany Bay: An Essay in Spatial History*, London: Faber and Faber, 1987, p. 74.
45 On Western Australia, thinking was more advanced than elsewhere. See Colin Forster, *France and Botany Bay: The Lure of a Penal Colony*, Melbourne: Melbourne University Press, 1996, and Leslie Marchant, *France Australe: A Study of French Explorations and Attempts to Found a Penal Colony and Strategic Base in South Western Australia, 1503–1826*, Perth: Artlook Books, 1982.
46 Jules Verne, *Mistress Branican* [1891], Paris: Gautier-Languereau, 1978, p. 299.
47 See, for example, the 1826 map by Adrien-Hubert Brué, a midshipman on the Baudin expedition who later became the Royal Geographer, and who continued to show French rights of discovery over 'Terre Napoléon' while changing its name to 'Terre de Baudin'. The Arrowsmith map of Australia of 1842 marks this same territory as 'Bonny Land', thus retaining the reference to Napoleon Bonaparte.

Chapter 3 | Wakefield Revisited Again

1. See, for example, Robert Harrison, *Colonial Sketches, or Five Years in South Australia*, London: Hall, Virtue & Co., 1862, pp. 1–10; and the survey of opinion in J.D. Young, 'South Australian Historians and Wakefield's Scheme', *Historical Studies*, vol. 14, no. 53, 1969, pp. 32–53.
2. Colin Kerr, *Archie: The Biography of Sir Archibald Grenfell Price*, Melbourne: Macmillan, 1983, p. 11.
3. For the criticisms reported in this and the following paragraph, see D.H. Pike reviewing M.F. Lloyd Prichard's *Collected Works of Edward Gibbon Wakefield*, in *Historical Studies*, vol. 14, no. 53, 1969, pp. 109–10; and Pike, *Paradise of Dissent: South Australia 1829–1857*, Melbourne: Melbourne University Press, 1957, esp. pp. 75–6.
4. These and the following observations are from P.A. Howell, 'Cleaning the Cobwebs: A Reconsideration of the Beginnings of the Province of South Australia', *History Forum*, vol. 13, no. 1, 1991, esp. pp. 7–10.
5. This agrees with Gordon Buxton's interpretation that by the 1860s '[t]he wealthy had long since picked the eyes out of the state' by special surveys and peacocking. See Buxton, *The South Australian Land Acts, 1869–1885*, Adelaide: Libraries Board of South Australia, 1966, p. 15.
6. The responsibility for failure and success in South Australia is a convoluted matter. Wakefield himself claimed that his ideas were never put into practice in the province, and his defenders blamed the 1841 debacle on the Colonial Office, on personal jealousies and the division of authority in Adelaide, and on the unworkable Act of Parliament. (See Young, 'South Australian Historians', pp. 33–4.) The economic downturn of 1841–2 was one of the worst of the nineteenth century, and devastated all the colonies, systematic and unsystematic alike. Contemporaries certainly used Wakefield as a scapegoat for colonial discontents.
7. Howell, 'Cleaning the Cobwebs', *passim*; and Howell, *South Australia and Federation*, Adelaide: Wakefield Press, 2002, pp. 74–7.
8. Even Wakefield's most appreciative contemporaries were sceptical of his obsession with 'concentration'. Herman Merivale said that it was 'cramping it, like some Chinese lady's foot, according to some imaginary standard of elegant proportion'. See Merivale, *Lectures on Colonization and Colonies Delivered before the University of Oxford in 1839, 1840 & 1841*, new edition, London: Longman, 1861, p. 426.
9. Wakefield, evidence before the House of Commons, *Report of Select Committee on the Disposal of Waste Lands in the British Colonies*, London, 1836, p. 90.
10. Douglas Pike, *Australia: The Quiet Continent*, 2nd ed., London: Cambridge University Press, 1970, p. 75.
11. Pike, *Paradise*, pp. 184–6.
12. See, for example, R.B. Madgwick, *Immigration into Eastern Australia, 1788–1851*, London: Longmans, Green & Co., 1937; R.M. Crawford, *Australia*, London: Hutchinson, 1952. This contention is refuted by Robin Haines in *Emigration and the Labouring Poor: Australian Recruitment in Britain and Ireland, 1831–60*, London: Macmillan, 1997, pp. 11–13.
13. Pike, *Australia*, p. 148.
14. J.W. McCarty, review of books by Burroughs and Macmillan in *Business History*, vol. 10, no. 2, 1968, pp. 135–6.
15. Peter Burroughs, 'Wakefield and the Ripon Land Regulations of 1831', *Historical Studies*, vol. 11, no. 44, 1965, pp. 465–6.
16. F.G. Clarke, *The Land of Contrarieties: British Attitudes to the Australian Colonies, 1828–1855*, Melbourne: Melbourne University Press, 1977, p. 135.
17. Quoted in D.N. Jeans, 'The Impress of Central Authority upon the Landscape: South-Eastern Australia, 1788–1850', in J.M. Powell and M. Williams (eds), *Australian Space,*

Australian Time: Geographical Perspectives, 1788–1914, Melbourne: Oxford University Press, 1975, p. 11.
18 See M.F. Lloyd Pritchard (ed.), *Collected Works of Edward Gibbon Wakefield*, Glasgow: Collins, 1968, p. 954; and D.H. Pike, 'Wakefield, Waste Land and Empire', *Tasmanian Historical Research Association Papers and Proceedings*, vol. 12, no. 3, 1965, p. 82. Many of these issues are well-summarised by Giancarlo de Vivo in his 'Introduction' to Robert Torrens, *Colonization of South Australia*, volume IV of the *Collected Works of Robert Torrens*, Bristol: Thoemmes, 2000, pp. vii-xxvii.
19 See, for example, Jan Kociumbas, *The Oxford History of Australia, Volume 2: Possessions, 1770–1860,* Melbourne: Oxford University Press, 1992.
20 Michael Williams, 'The Spread of Settlement in South Australia', in F. Gale and G.H. Lawton (eds), *Settlement and Encounter: Geographical Studies Presented to Sir Grenfell Price*, Melbourne: Oxford University Press, 1969, pp. 14, 25. See also Jeans, 'The Impress of Central Authority', *passim*. J.M. Powell argues that the imperatives of squatting, and the difficulty of fostering small farming in compact settlement patterns, prevailed over Wakefieldian prescriptions, except on the Adelaide Plains. See Powell, *The Public Lands of Australia: Settlement and Land Appraisal in Victoria 1834–91 with Special Reference to the Western Plains*, Melbourne: Oxford University Press, 1970, pp. 145–6.
21 See Beverley Anne Cocker, 'Special Surveys and the Wakefield Theory', BA Hons thesis, University of Adelaide, 1967; Williams, 'Spirit of Settlement', p. 25; Pike, 'The Smallholders' Place in the Australian Tradition', *Tasmanian Historical Research Association Papers and Proceedings*, vol. 10, no. 2, 1962, pp. 28–33; and Ann Herraman, 'The People of Mount Barker', PhD thesis, Flinders University, 2010, *passim*.
22 See Howell, 'Clearing the Cobwebs', pp. 8–9.
23 Helen Taft Manning, 'The Present State of Wakefield Studies', *Historical Studies*, vol. 16, no. 63, 1974, pp. 277–85.
24 See H.O. Pappe, 'Wakefield and Marx', *The Economic History Review*, vol. 4, no. 1, 1951, pp. 88–97.
25 K. Buckley, 'E.G. Wakefield and the Alienation of Crown Land in New South Wales in 1847', *Economic Record*, vol. 33, no. 64, 1957, p. 80. Coghlan believed that South Australia was flooded with working-class immigrants expressly to prevent the possibility of upward mobility through decent wages. See Howell, *South Australia and Federation*, p. 76.
26 The rapid acquisition of land by newly arrived labouring immigrants, and the consequent shortage of labour, was clearly a serious problem in contemporaneous Ohio as reported, for instance, by D. Griffiths, Jr, *Two Years in the New Settlements of Ohio, North America: With Directions for Emigrants*, London: Westley and Davis, 1835, pp. 54–8. The essential point had been most cogently enunciated in 1776 by Wakefield's own inspirer, Adam Smith, in *Wealth of Nations*, New York: Random House Modern Library, 1937, pp. 531–3.
27 See John Manning Ward, *James Macarthur: Colonial Conservative, 1798–1867*, Sydney: Sydney University Press, 1981, p. 48, and Buckley, 'Wakefield and Alienation', *passim*.
28 Quoted in Geoffrey Dutton, *Founder of a City: The Life of Colonel William Light, first Surveyor-General of the Colony of South Australia, founder of Adelaide, 1786–1839*, Melbourne: Cheshire, 1960, p. 218.
28 See Edward Wakefield, *Letter from Sydney and other Writings on Colonization*, London: J.M. Dent, Everyman's Library, 1929, p. 92; and Geoffrey Serle, *The Golden Age: A History of the Colony of Victoria, 1851–1861*, Melbourne: Melbourne University Press, 1963, p. 40.
30 Much of the advocacy and consistency came from Gouger. See Douglas Pike, 'Wilmot Horton and the National Colonisation Society', *Historical Studies*, vol. 7, no. 26, 1956, p. 206. See also Peter Burroughs, *Britain and Australia 1831–1855:*

A Study in Imperial Relations and Crown Lands Administration, Oxford: Clarendon Press, 1967, p. 27.

31 Wakefield, *Art of Colonization*, p. 230. He advocated the dedication of the land fund to emigration in his evidence to the *Select Committee on the Disposal of Lands in the British Colonies* (London: 1836), p. 92, as did Torrens, *ibid.*, p. 123. Later, Wakefield came to regard 'the entire proceeds of land sales as sacrosanct for emigration'. See Pike, *Paradise*, p. 94.

32 Wakefield, *Letter from Sydney*, p. 55.

33 There was in fact no anticipation of the sheer scale of Australian land sales in the 1830s. Ripon, looking back from 1840, conceded that he had never intended to deprive future administrators of control over funds to such a degree. See Clarke, *Land of Contrarieties*, p. 93.

34 Between 1832 and 1842 land sales yielded £1,090,583 in revenue in New South Wales, of which £951,241 was spent on the introduction of 51,736 immigrants. This excluded those whose bounty had been refused. See Transcripts of Missing Despatches, Report to accompany Blue Book, 30 September 1842, State Library of NSW (Mitchell Library), A 1267–7.

35 The quotes from *Westminster Review*, Cobbett, McCulloch and Marx are from Craufurd D.W. Goodwin, *The Image of Australia: Perception of the Australian Economy from the Eighteenth to the Twentieth Century*, Durham, N.C.: Duke University Press, 1974, p. 7 (note 6) and p. 32.

36 See Oliver MacDonagh, *A Pattern of Government Growth, 1800–1860: The Passenger Acts and their Enforcement,* London: MacGibbon & Kee, 1961, p. 80.

37 Brian Fitzpatrick, *British Imperialism and Australia, 1783–1833: An Economic History of Australasia*, Sydney: Sydney University Press, 1971, p. 262.

38 See Jeans, 'The Impress of Central Authority'. Wakefield's impact on political economists is considered in A.G.L. Shaw, *The Economic Development of Australia*, 6th edition, Melbourne: Longman, 1973, pp. 33–6, 41.

39 Howell, 'Clearing the Cobwebs', p. 10.

40 Merivale, *Lectures*, p. 472. The employers' dilemma was expounded in James Macarthur, *New South Wales, Its Present State and Future Prospects,* London: D. Walther, 1837, p. 151.

41 In the American colonies of the eighteenth century the most effective mode of emigration was by indenture, whereby migrants contracted themselves into a form of waged bondage for three to seven years in return for a passage, paid by the receiving employers. The Australian colonies were generally opposed to contract migration, with the main exception of the Chinese on the goldfields of the 1850s and the Pacific Island Kanaka system in the Queensland sugar industry from the 1870s. In Australia freedom of contract was a cardinal principle and one of the ways that the colonies attracted immigrants, who were generally completely free once they arrived. In any case, there was no realistic problem of retaining immigrants once they had arrived – the cost of return was too great to present a difficulty. Indenturing tended to negate any system of chain migration or the delivery of remittances, which became important elements in the Australian version of international migration.

42 *Port Phillip Patriot*, 15 March 1841, quoted in R.M. Hartwell, 'The Pastoral Ascendancy', in Gordon Greenwood (ed.), *Australia: A Social and Political History*, Sydney: Angus and Robertson, 1955, p. 80.

43 Evidence before the *Select Committee of the House of Lords on Colonisation from Ireland*, 1848, p. 63. This view was questioned by June Philip in 'The Wakefieldian Influence on New South Wales, 1830–1832', *Historical Studies*, vol. 9, no. 34, 1960, pp. 177–8.

44 Resistance by colonists to the Wakefieldian prescriptions is considered in Goodwin, *Image of Australia*, pp. 66–7.

45 See Herman Merivale, *Lectures on Colonization and Colonies,* vol. 2, London: Longman, 1842, p. 116.
46 Wakefield, *Letter from Sydney,* p. 92.
47 See Eric Richards, *The Genesis of International Migration: The British Case, 1750–1900,* Manchester: Manchester University Press, 2018.
48 Governor's Despatches, May-August 1839, p. 91, State Library of NSW (Mitchell Library), A1280.
49 Frank Broeze suggested that the merchants provided the main dynamic for the expansion of free emigration to Australia in the 1830s. (See Broeze, *Mr Brooks and the Australian Trade: Imperial Business in the Nineteenth Century,* Melbourne: Melbourne University Press, 1993, p. 136.) The opposing argument is that the shippers emerged in response to the Wakefield system; they were not themselves the initiating force.
50 See Alan Beever, 'From a Place of "Horrible Destitution" to a Paradise of the Working Class: The Transformation of British Working Class Attitudes to Australia, 1841–1851', *Labour History,* vol. 4, 1980, pp. 1–15. Even Pike conceded that Wakefield was 'responsible for removing from emigration the stigma that had turned the middle classes against it'. Pike, *Paradise,* p. 74.
51 Evidence for these assertions, and those in the following paragraph, can be found in Eric Richards, 'An Australian Map of British and Irish Literacy in 1841', *Population Studies,* vol. 53, no. 3, 1999, pp. 345–59; Robin Haines, *Emigration and the Labouring Poor: Australian Recruitment in Britain and Ireland, 1831–60,* London: Macmillan, 1997, *passim*; Robin Haines, Deborah Oxley, Margrette Kleinig and Eric Richards, 'Migration and Opportunity: An Antipodean Perspective', *International Review of Social History,* vol. 43, 1998, pp. 235–63; and John McDonald and Eric Richards, 'The Great Emigration of 1841: British and Irish Emigrants Assisted to New South Wales in 1841', *Population Studies,* vol. 51, no. 3, 1997, pp. 337–55.
52 *Ibid.*
53 See Wakefield, *Letter from Sydney,* Preface.
54 Manning, 'The Present State of Wakefield Studies', p. 284.
55 K.N. Bell and W.P. Morrell (eds), *Select Documents on British Colonial Policy 1830–1860,* Oxford: Clarendon Press, 1928, p. xxxiii.

Chapter 4 | Born Free: Wage-slaves and Chattel-slaves

1 Karl Marx, *The Poverty of Philosophy,* in *Marx-Engels Collected Works,* vol. 6, London: Lawrence & Wishart, 1976, p. 167.
2 Eric Williams, *Capitalism & Slavery* [1944], New York: Capricorn Books, 1966, p. 131.
3 H.O. Pappe, 'Wakefield and Marx', *The Economic History Review,* New Series, vol. 4, no. 1, 1951, pp. 88–97; Lionel Robbins, *Robert Torrens and the Evolution of Classical Economics,* London: Macmillan, 1958, pp. 153–73; Karl Marx, *Theories of Surplus-Value,* Part III, Moscow: Progress Publishers, 1971, pp. 71ff.
4 Karl Marx, *Capital,* Volume I, London: Penguin, 1976, pp. 932–3.
5 Marx, *Capital,* I, p. 932.
6 R.A. Bryer, 'Accounting for the Social Relations of Feudalism', *Accounting and Business Research,* vol. 24, no. 95, 1994, pp. 218ff.; R.A. Bryer, 'The History of Accounting and the Transition to Capitalism. Part One: Theory', *Accounting, Organizations and Society,* vol. 25, no. 2, 2000, pp. 131–61; R.A. Bryer, 'The History of Accounting and the Transition to Capitalism. Part Two: Evidence', *Accounting, Organizations and Society,* vol. 25, no. 4/5, 2000, pp. 327–81.
7 Marx, *Capital,* I, pp. 936–7.
8 Eugene D. Genovese, *In Red and Black: Marxian Explorations in Southern and Afro-American History,* New York: Vintage, 1972; Eric A. Nilsson, 'Empirical Evidence that

the Social Relations of Production Matter: The Case of the Ante-Bellum US South', *Cambridge Journal of Economics*, vol. 18, no. 3, 1994, pp. 259–77.
9   Charles Post, 'The American Road to Capitalism', *New Left Review*, no. 133, 1982, pp. 30–51; Michael Merrill, 'The Anticapitalist Origins of the United States', *Review (Fernand Braudel Center)*, vol. 13, no. 4, 1990, pp. 465–97; Michael Merrill, 'Putting "Capitalism" in its Place: A Review of Recent Literature', *The William and Mary Quarterly*, Third Series, vol. 52, no. 2, 1995, pp. 315–26.
10 Peter Temin, 'The Anglo-American Business Cycle, 1820–60', *The Economic History Review*, New Series, vol. 27, no. 2, 1974, pp. 207–21; Alasdair Roberts, *America's First Great Depression: Economic Crisis and Political Disorder after the Panic of 1837*, Ithaca: Cornell University Press, 2012.
11 *Capital*, I, p. 580, note 56 (cf. p. 931, note 1).
12 Rob A. Bryer, 'Part 1: Was America Born Capitalist?', *Critical Perspectives on Accounting*, vol. 23, no. 7/8, 2012, pp. 511–55. For more on Bryer, see my 'Accounting for Capital', http://www.surplusvalue.org.au/McQueen/capital/capital_accounting_for_capital.html.
13 Marx, *Capital*, I, p. 876.
14 Marx to Ludwig Kugelmann, 27 June 1870, in *Marx-Engels Collected Works*, vol. 43, London: Lawrence & Wishart, 1988, p. 527.
15 For my penny's worth, see 'Afterword', *A New Britannia: An Argument Concerning the Social Origins of Australian Radicalism and Nationalism*, Brisbane: University of Queensland Press, 2004, pp. 253–67.
16 K.M. Dallas, 'Slavery in Australia – Convicts, Emigrants, Aborigines', Special Issue, *Papers and Proceedings, Tasmanian Historical Research Association*, vol. 16, no. 2, 1968, pp. 61–76.
17 Liz Humphries, 'The Birth of Australia: Non-Capitalist Social Relations in a Capitalist Mode of Production?', *Journal of Australian Political Economy*, no. 70, 2012–13, pp. 110–29.
18 Ken Buckley, 'Primary Accumulation: The Genesis of Australian Capitalism', E.L. Wheelwright and Ken Buckley (eds), *Essays in the Political Economy of Australian Capitalism*, Volume 1, Sydney: ANZ Books, 1975, pp. 12–32.
19 G.J. Abbott, 'Economic Growth', in G.J. Abbott and N.B. Nairn (eds), *Economic Growth in Australia 1788–1821*, Melbourne: Melbourne University Press, 1969, pp. 139–61; M.J.E. Steven, 'The Changing Pattern of Commerce', in the same volume, accepts the 1820s (see p. 176).
20 For elaboration, see Humphrey McQueen, 'Marxism – Capital Refined', Surplus Value, www.surplusvalue.org.au/McQueen/Marxism/Marx_capital_refined.htm.
21 Michael Dunn, 'Early Australia: Wage Labour or Slave Society', in E.L. Wheelwright and Ken Buckley (eds), *Essays in the Political Economy of Australian Capitalism*, Volume 1, Sydney: ANZ Books, 1975, pp. 33–46.
22 D.W.A. Baker, 'The Origins of the Robertson's Land Acts', *Historical Studies*, vol. 8, no. 30, 1958, pp. 166–82; J.N. Connolly, 'The Middling-Class Victory in New South Wales, 1853–62: A Critique of the Bourgeois-Pastoralist Dichotomy', *Historical Studies*, vol. 19, no. 76, 1981, pp. 369–87; Joe Collins, *The Political Economy of Global Mining*, PhD Thesis, University of Western Sydney, 2016; Karl Marx, *Capital*, III, London: Penguin, 1981, Part VI.
23 Marx, *Capital*, I, pp. 254, 298, 342, 739, 989 and 1054.
24 None of the contributors to the first volume of *The Cambridge History of Capitalism from Ancient Origins to 1848* [2014] attempts to define that of which he or she is supposedly writing. See my review at: http://www.surplusvalue.org.au/McQueen/history/Review_of_Cambridge_History_of_Capitalism_V1.pdf.
25 R. Torrens, *An Essay on the Production of Wealth* [1821], pp. 70–1, quoted Marx, *Capital*, I, p. 291, note 10; S.A. Meenai, 'Robert Torrens, 1780–1864', *Economica*,

New Series, vol. 23, no. 89, 1956, pp. 49–61; Frank Whitson Fetter, 'Robert Torrens: Colonel of Marines and Political Economist', *Economica*, New Series, vol. 29, no. 114, 1962, pp. 152–65.
26 Adam Smith, *Inquiry into the Nature and Causes of the Wealth of Nations*, Oxford: Clarendon Press, 1976, p. 25.
27 For a recent instance of a-historical incapacity, see Phillip Roberts, 'Revisiting the Mount William Greenstone Quarry: Employment Specialisation and a Market Economy in Early Contract Hunter-Gatherer Society', *Australian Aboriginal Studies*, no. 2, 2017, pp. 14–27.
28 Marx, *Capital*, I, pp. 96–7, and Volume III, p. 681.
29 Arthur D. Gayer et al., *The Growth and Fluctuation of the British Economy, 1790–1850*, Oxford: Clarendon Press, 1953, pp. 171–210.
30 W.E. Cheong, 'China Houses and the Bank of England Crisis of 1825', *Business History*, vol. 15, no. 1, 1973, pp. 56–73.
31 Edwin Hodder, *George Fife Angas, Father and Founder of South Australia*, London: Hodder and Stoughton, 1896, p. 31. Also see P.A. Howell, 'Angas, George Fife (1789–1879), promoter of the colonization of South Australia', *Oxford Dictionary of National Biography*, https://doi.org/10.1093/ref:odnb/537.
32 Max Weber, *Roscher and Knies: The Logical Problems of Historical Economics*, New York: Free Press, 1975, p. 193; Marx, *Capital*, I, p. 990; *Capital*, III, p. 374; cf. *Capital*, II, London: Penguin, 1978, pp. 185–7.
33 Max Weber, *The Protestant Ethic and the 'Spirit' of Capitalism*, London: Penguin, 2005, pp. 362–4.
34 Marx, *Capital*, I, p. 176, note 35. Marx raises the bar when he observes that it is 'much easier to discover by analysis the earthly kernel of the misty creations of religion than to do the opposite, i.e. to develop from the actual, given relations of life the forms in which these have been apotheosised. The latter method is the only materialist, and therefore the only scientific one.' (p. 494, note 4)
35 Jim Main, 'Men of Capital', in Eric Richards (ed.), *The Flinders History of South Australia: Social History*, Adelaide: Wakefield, 1986, pp. 96–104.
36 P.W. Ireland, 'The Rise of the Limited Liability Company', *International Journal of the Sociology of Law*, vol. 12, no. 3, 1984, pp. 239–60; R.A. Bryer, 'The Mercantile Laws Commission of 1854 and the Political Economy of Limited Liability', *The Economic History Review*, New Series, vol. 50, no. 1, 1997, pp. 37–56.
37 Its fleeting appearance was par for the course since many were launched but few went on to operate. Official figures between the 1844 Companies Registration Act and Joint Stock Companies Act of 1856 show that of the nearly 4,000 companies that sought provisional registration only 956 obtained full registration. See Bishop Carleton Hunt, *The Development of the Business Corporation in England 1800–1867*, Cambridge, Mass.: Harvard University Press, 1936, pp. 15 and 87–89; Bernard Rudden, *The New River: A Legal History*, Oxford: Clarendon Press, 1985, p. 212.
38 In New South Wales, six unincorporated large partnerships were operating before 1836, with fifteen more by 1839. See G.J. Abbott, 'The Formation of Joint-Stock Companies in Sydney during the Second Half of the 1830s', *The Push from the Bush*, no. 14, 1983, pp. 4–27.
39 Marx, *Capital*, I, p. 742: 'Accumulate! accumulate! That is Moses and the Prophets.'
40 P.L. Cottrell, *Industrial Finance 1830–1914*, London: Methuen, 1980, pp. 39–40.
41 Cottrell, *Industrial Finance*, p. 2; Rudden, *The New River*, pp. 199–200 and 211.
42 Chantal Stebbings, 'The Legal Nature of Shares in Landowning Joint Stock Companies in the Nineteenth Century', *The Journal of Legal History*, vol. 8, no. 1, 1987, pp. 25–35; Rudden, *The New River*, pp. 212–3 and 221–38 *passim*; Hunt, *The Development of the Business Corporation*, pp. 39–45 and 83.
43 Cottrell, *Industrial Finance*, pp. 39–40.

44 Rudden, *The New River*, pp. 212–3 and 224ff.
45 *Ibid.*, pp. 233 and 244.
46 J. Robertson Christie, 'Joint-Stock Enterprise in Scotland before the Companies Act', *Juridical Review*, vol. XXI, no. 1, 1921, pp. 128–47; R.H. Campbell, 'The Law and the Joint-Stock Company in Scotland', in Peter L. Payne (ed.), *Studies in Scottish Business History*, London: Frank Cass, 1967, pp. 136–51; Arthur Herman, *The Scottish Enlightenment: The Scots' Invention of the Modern World,* London: Fourth Estate, 2001, pp. 82–96. Scone-born and Perth-educated Chief Justice Mansfield (1705–93) did what he could to bend the Common Law to the needs of commerce. See Norman S. Poser, *Lord Mansfield: Justice in the Age of Reason*, Montreal: McGill-Queen's University Press, 2014.
47 James P. Henderson, 'Agency or Alienation? Smith, Mill, and Marx on the Joint-Stock Company', *History of Political Economy*, vol. 18, no. 1, 1986, pp. 111–31.
48 Hunt, *The Development of the Business Corporation*, pp. 19, 38–9, 42, 56, 61 and 84; Ron Harris, 'Political Economy, Interest Groups, Legal Institutions, and the Repeal of the Bubble Act in 1825', *The Economic History Review*, New Series, vol. 50, no. 4, 1997, pp. 675–96. In the British parliament, the 'Law Lords' were members of the House of Lords qualified to perform its legal work.
49 Marx, *Capital*, I, p. 780.
50 Marx calls this worldview 'parliamentary cretinism'. See Karl Marx, 'The Eighteenth Brumaire of Louis Bonaparte', in *Marx-Engels Collected Works*, vol. 11, London: Lawrence & Wishart, 1979, p. 161.
51 Hodder, *George Fife Angas*, p. 132.
52 S.J. Butlin, *Foundations of the Australian Monetary System, 1788–1850*, Sydney: Sydney University Press, 1953, pp. 268–70.
53 *Ibid.*, p. 454; Hodder, *George Fife Angas*, p. 289.
54 Ian Bowen, 'Country Banking, The Note Issues and Banking Controversies in 1825', *Economic History*, vol. III, no. 13, 1938, pp. 68–88; Dieter Ziegler, 'Central Banking in the English Provinces in the Second Quarter of the Nineteenth Century', *Business History*, vol. 31, no. 4, 1989, pp. 33–47.
55 S.D. Chapman, 'The Foundation of the English Rothschilds: N.M. Rothschild as a Textile Merchant', *Textile History*, no. 18, 1977, pp. 99–115; Stuart Jones, 'The Manchester Cotton Magnates' Move into Banking, 1826–1850', *Textile History*, no. 9, 1978, pp. 90–111. For Marx on the changes in merchant capital from proto-capitalism, see *Capital*, III, chapters 16 to 20.
56 Hodder, *George Fife Angas*, pp. 85–7 and 254. Thomas Joplin was as influential in promoting the Currency School, which led to Robert Peel's disastrous 1844 Bank Act, as Wakefield was in publicising Systematic Colonisation. See Hunt, *The Development of the Business Corporation*, p. 64 (note 29), and p. 69 (note 45); J.H. Clapham, *The Bank of England: A History*, Cambridge: Cambridge University Press, 1944, pp. 11 and 92–4; Frank Whiston Fetter, *Development of British Monetary Orthodoxy, 1797–1875*, Cambridge, Mass.: Harvard University Press, 1965, pp. 110–11, 116 and 119ff.; A.S.J. Baster, *The Imperial Banks*, London: P.S. King and Son, 1929, pp. 56–8, 79, 120–1.
57 David Kynaston, *The City of London. Volume I: A World of Its Own*, London: Pimlico, 1995, p. 137; Iain S. Black, 'Money, Information and Space: Banking in Early-Nineteenth-Century England and Wales', *Journal of Historical Geography*, vol. 21, no. 4, 1995, pp. 398–403.
58 David Kynaston, *Till Time's Last Sand: A History of the Bank of England 1694–2013*, London: Bloomsbury, 2016, chapter 5. The compliance burdens imposed by Board of Trade for the chartering of imperial banks prompted Sir James Stephen to observe in 1834 that '[t]he Merchants on the Royal Exchange would be tenfold better Authorities than all the four Courts united.' See Hunt, *The Development of the Business Corporation*, p. 59, note 12.

59 Butlin, *Foundations,* pp. 546–7.
60 S.J. Butlin, *Australia and New Zealand Bank (ANZ),* London: Longmans, 1961, p. 22.
61 *Ibid.,* pp. 51–7; Butlin, *Foundations,* pp. 271ff.; Baster, *The Imperial Banks,* pp. 63–7.
62 E.A. Beever, *Launceston Bank for Savings, 1835–1970: A History of Australia's Oldest Savings Bank,* Melbourne: Melbourne University Press, 1972, pp. 5–18 *passim*; Butlin, *ANZ,* pp. 18–19 and 47–50; Isabella J. Mead, 'Philip Oakden', *Australian Dictionary of Biography,* Volume 2, Melbourne: Melbourne University Press, 1967, p. 290.
63 Alan Atkinson and Marian Aveling (eds), *Australians 1838,* Sydney: Fairfax, Syme & Weldon Associates, 1988, p. 130.
64 Baster, *The Imperial Banks,* pp. 32–3.
65 Hodder, *George Fife Angas,* pp. 129–31.
66 Butlin, *Foundations,* pp. 268–70.
67 Their situation had nothing to do with the current misconception of how British law considered the Indigenous inhabitants. See Andrew Fitzmaurice, 'The Genealogy of Terra Nullius', *Australian Historical Studies,* no. 129, 2007, pp. 1–15.
68 M.I. Finley, *The Ancient Economy,* Berkeley: University of California Press, 1973, chapter 1. Also see Karl Polanyi, *The Great Transformation: The Political and Economic Origins of Our Time,* Boston: Beacon Press, 1957.
69 V. Gordon Childe, *Man Makes Himself,* London: Watts, 1936, p. 62. Bill Gammage explores the magical dimensions in *The Biggest Estate on Earth: How Aborigines Made Australia,* Sydney: Allen & Unwin, 2011, chapter 4.
70 D.H. Pike (ed.), 'The Diary of James Coutts Crawford: Extracts on Aborigines and Adelaide, 1839 and 1841', *South Australiana,* vol. IV, no. 1, 1965, pp. 3–15; Geoffrey Dutton, *The Hero as Murderer: The Life of Edward John Eyre,* Melbourne: Cheshire, 1967, chapters 3 to 9; Gillian Hibbins, 'A Close Encounter of the First Kind – A Plea to Read the Overlanders', *Push From the Bush,* no. 9, 1981, pp. 87–95; Margaret Carnegie, 'Overlanders in 1838 Charles Sturt and David Reid', *Push From the Bush,* no. 14, 1983, pp. 56–64.
71 Douglas Pike, *Paradise of Dissent: South Australia 1829–1857,* 2nd edition, Melbourne: Melbourne University Press, 1967, pp. 102–3.
72 Fergus Robinson and Barry York, *The Black Resistance: An Introduction to the History of the Aborigines' Struggle against British Colonialism,* Melbourne: Widescope, 1977, chapter 6.
73 Marx, *Capital,* I, p. 926.
74 Peter Moore, 'Fatal Letter: Robert Torrens and Native Title', *Journal of the Historical Society of South Australia,* no. 40, 2012, pp. 27–40.
75 G.L. Fischer, 'South Australian Colonisation Act, and other related Constitutional Documents', *Adelaide Law Review,* vol. 3, no. 1, 1966, pp. 368–70.
76 Hodder, *George Fife Angas,* pp. 141ff.
77 June Philipp, 'Wakefieldian Influence and New South Wales, 1830–1832', *Historical Studies,* vol. 9, no. 34, 1960, pp. 173–80.
78 J.R. Wordie, 'The Chronology of English Enclosure, 1500–1914', *The Economic History Review,* New Series, vol. 36, no. 4, 1983, pp. 483–505; E.G. Wakefield, 'Proofs of the Rapidity with which Waste Land Rises in Value, Whenever People Congregate in Colonies', in M.F. Lloyd Prichard (ed.), *The Collected Works of Edward Gibbon Wakefield,* Glasgow: Collins, 1968, pp. 589–614.
79 Quoted in P.A. Howell, 'The South Australia Act, 1934', in Dean Jaensch (ed.), *Flinders History of South Australia: Political History,* Adelaide: Wakefield Press, 1986, p. 48. Also see Rob Linn, 'First Settlers' Perceptions of the Physical and Social Environment of South Australia', *The Push from the Bush,* no. 12, 1982, pp. 41–57; Ronald Parsons, *Hindmarsh Town,* Adelaide: The Corporation of the Town of Hindmarsh, 1974, pp. 1–23.

80 Douglas Pike, 'Introduction of the Real Property Act in South Australia', *Adelaide Law Review*, vol. 1, no. 2, 1960–62, pp. 169–89.
81 Rudden, *The New River*, pp. 209ff.
82 Henry Reynolds, 'That Hated Stain: The Aftermath of Transportation in Tasmania', *Historical Studies*, vol. 14, no. 53, 1969, pp. 19–31.
83 Unlike the Classical School, its successors never penetrated the phenomenal appearance to the dynamics of capital expansion, which is the essence of science in every realm. See Marx, *Capital*, I, pp. 174–5, note 34.
84 Marx, *Capital*, I, p. 644; *Capital*, II, p. 185.
85 George Nicholls quoted in *South Australian Gazette and Colonial Register*, 16 June 1838.
86 John Cashen, 'Masters and Servants in South Australia, 1837–1860', *Journal of the Historical Society of South Australia*, no. 10, 1982, pp. 32–43; John Cashen, 'Social Foundations of South Australia II: "Owners of Labour"', in Eric Richards (ed.), *The Flinders History of South Australia: Social History*, Adelaide: Wakefield Press, 1986, pp. 105–14. For the wider context see Douglas Hay and Paul Craven, *Masters, Servants, and Magistrates in Britain and the Empire, 1562–1955*, Chapel Hill: University of North Carolina Press, 2004.
87 Smith, *The Wealth of Nations*, p. 85.
88 Max Weber, *Critique of Stammler*, trans. Guy Oakes, New York: Free Press, 1977, pp. 100–1; Max Weber, 'R. Stammler's "Surmounting" of the Materialist Conception of History, Part 2' (trans and edited by Martin Albrow), *British Journal of Law and Society*, vol. 3, no. 1, 1976, p. 18.
89 Jim Moss, *Sound of Trumpets: History of the Labour Movement in South Australia*, Adelaide: Wakefield Press, 1985, pp. 1–11; David Faber, '"The Industrial Classes" in a Liberal Utopia: "The Industrial Principle" in the Inaugural 1851 South Australian Legislative Council Election', *Journal of the Historical Society of South Australia*, no. 43, 2015, pp. 111–21; George W. Hilton, *The Truck System including a History of the British Truck Acts, 1465–1960*, Cambridge: W. Heffer & Sons, 1960, chapters 5 and 6.
90 Michael Roe, *The Quest for Authority in Eastern Australia, 1835–1851*, Melbourne: Melbourne University Press, 1965.
91 E.A. Wrigley, 'The Transition to an Advanced Organic Economy: Half a Millennium of English Agriculture', *The Economic History Review*, New Series, vol. 59, no. 3, 2006, pp. 470–1.
92 Thomas N. Tyson et al., 'Accounting, Coercion and Social Control During Apprenticeship: Converting Slave Workers to Wage Workers in the British West Indies, c. 1834–1838', *The Accounting Historians Journal*, vol. 32, no. 2, 2005, pp. 201–31.
93 Hugh Tinker, *A New System of Slavery: The Export of Indian Labour Overseas 1830–1920*, London: Oxford University Press, 1974; Robert J. Steinfeld, *Coercion, Contract and Free Labour in the Nineteenth Century*, Cambridge: Cambridge University Press, 2001. Clare Anderson integrates convict with contract labour but fails to see that similar issues arise by her separating both from 'free labour' and wage-slavery, and the latter pair from each other. See Anderson, 'Convicts and Coolies: Rethinking Indentured Labour in the Nineteenth Century', *Slavery & Abolition*, vol. 30, no. 1, 2009, pp. 93–109.
94 Heather Foster, 'The First Indians: The Bruce and Gleeson Indentured Labourers in Nineteenth Century South Australia', *Journal of the Historical Society of South Australia*, vol. 39, 2011, pp. 21–30.
95 Howell, 'The South Australia Act', p. 29.
96 Weber, *The Protestant Ethic*, p. 57.

97 Ian Harmstorf, 'The Germans', in James Jupp (ed.), *The Australian People: An Encyclopedia of the Nation, its People and their Origins*, Melbourne: Cambridge University Press, 2001, pp. 360–2.
98 L.J. Jones, 'Engineering Considerations in an Historical Argument – The Ridley-Bull "Stripper" Controversy', Preprints of Papers for the Second National Conference on Engineering Heritage, Canberra: Institution of Engineers, Australia, 1985, p. 79.
99 Edgars Dunsdorf, *The Australian Wheat-Growing Industry 1788–1948*, Melbourne: Melbourne University Press, 1956, pp. 101–3, noting also that wages had to be higher than in England to attract more labourers to the colony.
100 Frances Wheelhouse, *Digging Stick to Rotary Hoe: Men and Machines in Rural Australia*, Melbourne: Cassell, 1966, pp. 51–61; Jones, 'Engineering Considerations', pp. 79–84; L.J. Jones, 'The Early History of Mechanical Harvesting', in A. Rupert Hall and Norman Smith (eds), *History of Technology*, Fourth Annual Volume, London: Mansell, 1979, pp. 135–48.
101 Marx, *Capital*, I, p. 492.
102 Sir Samuel Griffith, 'The Distribution of Wealth', *The Centennial Magazine*, vol. 1, no. 12, 1889, pp. 833–42.
103 Anon. (D.H. Pike?), 'Angas, George Fife', in Douglas Pike (ed.), *Australian Dictionary of Biography (ADB)*, Volume 1, Melbourne: Melbourne University Press, 1966, p. 15. On the heavy losses, see Hodder, *George Fife Angas*, p. 31, who implies a year or two earlier.
104 Hodder, *George Fife Angas*, pp. 21–3; Adam Bowett, 'The English Mahogany Trade 1700–1793', PhD thesis, Brunel University, 1996, pp. 184–92 and 205–8; Craig Stephen Revels, 'Timber, Trade, and Transformation: A Historical Geography of Mahogany in Honduras', PhD thesis, Louisiana State University, 2002, https://digitalcommons.lsu.edu/gradschool_dissertations/1285/; O. Nigel Bolland, *The Foundation of a Colonial Society: Belize, from Conquest to Crown Colony*, Baltimore: Johns Hopkins Press, 1977; and O. Nigel Bolland and Assad Shoman, *Land in Belize, 1765–1871*, Kingston: Institute of Social and Economic Research, University of the West Indies, 1977.
105 Hodder, *George Fife Angas*, p. 30.
106 Robin Blackburn, *The Making of New World Slavery: From the Baroque to the Modern 1492–1800*, London: Verso, 1997, chapter 7; Catherine Hall, Nicholas Draper and Keith McClelland (eds), *Emancipation and the Remaking of the British Imperial World*, Manchester: Manchester University Press, 2014.
107 Hodder, *George Fife Angas*, pp. 30–6. A.G.L. Shaw, *Sir George Arthur, 1784–1854*, Melbourne: Melbourne University Press, 1980, makes no mention of Angas although he was superintendent and commandant in British Honduras from 1814 to 1822. Competing claims over jurisdiction and uncertain borders make it hard to be sure which of Angas's business and missionary acts were in Belize and which in British Honduras.
108 The Centre for the Study of the Legacies of British Slave-Ownership at University College London records Angas's signing claims no. 51 for £686, no. 199 for £1,643, no. 231 for £2,177, and no. 244 for £2,439 (see www.UCL.ac.uk/lbs). Newspapers feel obliged to pretend that their total is around £5 million in today's money; a sounder comparison is with the British budget at the time (£40 million), a seven-storey Arkwright mill (£15,000), or the wage of an agricultural labourer, being less than ten shillings a week.
109 Although Britain abolished the trade in slaves out of Africa in 1807, dealing in the already enslaved and their offspring continued around the Americas, officially until the mid-1830s, to be winked at for decades thereafter by Whitehall to get cheap sugar from Cuba and Brazil. See Eric Williams, 'The British West Indian Slave Trade After Its Abolition', *The Journal of Negro History*, vol. 27, no 2, 1942, pp. 175–91; D. Eltis, 'The Traffic in Slaves between the British West Indian Colonies, 1807–1833', *The Economic History Review*, New Series, vol. 25, no. 1, 1972, pp. 55–64.

110 Israel Getzler, 'Joseph Barrow Montefiore', *Australian Dictionary of Biography*, Volume 2, Melbourne: Melbourne University Press, 1967, pp. 250–1.
111 Eli Faber, *Jews, Slaves, and the Slave Trade: Setting the Record Straight*, New York: New York University Press, 1998, p. 130.
112 L. Loewe (ed.), *Diaries of Sir Moses and Lady Montefiore*, Volume I, Chicago: Belford-Clarke, 1890, p. 94.
113 In partnership with Rothschild, Baring and Gurney, Montefiore formed the Alliance Assurance in 1824 with capital of £5 million for its worldwide operations, including marine insurance, after the London Assurance and the Royal Exchange lost their 100-year duopoly over Bottomry. See William Schooling, *Alliance Assurance (1824–1924)*, London: Alliance Assurance, 1924, pp. 1–2, 10–13.
114 For the terms see Loewe (ed.), *Diaries*, pp. 98–9. The government had to borrow a total of £20 million and passed an Act late in 1837 to restructure the debt. Kynaston makes no mention of the loan in either of his books covering the period. No mention of these dealings appears in the *Dictionary of National Biography* entry for Moses Montefiore, or in the *Jewish Encyclopedia*, Volume VIII, New York: Funk & Wagnells, 1904, pp. 668–71.
115 Hirsch Munz, *Jews in South Australia*, Adelaide: n.p., 1936, pp. 12–14, reprints an extract from *The Observer*, 1 January 1887.
116 Munz, *Jews in South Australia*, pp. 11–17; A. Fabian, 'Early Days of South Australian Jewry', *Australian Jewish Historical Society Journal*, vol. 2, 1944–48, pp. 140–2; D.J. Benjamin, 'The First Montefiore in Australia', *Australian Jewish Historical Society Journal*, vol. 2, 1944–48, pp. 467–71.
117 Pike, *Paradise of Dissent*, pp. 122 and 187.
118 A.H. John, 'The London Assurance Company and the Marine Insurance Market of the Eighteenth Century', *Economica*, New Series, vol. 25, no. 98, 1958, pp. 126–41; Clive Trebilcock, *Phoenix Assurance*, Volume I, Cambridge: Cambridge University Press, 1985, pp. 96–112; Robin Pearson and David Richardson, 'Business Networking in the Industrial Revolution', *The Economic History Review*, New Series, vol. 54, no. 4, 2001, pp. 657–79. For the Montefiore involvements, see Nicholas Draper, 'Helping to Make Britain Great', in Catherine Hall, Nicholas Draper and Keith McClelland (eds), *Legacies of British Slave Ownership*, Cambridge: Cambridge University Press, 2014, p. 107.
119 'Fidelia Hill (née Munkhouse)', Legacies of British Slave-Ownership database, University College London, https://www.ucl.ac.uk/lbs/person/view/-584002331.
120 Draper is wrong about the Montefiore brothers receiving compensation. See Hall, Draper and McClelland (eds), *Legacies*, p. 63.
121 Ian Duffield, 'From Slave Colonies to Penal Colonies: The West Indian Convict Transportees to Australia', *Slavery & Abolition*, vol. 7, no. 1, 1986, p. 31.
122 R.B. Sheridan, 'The Commercial and Financial Organisation of the British Slave Trade, 1750–1807', *The Economic History Review*, vol. 11, no. 2, 1958, pp. 249–63; Joseph E. Inikori, 'The Credit Needs of the African Trade and the Development of the Credit Economy in England', *Explorations in Economic History*, vol. 27, no. 2, 1990, pp. 197–231.
123 T.M. Devine, *The Tobacco Lords: A Study of the Tobacco Merchants of Glasgow and their Trading Activities, 1740–1790*, Edinburgh: Donald, 1975; Carol Hill, 'Galloway Shipping and Regional Development, 1750–1850', *Scottish Economic and Social History*, vol. 19, no. 2, 1999, pp. 95–116.
124 Brian Southam, 'The Silence of the Bertrams: Slavery and the Chronology of *Mansfield Park*', *Times Literary Supplement*, 17 February 1995, pp. 13–14; Edward W. Said, *Culture & Imperialism*, London: Chatto & Windus, 1993, pp. 69–70 and 110–16. More to the liking of the Jane-ites is Marilyn Butler, *Jane Austen and the War of Ideas*, Oxford: Clarendon Press, 1975, which ignores slavery more thoroughly than did its subject.

125 Marx, *Capital*, I, p. 741.
126 Walter Benjamin, *Illuminations*, London: Fontana, 1973, p. 259. Also see my essay 'Barbarisms and Civilisations' in *Temper Democratic: How Exceptional is Australia?*, Adelaide: Wakefield Press, 1998, pp. 217–26. The Earl of Chatham thought it 'barabarism' not to 'consider the sugar colonies as the landed interest of this kingdom' (quoted in Williams, *Capitalism & Slavery*, p. 95).
127 Simon Haines, 'An Education Manifesto for Western Civilisation', *Quadrant*, vol. 61, no. 12, 2017, pp. 14–17. Its manner and matter would affront both Allan and Harold Bloom.
128 This line is taken from Kipling's poem 'Recessional', composed for Queen Victoria's Diamond Jubilee in 1897.
129 Peter Burroughs, 'The Mauritius Rebellion of 1832 and the Abolition of British Colonial Slavery', *Journal of Imperial and Commonwealth History*, vol. 4, no. 3, 1976, pp. 243–65.
130 *Daily Post*, 24 June 1916, p. 11.
131 David Richardson argues that by the 1790s at least 40 per cent of the income of Bristolians derived from slavery-related activities. See Richardson, 'Slavery and Bristol's "Golden Age"', *Slavery & Abolition*, vol. 26, no. 1, 2005, pp. 35–54.

Chapter 5 | True Lies: South Australia's Foundation, the Idea of 'Difference', and the Rights of Aboriginal People

1 Janna Thompson, *Taking Responsibility for the Past: Reparation and Historical Justice*, Cambridge: Polity Press, 2002, p. xvii.
2 *Ibid.*, p. xviii.
3 These basic principles are spelt out by Douglas Pike in chapter 1 of *Paradise of Dissent: South Australia 1829–1857*, Melbourne: Melbourne University Press, 1957, with the notable exception of Aboriginal protection. This aspect came to be associated with the founding principles in later works such as R.M. Gibbs, *A History of South Australia*, Adelaide: Balara Books, 1978 (first published in 1969), chapter 3.
4 Tellingly, C.D. Rowley's chapter on Aboriginal policy in colonial South Australia in his landmark volume, *The Destruction of Aboriginal Society*, Melbourne: Penguin, 1970, is entitled 'The Colony that was to be Different'. As the title indicates, Derek Whitelock's *Adelaide 1836–1976: A History of Difference*, Brisbane: University of Queensland Press, 1977, also reinforced this idea of South Australia's 'sense of difference'.
5 Letters Patent Erecting and Establishing the Province of South Australia and Fixing its Boundaries, State Records of South Australia [henceforth SRSA], GRG 2/64.
6 First Annual Report of the Colonization Commissioners of South Australia, *House of Commons, Sessional Papers*, 1836, vol. 39, no. 426, p. 8.
7 *Ibid.*, p. 9.
8 Colonial Secretary Robert Gouger's Draft of a Proclamation, popularly known as 'the Proclamation', as read by Governor Hindmarsh at Glenelg: Announcing the Establishment of the Government, SRSA, GRG24/90 (Miscellaneous records of historical interest, item 401).
9 *The South Australia Act*, 1834 (Act 4 and 5 William IV, Cap 95, An Act to Empower His Majesty to Erect South Australia into a British Province or Provinces, and to Provide for the Colonization and Government thereof, 15 August 1834).
10 Letter from George Arthur to Thomas Spring Rice, 27 January 1835, SRSA, Colonial Office 280/55.
11 Letter from George Grey to Robert Torrens, 15 December 1835, SRSA, CO 13/3.
12 John Brown, Diary, 17 December 1835, State Library of South Australia [henceforth SLSA], PRG 1002/2, p. 75.
13 Letter from Lord Glenelg to Robert Torrens, 11 January 1836, SRSA, CO 13/4.

14 Brown, diary, 12 January 1836, pp. 90–1.
15 For a discussion of this, see chapter 5 of Henry Reynolds, *The Law of the Land*, Melbourne: Penguin, 1987.
16 *Advertiser*, 7 May 1919, p. 6.
17 Minutes of the General Committee of the Aborigines Friends Association, 11 April 1924, SLSA, SRG 139/2–6.
18 *Daylight*, 31 March 1926.
19 J.C. Genders, A Statement by the Aborigines' Protection League explaining its basic principles and proposals, Adelaide, bound with Report to the State Executive of the Aborigines Protection League, Adelaide, 26 June 1929, p. 2. Located in SLSA.
20 Conference of Representatives of Missions, Societies, and Associations interested in the Welfare of Aboriginals to consider the Report and Recommendations submitted to the Commonwealth Government by J.W. Bleakley Esq., Report of Debates, Commonwealth of Australia, 12 April 1929, p. 12.
21 J.C. Genders, *The Australian Aborigines*, typescript manuscript, 4 January 1937, p. 2. Located in SLSA.
22 *Advertiser*, 19 August 1921.
23 *Ibid.*, 31 December 1929.
24 *Ibid.*, 14 November 1934.
25 *Ibid.*, 15 November 1935.
26 *Ibid.*, 28 November 1935.
27 Marilyn Lake, *Getting Equal: The History of Australian Feminism*, Sydney: Allen & Unwin, 1999, p. 133.
28 John Summers, 'Aborigines and Government in the Twentieth Century', in Eric Richards (ed.), *The Flinders History of South Australia: Social History*, Adelaide: Wakefield Press, 1986, p. 499.
29 Paul Havemann, 'The Rule of Law, Betrayal and Reparation', in Shaun Berg (ed.), *Coming to Terms: Aboriginal Title in South Australia*, Adelaide: Wakefield Press, 2010, p. 141.
30 *South Australian Parliamentary Debates*, 13 July 1966, p. 473.
31 *Ibid.*
32 *Ibid.*, p. 475.
33 *Ibid.*, p. 479.
34 John Summers, 'Aboriginal Policy', in Andrew Parkin and Allen Patience (eds), *The Dunstan Decade: Social Democracy at the State Level*, Melbourne: Longman Cheshire, 1981, p. 133.
35 *Ibid.*
36 *Ibid.*, p. 142.
37 Don Dunstan, *Felicia: The Political Memoirs of Don Dunstan*, Melbourne: Macmillan, 1981, p. 110.
38 Thompson, *Taking Responsibility*, p. xviii.

Chapter 6 | George Hamilton, the Bold and Dashing Bushman: The Politics of Colonial Compassion

1 Obituary, 'The Late Mr. George Hamilton', *Adelaide Observer*, 4 August 1883, p. 32.
2 Judith Butler, *Frames of War: When is Life Grievable?* London: Verso, 2010, pp. 74–5.
3 *Ibid.*, p. 51.
4 Jane Haggis and Margaret Allen, 'Imperial Emotions: Affective Communities of Mission in British Protestant Women's Missionary Publications c1880-1920', *Journal of Social History*, vol. 41, no. 3, 2008, pp. 691–716.

5   George Hamilton, *The Horse: Its Treatment in Australia,* Adelaide: J.T. Shawyer, 1864; George Hamilton, *An Appeal for the Horse,* Adelaide: David Gall, 1866.
6   Martha Sear, Kylie Carman-Brown, Elizabeth Knox and Jennifer Wilson, 'George Hamilton Horse Welfare Collection', no date, National Museum of Australia, http://www.nma.gov.au/collections/highlights/hamilton_horse_welfare; accessed 2 December 2017.
7   Hamilton, *An Appeal for the Horse,* p. 7.
8   *Ibid.*, p. 12.
9   *Ibid.*
10 *Ibid.*
11 *Ibid.*, pp. 46–7.
12 *Ibid.*, p. 49.
13 'Review of George Hamilton, An Appeal for the Horse', *South Australian Register,* 8 February 1866, p. 2.
14 J.H. Love, 'Hamilton, George (1812–1883)', *Australian Dictionary of Biography,* http://adb.anu.edu.au/biography/hamilton-george-12961/text23427; accessed 3 December 2017.
15 Design and Art Australia Online, 'Exhibition of Pictures; the Works of Colonial Artists', https://daao.library.unsw.edu.au/bio/event/exhibition-of-colonial-artists-in-adelaide; accessed 3 December 2017.
16 Love, 'Hamilton'.
17 George Grey, *Journals of Two Expeditions of Discovery in North-West and Western Australia, During the Years 1837, 1838, and 1839, Under the Authority of her Majesty's Government,* Volume 2, London: T. and W. Boone, 1841.
18 These comprise three journal accounts (seemingly re-written from original entries) held by the National Library of Australia (NLA) and a trilogy published in 1880: George Hamilton, 'The Journal of an Overlander, or, a Narrative of Journies in New South Wales and South Australia from 1836 to 1845, ca. 1845' [manuscript], National Library of Australia, MS 4299C; George Hamilton, *Experiences of a Colonist Forty Years Ago; A Journey from Port Phillip to South Australia in 1839; and A Voyage from Port Phillip to Adelaide in 1846, by An Old Hand,* Adelaide: J. Williams, 1880. Only one of the hand-written journals is published, titled 'Port Phillip to Adelaide Beginning 1839 May, Following a Route discovered by Charles Bonney'. The other two NLA journal accounts comprise journeys from Sydney to Port Phillip in 1837, and a journey from Adelaide to Melbourne between 4 June – 26 June 1845. The two other accounts published in 1880 comprise a fictionalised amalgam incorporating elements from a journey from Sydney to Port Phillip in 1837, and a journey from Melbourne to Adelaide in 1846.
19 Grey, *Journals of Two Expeditions of Discovery.*
20 Instead of travelling down the Murray he struck across country to the Grampians, followed the Wannon and Glenelg Rivers, turned west and moved parallel to the coast. Although the journey was shorter than the Murray route, water was scarce. Hamilton, 'The Journal of an Overlander'; Hamilton, *Experiences of a Colonist.*
21 Hamilton, 'The Journal of an Overlander', p. 4.
22 *Ibid.*
23 *Ibid.*
24 *Ibid.*, p. 70.
25 *Ibid.*, pp. 46–7.
26 Hamilton, 'Sydney to Port Phillip in 1837', in 'The Journal of an Overlander', p. 24.
27 *Ibid.*, p. 26.
28 Hamilton, 'The Journal of an Overlander'; Hamilton, *Experiences of a Colonist.* The Murray route was more likely to prompt violence: Heather Burke, Amy Roberts, Mick

Morrison, Vanessa Sullivan and the River Murray and Mallee Aboriginal Corporation (RMMAC), 'The Space of Conflict: Aboriginal/European Interactions and Frontier Violence on the Western Central Murray, South Australia, 1830–41', *Aboriginal History*, vol. 40, 2016, pp. 145–79.
29 Hamilton, *A Journey from Port Phillip to South Australia in 1839*, pp. 20–1.
30 Robert Reece, *Aborigines and Colonist: Aborigines and Colonial Society in New South Wales in the 1830s and 1840s*, Sydney: Sydney University Press, 1974; Marian Aveling and Lyndall Ryan, 'At the Boundaries', in Alan Atkinson and Marian Aveling (eds), *Australians 1838*, Sydney: Fairfax, Syme & Weldon, 1987, pp. 54–60; Roger Milliss, *Waterloo Creek: The Australia Day Massacre of 1838, George Gipps and the British Conquest of New South Wales*, Melbourne: McPhee Gribble, 1992; Jane Lydon and Lyndall Ryan (eds), *Remembering Myall Creek*, Sydney: NewSouth Books, 2018.
31 Amanda Nettelbeck, 'Mythologising Frontier: Narrative Versions of the Rufus River Conflict, 1841–1899', *Journal of Australian Studies*, vol. 23, no. 61, 1999, pp. 75–82. See also Robert Foster, Rick Hosking and Amanda Nettelbeck, *Fatal Collisions: The South Australian Frontier and the Violence of Memory*, Adelaide: Wakefield Press, 2001, pp. 29–43.
32 'Despatch from Mr Eyre', *Southern Australian*, 18 February 1842, p. 3.
33 *Ibid.*
34 *Ibid.*
35 Hamilton, *A Journey from Port Phillip to South Australia in 1839*, p. 21.
36 Jane Lydon, '"The Colonial Children Cry": Jo the Crossing-Sweeper Goes to the Colonies', *Journal of Victorian Culture*, vol. 20, no. 3, 2015, pp. 1–18.
37 'Adelaide to Melbourne, 4–26 June 1845', in Hamilton, 'The Journal of an Overlander', p. 13.
38 *Ibid.*, p. 14.
39 Rebecca Schneider, *Performing Remains: Art and War in Times of Theatrical Re-enactment*, London: Routledge, 2011.
40 Catriona Elder, 'Colonialism and Reenactment Television: Imagining Belonging in *Outback House*', in Vanessa Agnew and Jonathan Lamb (eds), *Settler and Creole Reenactment*, Basingstoke: Palgrave Macmillan, 2009, pp. 193–207.
41 Hamilton, *Experiences of a Colonist Forty Years Ago*, p. 6.
42 Grey, *Journals of Two Expeditions of Discovery*, p. 184.
43 Hamilton, *Experiences of a Colonist*, p. 24.
44 *Ibid.*, p. 37.
45 Anya Schwartz '"Not This Year!": Reenacting Contested Pasts Aboard *The Ship*', *Rethinking History*, vol. 11, no. 3, 2007, pp. 427–46.
46 'How Whites First Met Blacks', *Advertiser*, 13 January 1932, p. 3.

Chapter 7 | Walking the Line in Historical Fiction

1 Janna Thompson, *Intergenerational Justice: Rights and Responsibilities in an Intergenerational Polity*, London: Routledge, 2009, p. 1, cited in Amanda Nettelbeck and Robert Foster, *Out of the Silence: The History and Memory of South Australia's Frontier Wars*, Adelaide: Wakefield Press, 2012, p. 26.
2 Lucy Treloar, *Salt Creek*, Sydney: Pan Macmillan, 2015.
3 Tony Roberts, 'The Brutal Truth', *The Monthly*, November 2009, https://www.themonthly.com.au/issue/2009/november/1330478364/tony-roberts/brutal-truth; accessed 12 November 2017.
4 Anne Lamott, *Bird by Bird: Some Instructions on Writing and Life*, New York: Random House, 1994, p. 57.
5 Hilary Mantel, 'Can These Bones Live?', The Reith Lectures, BBC, http://www.bbc.co.uk/programmes/b08wp3g3; accessed 8 July 2017.

6. Joanne Jones, 'A Study of the Significance of the Australian Historical Novel in the Period of the History Wars, 1988 – present', PhD thesis, Curtin University, 2012, p. 73; Chris Conti, 'Grenville on the Frontier', *Sydney Review of Books*, 4 May 2017, https://sydneyreviewofbooks.com/kate-grenville-on-the-frontier-the-secret-river/; accessed 13 September 2017.
7. Inga Clendinnen, 'The History Question', *Quarterly Essay*, Melbourne: Black Inc., 2006, pp. 31–2.
8. Chris Conti, 'Grenville on the Frontier', *Sydney Review of Books*, 4 May 2017, https://sydneyreviewofbooks.com/kate-grenville-on-the-frontier-the-secret-river; accessed 4 September 2017.
9. *Ibid.*
10. *Ibid.*
11. Mark McKenna, 'Comfort History', *Weekend Australian*, 18 March 2006, cited in Conti, 'Grenville on the Frontier'.
12. Inga Clendinnen, *Dancing with Strangers*, Melbourne: Text Publishing, 2005, p. 12.
13. Clendinnen, 'The History Question', p. 21.
14. David Malouf, cited in Clendinnen, 'The History Question', p. 21.
15. *Ibid.*
16. Clendinnen, 'The History Question', p. 20.
17. *Ibid.*, p. 21.
18. Sue Kossew, 'Voicing "The Great Australian Silence": Kate Grenville's Narrative of Settlement in *The Secret River*', *Journal of Commonwealth Literature*, vol. 42, no. 2, 2007, cited in Conti, 'Grenville on the Frontier'.
19. *Ibid.*
20. Iola Hack, *Chequered Lives: John Barton Hack and Stephen Hack and the Early Days of South Australia*, Adelaide: Wakefield Press, 2014.
21. John Barton Hack, Report on the Select Committee of the Legislative Council Upon 'The Aborigines', Adelaide: Government Printer, 1860, p. 93, https://aiatsis.gov.au/sites/default/files/catalogue_resources/92284.pdf.
22. Charles Darwin, *The Voyage of the Beagle* [1839], New York: Cosimo Inc [facsimile edition], 2008, pp. 438–9.
23. *Ibid.*, p. 508.
24. L.P. Hartley, *The Go-Between*, London: Hamish Hamilton, 1953, p. 9.
25. Sarah Pinto, 'History, Fiction and *The Secret River*', in Sue Kossew (ed.), *Lighting Dark Places: Essays on Kate Grenville*, Amsterdam: Rodopi, 2010, pp. 179–97.
26. Susan Wyndham, 'Connections in Isolation', *Sydney Morning Herald*, 6 October 2012.
27. Kim Scott, *That Deadman Dance*, Sydney: Pan Macmillan, 2010.
28. Larissa Berendht, from personal notes taken at a panel discussion on foundation fictions of which I was part, Brisbane Writers Festival, 2016.
29. Shirley Barrett, *Rush Oh!*, Sydney: Pan Macmillan, 2015.
30. Mantel, 'Can These Bones Live?'.
31. Jeremy de Groot, discussion on Open Book, BBC Radio, 16 June 2016, http://www.bbc.co.uk/programmes/p03y9y5l; accessed 10 August 2017.
32. Mantel, 'Can These Bones Live?'.
33. Letters Patent Erecting and Establishing the Province of South Australia and Fixing its Boundaries, 19 February 1836, State Records of South Australia, GRG 2/64.
34. Catherine Helen Spence, *Clara Morrison* [1854], facsimile edition, Adelaide: Wakefield Press, 1986, p. 237.
35. Nettelbeck and Foster, *Out of the Silence*, p. 136.
36. Simpson Newland, *Paving the Way: A Romance of the Australian Bush*, London: Gay and Hancock, 1912, digitised version, University of California Libraries, https://archive.org/details/pavingwayromance00newlrich; accessed 9 September 2017.

37 *Ibid.*, p. 128.
38 Simpson Newland, *Blood Tracks of the Bush*, London: Gay and Bird, 1900.
39 I am indebted here to Tony Roberts's article, 'The Brutal Truth'.
40 Newland, *Paving the Way*, p. 165.
41 Jane Rawson, *From the Wreck*, Melbourne: Transit Lounge, 2017.
42 Cody Delistraty, 'The Psychological Comforts of Storytelling', *The Atlantic*, 2 November 2014, https://www.theatlantic.com/health/archive/2014/11/the-psychological-comforts-of-storytelling/381964; accessed 25 September 2017.
43 David Comer Kidd and Emanuele Castano, 'Reading Literary Fiction Improves Theory of Mind', *Science*, vol. 342, no. 6156, 18 October 2013, cited in Delistraty, 'The Psychological Comforts of Storytelling'.
44 Flannery O'Connor quoted in Joanne Halleran McMullen and Jon Parrish Peede (eds), *Inside the Church of Flannery O'Connor: Sacrament, Sacramental and the Sacred in her Fiction*, Macon: Mercer University Press, 2008, p. 46.
45 Hilary Mantel, 'Can These Bones Live?'.
46 Clendinnen, *Dancing with Strangers*, p. 13.
47 *Ibid.*, p. 14.
48 *Ibid.*, p. 15.
49 *Ibid.*, p. 16.
50 *Ibid.*, p. 17.
51 Clendinnen, 'The History Question', p. 11.
52 Treloar, *Salt Creek*, p. 252.
53 Clendinnen, 'The History Question', p. 18.
54 This quote and the ones that follow in this and the next paragraph are taken from Mark McKenna, *From the Edge: Australia's Lost Histories*, Melbourne: Melbourne University Publishing, 2016, pp. 14–16.
55 *Ibid.*, pp. xi–xviii.
56 *Ibid.*, pp. 1–63.
57 *Ibid.*, p. 37.
58 Rebe Taylor, 'The Wedge Collection and the Conundrum of Humane Colonisation', *Meanjin*, vol. 76, no. 4, 2017, pp. 34–55.
59 *Ibid.*, p. 34.
60 *Ibid.*, p. 36.
61 Interview with Rebe Taylor via email with Lucy Treloar, 20–24 January 2018.
62 *Ibid.*
63 Taylor, 'The Wedge Collection', p. 55.
64 Interview with Rebe Taylor.
65 Camilla Nelson and Christine de Matos, 'Fictional Histories and Historical Fictions: Writing History in the Twenty-First Century', *TEXT* Special Issue, no. 28, April 2015, p. 9.
66 Mark McKenna, *Looking for Blackfellas Point: An Australian History of Place*, Sydney: University of New South Wales Press, 2006, p. 108, cited in Nelson and de Matos, 'Fictional Histories and Historical Fictions', p. 9.
67 Phone interview with Ursula Le Guin, Paul Holdengräber, *Soundcloud*, 3 January 2018, https://soundcloud.com/lithub/a-conversation-with-ursula-k-le-guin?utm_source=soundcloud&utm_campaign=share&utm_medium=twitter; accessed 18 January 2018.

Chapter 8 | Legends of the Nineties: Literary Culture in Adelaide at the End of the Nineteenth Century

1. Arthur Jose, 'The Romantic 'Nineties. IX', *Brisbane Courier*, 23 July 1932, p. 19.
2. Arthur Jose, 'The Romantic 'Nineties. VII', *Brisbane Courier*, 9 July 1932, p. 19.
3. Vance Palmer, *The Legend of the Nineties*, Melbourne: Melbourne University Press, 1954; A.A. Phillips, *The Australian Tradition: Studies in a Colonial Culture*, Melbourne: Cheshire, 1958; Russel Ward, *The Australian Legend*, Melbourne: Oxford University Press, 1958.
4. 'University of Adelaide', *Advertiser*, 19 December 1895, p. 7; 'Appendix B. Estimated Population of the Province of South Australia and of the City of Adelaide', in J.J. Pascoe (ed.), *History of Adelaide and Vicinity*, Adelaide: Hussey & Gillingham, 1901, p. 617.
5. 'General Committee Minutes', 21 August 1883 to 3 July 1889, South Australian Literary Societies' Union Papers, State Library of South Australia, SRG 45/1; Paul Depasquale, *A Critical History of South Australian Literature, 1836–1930*, Warradale, S.A.: Pioneer, 1978, p. 116.
6. 'University of Adelaide', p. 7.
7. 'Our Literary Societies' Federation: Its Past, Present, and Future', *Literary Societies' Year Book*, 1899, pp. 5–6.
8. 'General Committee Minutes', South Australian Literary Societies' Union Papers.
9. 'Australasian Home-Reading Union', *Advertiser*, 25 April 1893, p. 6.
10. John Jenkin, 'The Australasian Home Reading Union: Spectacular Rise, Precipitous Fall', *Journal of the Historical Society of South Australia*, vol. 38, 2010, pp. 64, 70.
11. 'University of Adelaide', p. 7.
12. Leigh Dale, *The Enchantment of English: Professing English Literatures in Australian Universities*, Sydney: Sydney University Press, 2012, p. 45.
13. Catherine Helen Spence, 'An Autobiography', in Susan Magarey (ed.) with Barbara Wall, Mary Lyons and Maryan Beams, *Ever Yours, C.H. Spence*, Adelaide: Wakefield Press, 2005, p. 48.
14. 'What the People Read', *South Australian Register*, 25 September 1897, p. 5.
15. Carl Bridge, *A Trunk Full of Books: History of the State Library of South Australia and Its Forerunners*, Adelaide: Wakefield, 1986, p. 72.
16. 'What the People Read', p. 5.
17. 'A Remarkable Career', *Register*, 21 November 1906, pp. 5–6.
18. 'Madame Sarah Bernhardt', *Adelaide Observer*, 4 July 1891, p. 36. For the best overview of theatre during this period, see Gerald Fischer, 'The Professional Theatre in Adelaide, 1838–1922', *Australian Letters*, March 1960, pp. 79–97.
19. Unknown to Adelaide audiences, Joseph Conrad visited several times between 1889 and 1893, before his first novel had been published. See Joseph Conrad, *A Personal Record*, London: Nelson, 1916, pp. 51–5.
20. 'An Interview with Rudyard Kipling', *Advertiser*, 26 November 1891, p. 5.
21. 'New Australia', *South Australian Register*, 26 April 1893, p. 3.
22. 'Mark Twain at Home', *South Australian Register*, 14 October 1895, p. 6.
23. Frances McGuire, *Bright Morning: The Story of an Australian Family before 1914*, Adelaide: Rigby, 1975, p. 41.
24. 'The Burns Demonstration', *Evening Journal*, 7 May 1894, p. 4.
25. See, for example, Depasquale, *A Critical History*, p. 139.
26. 'Comin' 'Ome frum Shearin'', *Critic*, 12 February 1898, p. 8; 'The Cockie's Man', *Critic*, 19 February 1898, p. 5.
27. Thomas Gill, *Bibliography of South Australia*, Adelaide: Government Printer, 1886.
28. Douglas Sladen (ed.), *A Century of Australian Song*, London: Scott, 1888; Douglas Sladen (ed.), *Australian Ballads and Rhymes: Poems Inspired by Life and Scenery in*

Australia and New Zealand, London: Scott, 1888; Douglas Sladen (ed.), *Australian Poets: 1788–1888*, London: Griffith, Farran, Okeden and Welsh, 1888.
29   Sladen (ed.), *A Century*, pp. 27, 29.
30   'Agnes Neale' [Caroline Agnes Leane], *Shadows and Sunbeams*, Adelaide: Burden & Bonython, 1890, p. 76.
31   *An Australian Girl*, 3 volumes, London: Bentley, 1890.
32   Desmond Byrne, *Australian Writers*, London: Bentley, 1896, p. 25.
33   Spence, 'An Autobiography', pp. 116–17.
34   Susan Magarey, *Passions of the First Wave Feminists*, Sydney: UNSW Press, 2001, p. 44; Sharon Crozier-De Rosa, 'Identifying with the Frontier: Federation, New Woman, Nation and Empire', in Maggie Tonkin, Mandy Treagus, Madeleine Seys and Sharon Crozier-De Rosa (eds), *Changing the Victorian Subject*, Adelaide: University of Adelaide Press, 2014, p. 45.
35   Paul Eggert, 'Australian Classics and the Price of Books: The Puzzle of the 1890s', in Gillian Whitelock (ed.), *The Colonial Present: Australian Writing for the 21st Century*, *JASAL* Special Issue, 2008, p. 143.
36   See, for example, Sue Sheridan, '"Temper, romantic; bias offensively feminine": Australian Women Writers and Literary Nationalism', *Kunapipi*, vol. 7, no. 2, 1985, pp. 49–58.
37   See, for example, Crozier-De Rosa, 'Identifying with the Frontier', pp. 37–58.
38   Depasquale, *A Critical History*, p. 179.
39   Simpson Newland, *Paving the Way: A Romance of the Australian Bush* [1893], Adelaide: Rigby, 1954, p. 243.
40   *Ibid.*, p. 259.
41   Don Wright, 'Symon, Sir Josiah Henry (1846–1934), *Australian Dictionary of Biography*, http://adb.anu.edu.au/biography/symon-sir-josiah-henry-8734/text15293, published first in hardcopy 1990, accessed 8 February 2018.
42   Bridge, *A Trunk Full of Books*, pp. 10, 16–17.
43   'The Reconstruction of Society', *South Australian Register*, 16 February 1891, p. 6.
44   Philip Butterss, 'Building Literary Adelaide, 1836–60', *Journal of Australian Studies*, vol. 39, no. 3, 2015, pp. 348–9.
45   Alfred Chandler, *Songs of the Sunland*, Adelaide: E.S. Wigg, 1889.
46   Herbert Hall, *Lay of the Laborer*, Adelaide: n.p., 1899.
47   'Amusements. Theatre Royal', *Express and Telegraph*, 5 December 1890, p. 3.
48   'Theatre Royal. The Jonquille', *South Australian Register*, 15 August 1891, p. 6.
49   Depasquale, *A Critical History*, p. 196.
50   For a more detailed discussion, see Philip Butterss, 'The Tennysons in Literary Adelaide', *Australian Literary Studies*, vol. 30, no. 3, 2015, pp. 110–20.
51   'The New Governor', *South Australian Register*, 2 February 1899, p. 5.
52   Alexandra Hasluck (ed.), *Audrey Tennyson's Vice-Regal Days: The Australian Letters of Audrey Lady Tennyson to Her Mother Zacyntha Boyle, 1899–1903*, Canberra: National Library of Australia, 1978, p. 26.
53   'The Governor's Speech', *Advertiser*, 11 April 1899, p. 6.
54   Samuel Way to Reverend G.G. Coster, 19 June 1899, Samuel Way Papers, State Library of South Australia, PRG 30/5.
55   'Hear Here', *Quiz and the Lantern*, 13 April 1899, p. 8.
56   Mercutio, 'Unjointed Chat', *Sydney Morning Herald*, 19 April 1899, p. 8; 'Clackery', *Clipper*, 6 May 1899, p. 7; *Mount Alexander Mail*, 12 April 1899, p. 2.
57   Brian Samuels, 'Gawler, "the Colonial Athens", and South Australia's First Local History and First Public Museum', *Journal of the Historical Society of South Australia*, vol. 40, 2012, p. 41.

58 'Survey: City of Culture not Living up to its Name', *Canberra Times*, 26 June 1971, p. 11.
59 'Notes and Queries. A Statue of Gordon', *Register*, 29 August 1904, p. 6.
60 'A National Band', *Register*, 22 May 1925, p. 9.
61 Alison Broinowski, 'The Athens of the South', in Philip Butterss (ed.), *Adelaide: A Literary City*, Adelaide: University of Adelaide Press, 2013, pp. 159–60.

Chapter 9 | South Australia: The Pivotal State

1 J.B. Hirst, *Adelaide and the Country 1870–1917: Their Social and Political Relationship*, Melbourne: Melbourne University Press, 1973.
2 Robert Dare, 'History and Historians', in Wilfrid Prest, Kerrie Round and Carol Fort (eds), *The Wakefield Companion to South Australian History*, Adelaide: Wakefield Press, 2001, pp. 257–60.
3 J.B. Hirst, 'Distance in Australia – Was It a Tyrant?', *Historical Studies*, vol. 16, no. 64, 1975, pp. 435–47.
4 J.B. Hirst, 'The Pioneer Legend', *Historical Studies*, vol. 18, no. 71, 1978, pp. 316–37; J.B. Hirst, *Convict Society and its Enemies: A History of Early New South Wales*, Sydney: George Allen & Unwin, 1983; J.B. Hirst, *The Strange Birth of Colonial Democracy: New South Wales 1848–1884*, Sydney: Allen & Unwin, 1988.
5 See the collection republished as John Hirst, *Sense and Nonsense in Australian History*, Melbourne: Black Inc., 2005.
6 John Hirst, 'South Australia and Australia: Reflections on their Histories', in Robert Foster and Paul Sendziuk (eds), *Turning Points: Chapters in South Australian History*, Adelaide: Wakefield Press, 2012. This chapter was presented in a slightly different form as the History Council of South Australia Annual Lecture, University of Adelaide, 4 August 2011.
7 *Ibid.*, p. 124.
8 David Hackett Fischer, *Historians' Fallacies: Towards a Logic of Historical Thought*, New York: Harper, 1970.
9 David Hackett Fischer, *Albion's Seed: Four British Folkways in America*, New York: Oxford University Press, 1989.
10 Paul Sendziuk, 'No Convicts Here: Reconsidering South Australia's Foundation Myth', in Robert Foster and Paul Sendziuk (eds), *Turning Points: Chapters in South Australian History*, Adelaide: Wakefield Press, 2012, pp. 33–47.
11 Hirst, 'South Australia and Australia', p. 126.
12 *Ibid.*, p. 127.
13 John Hirst, *The Sentimental Nation: The Making of the Australian Commonwealth*, Melbourne: Oxford University Press, 2000.
14 Alfred Deakin, *The Federal Story: The Inner History of the Federal Cause 1880–1900*, J.A. La Nauze (ed.), Melbourne: Melbourne University Press, 1963, pp. 61–2, 79, 86.
15 John Bannon, 'South Australia: Federation sine qua non', *The New Federalist*, no. 8, December 2001, p. 35.
16 J.A. La Nauze, *The Making of the Australian Constitution*, Melbourne: Melbourne University Press, 1972, p. 146.
17 J.C. Bannon, 'South Australia', in Helen Irving (ed.), *The Centenary Companion to Australian Federation*, Cambridge: Cambridge University Press, 1999, p. 145.
18 La Nauze, *The Making of the Australian Constitution*, p. 190.
19 R. Norris, 'Economic Influences on the 1898 South Australian Federation Referendum', in A.W. Martin (ed.), *Essays in Australian Federation*, Melbourne: Melbourne University Press, 1969, pp. 13–40.
20 Bannon, 'South Australia', pp. 174, 178.
21 *Ibid.*, p. 177.

22 La Nauze, *The Making of the Australian Constitution*, p. 211.
23 *Equality in Diversity: History of the Commonwealth Grants Commission*, 2nd edition, Canberra: Australian Government Publishing Service, 1995, pp. 10–12.
24 See, for example, Paul Sendziuk, 'The Great Man of History: Industrialisation and the Playford Legend', in this volume, and David C. Rich, 'Tom's Vision? Playford and Industrialisation', in Bernard O'Neil, Judith Raftery and Kerrie Round (eds), *Playford's South Australia: Essays on the History of South Australia, 1933–1968*, Adelaide: Association of Professional Historians, 1996, pp. 91–116.
25 Carol S. Fort, '"Equality of Sacrifice"? War Work in Salisbury, South Australia', in Bernard O'Neil, Judith Raftery and Kerrie Round (eds), *Playford's South Australia: Essays on the History of South Australia, 1933–1968*, Adelaide: Association of Professional Historians, 1996, pp. 215–32; Paul Sendziuk and Robert Foster, *A History of South Australia*, Melbourne: Cambridge University Press, 2018, pp. 138–9.
26 S.J. Butlin and C.B. Schedvin, *War Economy 1942–1945*, Canberra: Australian War Memorial, 1977, p. 359.
27 Stuart Macintyre, *Australia's Boldest Experiment: War and Reconstruction in the 1940s*, Sydney: NewSouth, 2015, pp. 98–104.
28 Letter from Lloyd Dumas to Keith Murdoch, 1 and 9 December 1942, Dumas Papers, National Library of Australia [henceforth NLA], MS 4849, Box 6, Folder 41.
29 Hedley Cantril (ed.), *Public Opinion 1935–1946*, Princeton: Princeton University Press, 1951, p. 816.
30 Macintyre, *Australia's Boldest Experiment*, pp. 253–70.
31 Cantril (ed.), *Public Opinion*, pp. 740–1.
32 Referendum 1944, National Archives of Australia [henceforth NAA], A9816, 1944/162; Crisp Papers, NLA, MS 5243, series 11, folders 13–16. Also see L.F. Crisp, *The Parliamentary Government of the Commonwealth of Australia*, London: Longmans, Green, 1949, chapter 1.
33 Letter from Lloyd Dumas to Keith Murdoch, 14 December 1942, Dumas Papers, NLA, MS 4849, Box 6, Folder 41.
34 *Digest of Decisions and Announcements*, no. 14 (3–13 January 1942), p. 12; no. 31, 2–5 June 1942, p. 5.
35 'Unionist Speaks Out About Need for a National Ideal', *Mail*, 15 August 1942; Guy Pentreath, 'Creating a Better Post-War World', *Mail*, 29 August 1942.
36 'Alleged Disloyal Speech', *Sydney Morning Herald*, 22 October 1940.
37 G.V. Portus, 'The Origin and Aims of New South Australian Movement', *News*, 1 March 1943.
38 Common Cause prospectus sent by Sid Crawford to H.C. Coombs, Director-General of Post-War Reconstruction, March 1943, NAA, M448/1, 39.
39 'Middle Class Audience', *News*, 12 March 1945; 'Women's Section for Common Cause', *Advertiser*, 18 September 1943.
40 'Five Common Cause Schools', *Advertiser*, 4 April 1945.
41 *A Township Starts to Live: The Valley of Barossa, South Australia's New Community*, Adelaide: Common Cause, 1944; Letter from Roy Brown to Ben Chifley, 19 September 1944, Community Facilities Correspondence, NAA, A9816, 1944/334 PART 1.
42 Letter from Eric Wylde to Keith Murdoch, 7 May 1943, NLA, MS 4849, Box 6, Folder 43.
43 Keith Isles and Alex Ramsay, Letter to *Advertiser*, 19 May 1943; 'Communist and a Company Director', *News*, 11 June 1943.
44 Alf Watt, letter to *Advertiser*, 19 May 1943.
45 A.J. Hannan, 'Greater Evil', *News*, 6 May 1943.
46 Katharine Thornton, 'Arthur Godolphin Guy Carleton Pentreath', *Australian Dictionary of Biography*, vol. 18, Melbourne: Melbourne University Press, 2012, p. 274.

47 'Post-War Planning Needed Now', *News*, 2 April 1943; Edith Casely, secretary of Common Cause, letter to *Advertiser*, 15 June 1944.
48 Letter from Keith Murdoch to Lloyd Dumas, 10 February 1945, NLA, MS 4849, Box 7, Folder 44.

Chapter 10 | The Great Man of History: Industrialisation and the Playford Legend

1 Dean Jaensch, *The Government of South Australia*, Brisbane: University of Queensland Press, 1977, p. 12.
2 See Stewart Cockburn assisted by John Playford, *Playford: Benevolent Despot*, Adelaide: Axiom Publishing, 1991; and Nic Klaassen, 'The Battle for Leigh Creek', in Bernard O'Neil, Judith Raftery and Kerrie Round (eds), *Playford's South Australia: Essays on the History of South Australia 1933–1968*, Adelaide: Association of Professional Historians Inc., 1996, p. 138.
3 Cockburn, *Playford*; Walter Crocker, *Sir Thomas Playford: A Portrait*, Melbourne: Melbourne University Press, 1983; David Nicholas, *The Pacemaker: The Playford Story*, Adelaide: Brolga Books, 1969. I accept that not all historians and commentators share this view. For more nuanced accounts, closer to my own view, see T.J. Mitchell, 'J.W. Wainright [sic]: The Industrialisation of S.A., 1935–40', *Australian Journal of Politics and History*, vol. 8, no. 1, 1962, pp. 27–40; Michael Stutchbury, 'The Playford Legend and the Industrialisation of South Australia to 1945', *Australian Economic History Review*, vol. 24, no. 1, 1984, pp. 1–19; and David C. Rich, 'Tom's Vision? Playford and Industrialisation', in Bernard O'Neil, Judith Raftery and Kerrie Round (eds), *Playford's South Australia: Essays on the History of South Australia, 1933–1968,* Adelaide: Association of Professional Historians, 1996, pp. 91–116.
4 See, for example, R.L. Butler, 'Financial Statement of the Honourable Premier and Treasurer', 27 September 1934, *South Australian Parliamentary Paper*, No. 18, 1934.
5 Butler's government approved the construction of the bridge and it became operational in 1940. It spanned the Port River to connect Port Adelaide with the suburb of Birkenhead. Prior to its construction, for more than a century, transit across this stretch of the river had been achieved by oar-driven and motorised ferries. The bridge thus greatly facilitated accessibility to the suburbs, industrial complexes, depots and maritime infrastructure on either side of the river.
6 T.J. Mitchell, 'J.W. Wainright [sic]: The Industrialisation of S.A., 1935–40', *Australian Journal of Politics and History*, vol. 8, no. 1, 1962, p. 33.
7 The terms of the *Broken Hill Proprietary Company's Indenture Act, 1937*, were extremely generous. See Crocker, *Sir Thomas Playford*, p. 42. Also see *Northern Areas and Whyalla Water Supply Act, 1940*.
8 *South Australian Parliamentary Debates* (henceforth *SAPD*), House of Assembly (HoA), 19 October 1937, pp. 1125–7.
9 See *Broken Hill Proprietary Company's Steel Works Indenture Act*, 1958.
10 Michael Stutchbury, 'State Government Industrialisation Strategies', in Kyoko Sheridan (ed.), *The State as Developer: Public Enterprise in South Australia*, Adelaide: Royal Australian Institute of Public Administration and Wakefield Press, 1986, p. 71.
11 *Ibid.*, pp. 69–70.
12 *SAPD*, HoA, 10 November 1936, pp. 3313–4.
13 *SAPD*, HoA, 16 November 1936, pp. 2460–1.
14 These were the *Housing Improvement Act* (1940) and the *Homes Act* (1941). The *Housing Improvement Act* also made provision for the fixing (or capping) of rent payable for accommodation deemed to be of poor standard, which acted as an incentive for the landlord to improve the property or sell it.

15 Susan Marsden, 'The South Australian Housing Trust, Elizabeth and Twentieth Century Heritage', *Journal of the Historical Society of South Australia*, no. 28, 2000, pp. 49–61, p. 52.
16 For further discussion of the Trust's role in country areas, see Susan Marsden, *Business, Charity and Sentiment: The South Australian Housing Trust 1936–1986*, Adelaide: Wakefield Press, 1986, pp. 185–226.
17 Marsden, *Business, Charity and Sentiment*, pp. 428–9.
18 *Ibid.*, p. 88.
19 M.A. Jones, *Housing and Poverty in Australia*, Melbourne: Melbourne University Press, 1972, p. 16.
20 Susan Marsden, 'Playford's Metropolis', in Bernard O'Neil, Judith Raftery and Kerrie Round (eds), *Playford's South Australia: Essays on the History of South Australia, 1933–1968*, Adelaide: Association of Professional Historians, 1996, p. 127. See also Martin Shanahan, 'Dress Circle or Stalls? A Note on the Geography of Income-Distribution in Adelaide', *Flinders Journal of History and Politics*, no. 10, 1984, pp. 23–39.
21 Margaret Allen, 'Salisbury (S.A.) in Transition', MA thesis, University of Adelaide, 1975, p. 78.
22 Marsden, 'Playford's Metropolis', p. 123.
23 Marsden, *Business, Charity and Sentiment*, p. 236.
24 *Ibid.*, pp. 298–9.
25 Geoffrey Blainey, *The Steel Master: A Life of Essington Lewis*, Melbourne: Sun Books, 1981, pp. 120–41. BHP also began producing munitions and formed a syndicate with other companies to build aircraft.
26 P.A. Howell, 'Playford, Sir Thomas (Tom) (1896–1981)', *Australian Dictionary of Biography*, http://adb.anu.edu.au/biography/playford-sir-thomas-tom-15472/text26686, accessed 20 April 2013.
27 Carol S. Fort, '"Equality of sacrifice"? War Work in Salisbury, South Australia', in Bernard O'Neil, Judith Raftery and Kerrie Round (eds), *Playford's South Australia: Essays on the History of South Australia 1933–1968*, Adelaide: Association of Professional Historians Inc., 1996, pp. 216–7; Carol Fort, 'World War II', in Wilfrid Prest, Kerrie Round and Carol Fort (eds), *The Wakefield Companion to South Australian History*, Adelaide: Wakefield Press, 2001, p. 594.
28 'Another War Secret', *Chronicle*, 30 August 1945, p. 26. These events were kept secret from the public until after the war was over.
28 Fort, 'World War II', p. 594.
30 Fort, '"Equality of sacrifice"?', p. 215.
31 Susan Marsden, *A History of Woodville*, Adelaide: Corporation of the City of Woodville, 1977, pp. 215, 216.
32 Fort, 'World War II', p. 594.
33 Marsden, *A History of Woodville*, p. 228. As Marsden notes, most of the firms, especially those from interstate, like Tecalemit, or overseas, like Kelvinator, acknowledged the co-operation of the SA government and the Commonwealth government's Secondary Industries Commission in their transfer to premises in Finsbury. See, for example, 'English Firm for South Australia', *Advertiser*, 18 April 1946, p. 1.
34 Marsden, *A History of Woodville*, p. 231.
35 See speeches by J. Fletcher and R.S. Richards, *SAPD*, HoA, 13 October 1942, pp. 835, 847; 'Tension Over N.S.W. Strike', *Advertiser*, 17 October 1945, p. 1. About 53% of the total loss of working days due to strikes during the war occurred in coal mining, the majority of which was based in New South Wales. See S.J.C.L. Butlin, *Australia in the War of 1939–1945. Series 4 – Civil: Volume IV – War Economy 1942–1945*, 1st ed., Canberra: Australian War Memorial, 1977, p. 603.
36 Cockburn, *Playford*, pp. 109–11.

37 P.A. Howell, 'Cudmore, Sir Collier Robert (1885–1971)', *Australian Dictionary of Biography*, http://adb.anu.edu.au/biography/cudmore-sir-collier-robert-9873/text17471, accessed 24 January 2014.
38 Bruce Muirden, 'The Electricity Trust Affair', in Dean Jaensch (ed.), *The Flinders History of South Australia: Political History*, Adelaide: Wakefield Press, 1986, p. 276.
39 *Ibid.*, pp. 276–7.
40 *Ibid.*, p. 280. Playford's personal risk and stake in achieving the nationalisation of AESC and developing the Leigh Creek coalfield is evocatively told by Klaassen, 'The Battle for Leigh Creek', pp. 135–54.
41 Murray McCaskill, '1950: Forging an Industrial State', in Trevor Griffin and Murray McCaskill (eds), *Atlas of South Australia*, Adelaide: SA Government Printing Division and Wakefield Press, 1986, p. 28; and Stutchbury, 'State Government Industrialisation Strategies', pp. 70–1.
42 Muirden, 'The Electricity Trust Affair', p. 280.
43 Australian Bureau of Statistics (henceforth ABS), *Labour Report No. 58, 1973*, cat. no. 6101.0, 1973, pp. 348–50; ABS, *Labour Statistics, Australia, 1990*, cat no. 6101.0, 1990, p. 116; ABS, *Labour Statistics, Australia, 1997*, cat. no. 6101.0, 1997, p. 175.
44 John Wanna, 'The State and Industrial Relations', in Kyoko Sheridan (ed.), *The State as Developer: Public Enterprise in South Australia*, Adelaide: Royal Australian Institute of Public Administration and Wakefield Press, 1986, p. 138.
45 *Ibid.*, p. 135. For elaboration of these and other factors, see John Wanna, 'A Paradigm of Consent: Explanations of Working Class Moderation in South Australia', *Labour History*, no. 53, 1987, pp. 54–72.
46 Wanna, 'A Paradigm of Consent', p. 64.
47 Mitchell, 'J.W. Wainright [sic]', p. 30.
48 P.A. Howell, 'Playford, Sir Thomas'. In an interview with Hugh Stretton conducted nearly 40 years after these events, Playford named Eric O'Connor as the union official; however Howell is adamant that this man was Clyde Cameron based on a personal conversation with Cameron.
49 Mitchell, 'J.W. Wainright [sic]', p. 36.
50 *Ibid.*, p. 32.
51 Jim Moss, *Sound of Trumpets: History of the Labour Movement in South Australia*, Adelaide: Wakefield Press, 1985, p. 362.
52 Malcolm Saunders, 'Playford, Cavanagh, and the Plasterers' Society of South Australia 1945–63', *Journal of the Historical Society of South Australia*, no. 32, 2004, pp. 95–109.
53 Cockburn, *Playford*, pp. 217–18.
54 *Ibid.*, p. 218.
55 Some of the country electorates had as few as 4,000 people, while those in the city were more than four times as large. The boundaries of these electorates were not readjusted for two decades; hence as the city became bigger and rural areas stripped of population, the malapportionment became more pronounced. See Jenny Tilby Stock, 'The "Playmander": Its Origins, Operation and Effect on South Australia', in Bernard O'Neil, Judith Raftery and Kerrie Round (eds), *Playford's South Australia: Essays on the History of South Australia, 1933–1968*, Adelaide: Association of Professional Historians, 1996, pp. 73–90.
56 The biographies of Playford published in the 1980s and 1990s reflect this trend. For a recent example, see Bob Byrne, 'Adelaide, Remember When … Tom Playford Ruled South Australia?', *Advertiser*, 14 March 2014, accessible at http://www.adelaidenow.com.au/news/south-australia/adelaide-remember-when-tom-playford-ruled-south-australia/story-fni6uo1m-1226855067404.

57 Further discussion of Cartledge and Ramsay's contributions is offered by Marsden, *Business, Charity and Sentiment*; and Hugh Stretton 'Obituary: A.M. Ramsay and the Conventional Wisdom', *Australian Quarterly*, vol. 50, no. 3, 1978, pp. 90–100.
58 See, for example, Stutchbury, 'State Government Industrialisation Strategies', pp. 72–3.
59 Marsden, 'Playford's Metropolis', p. 130.
60 Stock, 'The "Playmander"', pp. 87–89.
61 Clare Parker, 'What Have the Arts Ever Done for Us? The Transformation of the Performing Arts in Don Dunstan's South Australia', BA(Hons) thesis, School of History and Politics, The University of Adelaide, 2009, pp. 13–18. Also see Cockburn, *Playford*, pp. 188–90.
62 P.A. Howell, 'Playford, Politics and Parliament', in Bernard O'Neil, Judith Raftery and Kerrie Round (eds), *Playford's South Australia: Essays on the History of South Australia, 1933–1968,* Adelaide: Association of Professional Historians, 1996, p. 48.
63 Cockburn, *Playford*, p. 194.
65 See, for example, Cockburn, *Playford*, pp. 329–30; Kerrie Round, 'A Deputation for a National Trust', in Bernard O'Neil, Judith Raftery and Kerrie Round (eds), *Playford's South Australia: Essays on the History of South Australia, 1933–1968,* Adelaide: Association of Professional Historians, 1996, pp. 325–6.
65 See Jaensch, *The Government of South Australia*, pp. 13–14.
66 Carlyle's 'great man' theory of history runs through much of his historical writing, but is best articulated in his book *On Heroes, Hero-Worship and the Heroic in History* [1840], which sees history as having turned on the decisions of 'heroes' and provides detailed analysis of the influence of several such men, including Muhammad, Shakespeare, Luther and Napoleon.

Chapter 11 | Nineteenth Century Dreams, Twentieth Century Realities: Reframing the Abolition of Capital Punishment in South Australia

1 This is the date of assent; see South Australia, *Statues Amendment (Capital Punishment Abolition) Act*, no. 115 of 1976. Australian jurisdictions abolished capital punishment in the following order: Queensland (1922), Tasmania (1968), the Commonwealth of Australia (1973), Victoria (1975), South Australia (1976), Australian Capital Territory (1983), Western Australia (1984) and New South Wales (1985). See Sam Garkawe, 'The Reintroduction of the Death Penalty in Australia? – Political and Legal Considerations', *Criminal Law Journal*, vol. 24, no. 2, 2002, pp. 101–8.
2 Andrew Russ and Bianca Zanatta, 'The Application and Eventual Abolition of the Death Penalty in South Australia', South Australian Parliament Research Library, 2017, pp. 32–5.
3 David McLaren, 'Lecture on the abolition of capital punishments delivered by David McLaren to the Literary and Scientific Association and Mechanic's Institute, at Adelaide, December 18, 1840', reprinted in Nathaniel Lipscomb Kentish, *Essay on Capital Punishment: With an earnest appeal ... for the abolition ... of ... laws which sanction the taking of human life ...*, Hobart: S.A. Tegg, 1842, pp. 22–37, National Library of Australia, FRM F3431. Hereafter the short citation of McLaren's lecture will carry the year the lecture was delivered (1840), not publication date of Kentish's work (1842). Note the reprint that appears in Kentish's work erroneously states that the lecture was delivered on 18 December but it was actually 10 December. See *Southern Australian*, 8 December 1840, p. 3, for an advertisement of the original talk.
4 William H. Burford, *Lecture on Capital Punishment, viewed in its Social, Political, and Scriptural Aspects*, Adelaide: William Kyffin Thomas Printer, 1874, p. 29, State Library of South Australia, South Australiana Pamphlets, 364.66 B953.

5   For allowing me the time and resources to research colonial capital punishment abolition literature in depth, I am indebted to the Norman McCann Summer Scholarship awarded to me by the National Library of Australia in 2013.
6   Ralph M. Hague, *Hague's History of the Law in South Australia, 1837–1867*, 2 volumes, Adelaide: The University of Adelaide Barr Smith Press, 2005; Mark Finnane, 'Crime', in Wilfrid Prest, Kerrie Round and Carol Fort (eds), *The Wakefield Companion to South Australian History*, Adelaide: Wakefield Press, 2001, pp. 133–6; Alex C. Castles and Michael C. Harris, *Lawmakers and Wayward Whigs*, Adelaide: Wakefield Press, 1987, pp. 353–5.
7   A.R.G. Griffiths, 'Capital Punishment in South Australia 1836–1964', *Australian & New Zealand Journal of Criminology*, vol. 3, no. 4, 1970, pp. 214–22; David J. Towler and Trevor J. Porter, *The Hempen Collar: Executions in South Australia, 1838–1964, A Collection of Eyewitness Accounts*, Adelaide: The Wednesday Press, 1990.
8   Alan Pope, *One Law for All?: Aboriginal People and Criminal Law in Early South Australia*, Canberra: Aboriginal Studies Press, 2011.
9   Robert Foster, Rick Hosking and Amanda Nettelbeck, *Fatal Collisions: The South Australian Frontier and the Violence of Memory*, Adelaide: Wakefield Press, 2001, pp. 13–28; Judy Hamann, 'The Coorong Massacre: A Study in Early Race Relations in South Australia', *Flinders Journal of History and Politics*, vol. 3, 1979, pp. 1–9; Peter Liddy, *The Rainberd Murders: 1861*, Adelaide: Peacock Publications, 1993; Jean Schamaal, 'The Rainberd Story', *The Police Journal of South Australia*, vol. 56, no. 3, 1975, pp. 17–19; Allan L. Peters, *Dead Woman Walking: Was an Innocent Woman Hanged?*, Adelaide: Bas Publishing, 2008.
10 Steven Anderson, 'Death of a Spectacle: The Transition from Public to Private Executions in Colonial Australia', unpublished PhD thesis, The University of Adelaide, 2016.
11 Steven Anderson, 'Punishment as Pacification: The Role of Indigenous Executions on the South Australian Frontier, 1836–1862', *Aboriginal History*, vol. 39, 2015, pp. 3–26; Steven Anderson and Paul Sendziuk, 'Hang the Convicts: Capital Punishment and the Reaffirmation of South Australia's Foundation Principles', *Journal of Australian Colonial History*, vol. 16, 2014, pp. 83–111.
12 James Gregory, *Victorians Against the Gallows: Capital Punishment and the Abolitionist Movement in Nineteenth Century Britain*, London: I.B. Tauris, 2012, pp. 40–6.
13 Russ and Zanatta, 'The Application and Eventual Abolition of the Death Penalty in South Australia'.
14 'McLaren, David (1785–1850)', *Australian Dictionary of Biography*, http://adb.anu.edu.au/biography/mclaren-david-2412, accessed 22 November 2017. An extended, though dated, biography of McLaren is also available. See E.T. McLaren, *Dr McLaren of Manchester: A Sketch*, London: Hodder and Stoughton, 1911.
15 'McLaren, David (1785–1850)', *Australian Dictionary of Biography*, http://adb.anu.edu.au/biography/mclaren-david-2412, accessed 22 November 2017.
16 Herbert R. Taylor, 'Burford, William Henville (1807–1895)', *Australian Dictionary of Biography*, http://adb.anu.edu.au/biography/burford-william-henville-1851, accessed 20 November 2017. For Burford's obituary, see *The Advertiser*, 10 April 1896, p. 4.
17 According to one local church historian, William H. Burford and his son, 'stand high in the roll of honour of the worthy Christian men who laid the foundation and helped to establish Churches of Christ in South Australia'. See Herbert R. Taylor, *The History of Churches of Christ in South Australia, 1846–1959*, Adelaide: The Churches of Christ Evangelistic Union Inc., 1959, pp. 174–6.
18 'Former Member of Parliament Details: Mr William Burford', Parliament of South Australia, 2010, http://www.parliament.sa.gov.au/Members/FormerMembers/Pages/default.aspx, accessed 8 December 2017.

19 Douglas Pike, *Paradise of Dissent: South Australia, 1829–1857*, Melbourne: Melbourne University Press, 1967.
20 Genesis 9:6 reads 'Whoso sheddeth man's blood, by man shall his blood be shed' while Leviticus 24:17 says that 'And he that killeth any man shall surely be put to death'. All Bible translations in this chapter are taken from the King James Bible.
21 McLaren, 'Lecture on the abolition of capital punishments', p. 24.
22 Burford, *Lecture on Capital Punishment*, p. 29.
23 McLaren, 'Lecture on the abolition of capital punishments', p. 27.
24 *Ibid.*, pp. 24–5.
25 Burford, *Lecture on Capital Punishment*, p. 28.
26 *Ibid.*, pp. 24–5.
27 McLaren, 'Lecture on the abolition of capital punishments', p. 28.
28 Burford, *Lecture on Capital Punishment*, p. 22.
29 *Ibid.*, p. 15; McLaren, 'Lecture on the abolition of capital punishments', p. 28.
30 Both Burford and McLaren's entries in the *Australian Dictionary of Biography* offer a summary of their religious affiliations; see 'McLaren, David (1785–1850)', *Australian Dictionary of Biography*, http://adb.anu.edu.au/biography/mclaren-david-2412, and Herbert R. Taylor, 'Burford, William Henville (1807–1895)', *Australian Dictionary of Biography*, http://adb.anu.edu.au/biography/burford-william-henville-1851.
31 For evidence of their religious affiliations, see A.W. Martin, 'Parkes, Sir Henry (1815–1896)', *Australian Dictionary of Biography*, http://adb.anu.edu.au/biography/parkes-sir-henry-4366, accessed 11 December 2017; Michael Roe, 'Taylor, Alfred Joseph (1849–1921)', *Australian Dictionary of Biography*, http://adb.anu.edu.au/biography/taylor-alfred-joseph-4691, accessed 11 December 2017.
32 John J. Ford, *Capital Punishment*, Melbourne: The Australian Catholic Truth Society, 18-? [exact publication date is unknown], State Library of New South Wales, Mitchell Library, 179.7/F.
33 McLaren, 'Lecture on the abolition of capital punishments', p. 29.
34 Burford, *Lecture on Capital Punishment*, pp. 18–19.
35 McLaren, 'Lecture on the abolition of capital punishments', p. 29.
36 McLaren singles out Beccaria by name as a thinker in possession of 'powerful reasoning'; see McLaren, 'Lecture on the abolition of capital punishments', p. 32. For the influential passage where he outlines his position on capital punishment, see Cesare Beccaria, *On Crimes and Punishments and Other Writings* [1764], R. Bellamy (ed.), Cambridge: Cambridge University Press, 1995.
37 Burford, *Lecture on Capital Punishment*, p. 10.
38 *Ibid.*
39 William Blackstone quoted in Burford, *Lecture on Capital Punishment*, p. 10. To locate this passage in Blackstone's original text, see William Blackstone, *Commentaries on the Laws of England* [1765–1769], Chicago: Callaghan and Cockcroft, 1871, p. 309.
40 Burford, *Lecture on Capital Punishment*, p. 10.
41 McLaren, 'Lecture on the abolition of capital punishments', p. 35.
42 *Ibid.*
43 *Ibid.*
44 Burford, *Lecture on Capital Punishment*, pp. 11–13.
45 *Ibid.*
46 *Ibid.*
47 McLaren, 'Lecture on the abolition of capital punishments', p. 31.
48 *Ibid.*
49 *Ibid.*, p. 30.
50 *South Australian Parliamentary Debates*, 21 September 1858, p. 173.

51 Burford, *Lecture on Capital Punishment*, p. 4.
52 *Ibid.*, p. 10.
53 McLaren, 'Lecture on the abolition of capital punishments', pp. 32–3.
54 *Ibid.*, p. 32; Burford, *Lecture on Capital Punishment*, p. 8.
55 Burford, *Lecture on Capital Punishment*, pp. 6–7.
56 McLaren, 'Lecture on the abolition of capital punishments', p. 33.
57 For references to the first reading of Henry Parkes' unsuccessful Bills to abolish capital punishment in New South Wales Parliament during the 1860s, see New South Wales, *Votes and Proceedings of the Legislative Council*, no. 12 of 1860, 12 October 1860, p. 55; New South Wales, *Votes and Proceedings of the Legislative Council*, no. 4 of 1861, 15 January 1861, p. 19.
58 New South Wales, *Votes and Proceedings of the Legislative Assembly*, no. 15 of 1872, 29 November 1872, p. 54.
59 For some, but not all, of the advertisements to buy Lee's publication, see *South Australian Advertiser*, 8 July 1864, p. 1; 20 July 1864, p. 1; 27 July 1864, p. 1; 29 August 1864, p. 1. For a copy of Lee's lecture, see Fredrick Lee, *Abolition of Capital Punishment: A Lecture, Delivered in the School of Arts, Sydney, New South Wales, on Thursday, May 26, 1864*, Sydney: Hanson and Bennet Printers, 1864, National Library of Australia, NP 343.23 LEE.
60 For an advertisement to purchase the work locally, see *Adelaide Observer*, 2 September 1843, p. 4.
61 McLaren, 'Lecture on the abolition of capital punishments', pp. 33–4.
62 Penny Russell, *Savage or Civilized?: Manners in Colonial Australia*, Sydney: University of New South Wales Press, 2010, p. 108.
63 McLaren, 'Lecture on the abolition of capital punishments', p. 36.
64 *Ibid.*, p. 22. For a brief overview of the Maria Massacre, see Foster, Hosking and Nettelbeck, *Fatal Collisions,* pp. 13–29.
65 For an early mention of the Society in 1844 advocating to commute the sentence of death upon two criminals, see *South Australian Register*, 22 March 1845, p. 3. For the last mention of the Society in the newspapers, see *South Australian*, 19 March 1847, p. 3.
66 William Anderson Cawthorne, 'Minutes of the Society for the Abolition of Capital Punishment, 26 September 1844 – 25 April 1845', in 'Rough Notes on the Manners and Customs of the Natives', State Library of South Australia, PRG 489/3.
67 *South Australian Advertiser*, 9 January 1874, p. 2. Burford helped form this 'Committee' and remarked how he had been involved in the earlier 'Society for the Abolition of Capital Punishment' during the 1840s as well. To quote Burford directly: 'Some years ago – about 30 years ago – several gentlemen, amongst whom was himself, associated together in a similar movement to the present, but they could not make headway'.
68 The following are a list of community groups that participated in discussions (mostly in a debate format) for and against capital punishment during the nineteenth century: Adelaide Debating Society (October 1853), Adelaide Literary and Scientific Debating Society (October 1853), Wallaroo Mutual Improvement Association (October 1868), Port Adelaide Young Men's Society (November 1878), North Adelaide Young Men's Society (April 1884), Rose Park Young Men's Society (October 1884), Adelaide Literary Society (October 1884), Gawler Literary Society (July 1892), St. George's Society (July 1892), M.C.A. (December 1893), St. Ignatius Society (December 1893), Narracoorte Debating Club (January 1894). For evidence of these meetings taking place, see *South Australian Register*, 8 October 1853, p. 4; *Adelaide Times*, 10 October 1853, p. 3; *The Wallaroo Times and Mining Journal*, 21 October 1868, p. 1; *The Express and Telegraph*, 2 November 1878, p. 1; *South Australian Register*, 21 April 1884, p. 2; *South Australian Register*, 21 October 1884,

p. 2; *Bunyip*, 22 July 1892, p. 3; *South Australian Register*, 14 December 1893, p. 5; *The Narracoorte Herald*, 16 January 1894, p. 3.
69   *Evening Journal*, 27 August 1892, p. 4; *South Australian Register*, 21 March 1891, p. 2; *South Australian Register*, 1 September 1894, p. 2; *The Wallaroo Times and Mining Journal*, 27 September 1879, p. 2.
70   *Evening Journal*, 18 November 1897, p. 4.
71   Russ and Zanatta, 'The Application and Eventual Abolition of the Death Penalty in South Australia', pp. 22–3.
72   South Australia, *Act to Regulate the Execution of Criminals*, no. 23 of 1858.
73   South Australia, *Act to amend an Act, no. 23 of 22nd Victoria, intituled 'An Act to Regulate the Execution of Criminals'*, no. 1 of 1861. For further discussion on this amendment, see Anderson, 'Punishment as Pacification', pp. 17–21.
74   For the 1875 petitions, see *South Australian Advertiser*, 8 September 1875, p. 6. For evidence of a petition organised by the Quakers being received in 1891, see Parliament of South Australia, *Index to the Votes and Proceedings of the House of Assembly from the Beginning of Year 1874 to the End of Year 1900*, p. 34. For another Quaker petition in 1894, see Parliament of South Australia, *Index to Papers Laid Before Both Houses and Printed Petitions from June, 1881 to the End of Year 1900*, p. 85.
75   See, for example, Worthy Worthington George Nicholls, 'The petition of Worthy Worthington George Nicholls, to His Excellency Governor Gawler concerning Joseph Stagg, 1840', held at the State Library of South Australia, 364.66 N615 c++.
76   Parliament of South Australia, *Index to the Votes and Proceedings of the House of Assembly from the Beginning of Year 1874 to the End of Year 1900*, p. 13.
77   Jo Lennan and George Williams, 'The Death Penalty in Australian Law', *Sydney Law Review*, vol. 34, 2012, p. 668. The two major blows to South Australia's capital code came in 1842 and 1876. In 1842 Governor George Grey adopted an Act of British Parliament (first passed in 1837) that prevented a number of lesser crimes from being punishable by death. Later in 1876, when the colony consolidated its criminal law for the first time, South Australia's capital code was further narrowed. See South Australia, *An Act for adopting certain Acts of Parliament passed in the First year of the Reign of Her Majesty Queen Victoria in the Administration of Justice in South Australia in like manner as other laws of England are applied therein*, no. 14 of 1842. For the 1876 consolidation of the criminal law and the passages therein that pertain to capital punishment, see South Australia, *Criminal Law Consolidation Act*, no. 38 of 1876, sections 5, 19, and 227.
78   Russ and Zanatta, 'The Application and Eventual Abolition of the Death Penalty in South Australia', p. 22.
79   *South Australian Register*, 24 July 1857, p. 3.

Chapter 12 | Sending Out an SOS: South Australia's Forgotten Anti-Conscription Crusaders

1   'Women Demonstrate: Silent Airport Vigil', *News*, 1 July 1965.
2   Audrey Potticary, 'Save Our Sons Remembered', in Beryl Miller and Susan Marsden (eds), *Years of Struggle: Reminiscences of the Union of Australian Women in South Australia, 1950–2005*, Adelaide: UAW and Susan Marsden, 2005, p. 46.
3   See, for example: Bob Scates, *'Draftmen Go Free': A History of the Anti-Conscription Movement in Australia*, Melbourne: R. Scates, 1988; Chris Guyatt, 'The Anti-Conscription Movement, 1964–1966', in Roy Forward and Bob Reece (eds), *Conscription in Australia*, Brisbane: University of Queensland Press, 1968, pp. 178–90; Barry York, *Student Revolt! La Trobe University 1967–73*, Canberra: Nicholas Press, 1989; Michael Hamel-Green, 'The Resisters: A History of the Anti-Conscription

Movement 1964–1972', in Peter King (ed.), *Australia's Vietnam*, Sydney: Allen &Unwin, 1983, pp. 100–28.

4   The ALP came to power in March 1965 under the leadership of Frank Walsh. Don Dunstan became Premier in a leadership ballot in June 1967 but Labor lost the 1968 election. He became Premier again after Labor won the May 1970 election, resigning in February 1979.

5   See, for example, Malcolm Saunders and Ralph Summy, *The Australian Peace Movement: A Short History*, Canberra: Peace Research Centre, Australian National University, 1986; Malcolm Saunders, 'The ALP's Response to the Anti-Vietnam War Movement: 1965–1973', *Labour History*, vol. 44, 1983, pp. 75–91; Malcolm Saunders, 'Opposition to the Vietnam War in South Australia, 1965–73', *Journal of the Historical Society of South Australia*, vol. 10, 1982, pp. 61–71; Malcolm Saunders, 'The Campaign for Peace in Vietnam (SA) 1967–1972', BA (Hons thesis), Flinders University, 1972; Malcolm Saunders, 'The Vietnam Moratorium Movement in Australia: 1969–1973', PhD thesis, Flinders University, 1977.

6   Three hundred trade unionists attended a meeting at Trades Hall in Adelaide in May 1965 to condemn the move by the Australian Government to send troops to Vietnam. 'Viet. Protest in All Capitals,' *Advertiser*, 24 May 1965.

7   SA SOS is discussed in Miller and Marsden (eds), *Years of Struggle: Reminiscences of the Union of Australian Women in South Australia, 1950–2005*. For the national movement, see, for example, Ann-Mari Jordens, 'Conscription and Dissent: The Genesis of Anti-War Protest', in Gregory Pemberton (ed.), *Vietnam Remembered*, Sydney: New Holland Publishers, 2009, pp. 60–81; Siobhan McHugh, *Minefields and Miniskirts: Australian Women and the Vietnam War*, Sydney: Doubleday, 1993, pp. 200–64; Ann Curthoys, '"Shut up, You Bourgeois Bitch": Sexual Identity and Political Action in the Anti-Vietnam War Movement', in Joy Damousi and Marilyn Lake (eds), *Gender and War: Australians at War in the Twentieth Century*, Cambridge: Cambridge University Press, 1995, pp. 311–41.

8   Dorothy Cora, *Noreen Hewett: Portrait of a Grassroots Activist*, Sydney: Older Women's Network of NSW, 2010, p. 24.

9   On 10 November 1964, Prime Minister Robert Menzies made a statement on defence to the House of Representatives in which he announced the introduction of a compulsory selective National Service Scheme. See *Commonwealth Parliamentary Debates*, House of Representatives, vol. 46, 10 November 1964, pp. 2715–24; 'Women in Black Hoods Fail to Shake Menzies at Poll Rally', *Sydney Morning Herald*, 24 November 1964.

10 See, Peter Edwards, *A Nation at War: Australian Politics, Society and Diplomacy during the Vietnam War 1965–1975*, Sydney: Allen & Unwin, 1997, pp. 76–7.

11 'Mothers Oppose Call-Up', *Australian*, 19 May 1965.

12 Sydney SOS, Press Statement, May 1965, National Library of Australia (henceforth NLA), MS 3821-25.

13 Sydney SOS, Statement of Aims, 1965, NLA, MS 3821-25.

14 'Viet. Key to Vote', *News*, 22 November 1966.

15 Edwards, *A Nation at War*, p. 82; John Murphy, *Harvest of Fear: A History of Australia's Vietnam War*, Sydney: Allen & Unwin, 1993, p. 142.

16 Irene Miller interviewed by the author, 31 July 2014.

17 Carolyn Collins, 'Those Women with Banners: A History of the Save Our Sons Movement 1965–1973', PhD thesis, University of Adelaide, 2015.

18 Memo from Australia House, London, to ASIO, 20 July 1960, National Archives of Australia (henceforth NAA), A6119, 4102/2.

19 Cora, *Noreen Hewett*, p. 23.

20 *Ibid.*, p. 24.

21 ASIO report of Save Our Sons meeting, 1 July 1965, NAA, A6126, 1338/49.

22 ASIO report of SA SOS, 2 July 1965, NAA, A6122, 1813/2.
23 Barbara Curthoys and Audrey McDonald, *More Than a Hat and Glove Brigade: The Story of the Union of Australian Women*, Sydney: Union of Australian Women, 1996, p. 76.
24 UAW (SA), *Annual Report 1964–65*, State Library of South Australia (henceforth SLSA), SRG 781/261.
25 Beryl Miller interviewed by the author, 8 April 2014.
26 'Viet. Key to Vote', *News*, 22 November 1966.
27 *Ibid.*
28 ASIO report of SOS public meeting at Willard Hall, 25 September 1966, NAA, A6122, 1813/78.
29 Murphy, *Harvest of Fear*, p. 141.
30 Marion Henderson, 'History of SOS Perth,' n.d., NLA, MS 3821–2.
31 SA SOS Minutes, 24 June 1968, SLSA, SRG 555.
32 Eulalie Tapp, 'SOS South Australia', NLA, MS 9878–2.
33 'Report from SA branch UAW', 8 July 1965, NLA, MS 3821–19.
34 SA SOS Minutes, 13 September 1965, SLSA, SRG 555.
35 Eulalie Tapp, 'SOS South Australia', NLA, MS 9878–2.
36 'Vietnam' [advertisement], *News*, 29 November 1965.
37 Sydney SOS, 'Report on Canberra Deputation', 27 April 1966, NLA, MS 3821–12.
38 SA SOS Minutes, 31 October 1966, SLSA, SRG 555.
39 Sydney SOS, 'SOS Canberra Lobbying Mission Report', October 1965, NLA, MS 3821–12.
40 Letter from Audrey Potticary to Sydney SOS, 27 August 1968, NLA, MS 3821–19.
41 Letter from Ella Outhred to Adelaide SOS, 25 April 1966, NLA, MS 3821–19.
42 Sydney SOS, *Second Annual Report*, June 1967, NLA, MS 3821–23.
43 SOS, 'Christmas' [leaflet], December 1965, NLA, MS 9878–5.
44 SA SOS Minutes, 13 September 1965, SLSA, SRG 555.
45 SA SOS Minutes, 26 June 1965, SLSA, SRG 555.
46 'War Toys Losing the Sales Battle', *Sun News-Pictorial*, 12 March 1968.
47 Bill White cited in Greg Langley, *A Decade of Dissent: Vietnam and the Conflict on the Australian Homefront*, Sydney: Allen & Unwin, 1992, p. 61.
48 Sydney SOS Newsletter, December 1966, NLA, MS 3821–20.
49 Letter from Mrs Wharton to Sydney SOS, 16 December 1966, NLA, MS 3821–2.
50 SA SOS, 'Calling All Parents' [leaflet], date unknown, SLSA, SRG 555.
51 Letter from Adele Pert to Police Commissioner Bischof, 10 February 1967, NLA, MS 3821–5.
52 SA SOS Minutes, 20 March 1967, SLSA, SRG 555.
53 SA SOS Minutes, 28 November 1966, SLSA, SRG 555.
54 SA SOS Minutes, 27 February 1967, SLSA, SRG 555.
55 SA SOS Minutes, 27 February 1967, SLSA, SRG 555.
56 SA SOS, 'Letter to Prime Minister Gorton', SLSA, SRG 555.
57 'Viet. Objector Sent to Gaol', *Advertiser*, 26 September 1970.
58 SA SOS Minutes, 5 September 1967, SLSA, SRG 555.
59 Letter from Pat Ashcroft to Vilma Ward, 6 October 1965, NLA, MS 3821–5.
60 SA SOS Minutes, 24 June 1968, SLSA, SRG 555.
61 SA SOS Minutes, 3 May 1971, SLSA, SRG 555.
62 SA SOS Minutes, 27 November 1967, SLSA, SRG 555.
63 CPV and SOS, 'Some Won't Go' [leaflet], NAA, A6122, 1813/134.
64 Eulalie Tapp, 'SOS South Australia', NLA, MS 9878–2.

65 SA SOS Minutes, 3 February 1969 and 24 February 1969, SLSA, SRG 555.
66 SA SOS Minutes, 29 March 1969, SLSA, SRG 555.
67 'Students, Police Fight in City Streets', *Advertiser*, 12 April 1969.
68 '13 on Bail after City Fracas', *News*, 9 May 1969.
69 Letter from Sadie Pritchard re: Legal Aid Committee, 24 October 1971, Papers of Hal and Sadie Pritchard, SLSA, PRG 1561 92/1.
70 Eulalie Tapp, 'SOS South Australia', NLA, MS 9878-2.
71 SA SOS Minutes, 30 June 1969, SLSA, SRG 555.
72 Eulalie Tapp, 'SOS South Australia', NLA, MS 9878-2.
73 Audrey Potticary, 'Secretary's report', 28 July 1969, SLSA, SRG 555.
74 'Call-Up Protest Disrupts House', *Sydney Morning Herald*, 12 June 1970.
75 'Women Jailed for Trespass', *Canberra Times*, 9 April 1971.
76 'Police Called After Scuffle at Station', *Advertiser*, 13 May 1971.
77 Jim Cairns interviewed by Pauline Armstrong, 5 August 1990, NLA, MS 9878-3-2.
78 Eulalie Tapp, 'SOS South Australia', NLA, MS 9878-2.
79 Letter from Margaret Forte to SOS Sydney, 11 May 1970, NLA, MS 3821-2.
80 Letter from Sadie Pritchard to Janet Darling, 28 October 1970, SLSA, SRG781/25/4.
81 'Appeal to City – Play it Cool', *Advertiser*, 8 May 1970.
82 '600 Sing, Chant in City Protest', *Sunday Mail*, 9 May 1970.
83 '3 Soldiers on March Charges', *News*, 9 May 1970.
84 'Vietnam Moratorium Campaign', Brian Medlin Collection, Flinders University Library Special Collections.
85 Letter from Audrey Potticary to Adele Pert, 27 May 1970, NLA, MS 3821-2.
86 'Courts Guarded as 129 Charged', *News*, 19 September 1970.
87 'SA Inquiry Will Seek Cause of Protest Violence', *Sydney Morning Herald*, 22 September 1970.
88 SA SOS, Secretary's annual report 1970–71, SLSA, SRG 781/26/3.
89 Saunders, 'The Campaign for Peace in Vietnam', p. 134.
90 SA SOS, Secretary's annual report 1970–71, SLSA, SRG 781/26/3.
91 J.L. Darling, notes on SOS leaflet distributed to members, July 1970, SLSA, SRG 555.
92 SA SOS Minutes, 27 March 1972, SLSA, SRG 555.
93 *Ibid.*
94 Murray Goot and Rodney Tiffen, 'Public Opinion and the Politics of the Polls', in Peter King (ed.), *Australia's Vietnam*, Sydney: Allen & Unwin, 1983, p. 164.
95 Edwards, *A Nation at War*, p. 351.
96 Jean McLean interviewed by author, 2 October 2014.
97 Mac Gudgeon, email to author, 16 November 2012.
98 Jim Cairns interviewed by Pauline Armstrong, 5 August 1990, NLA, MS 9878-3-2.
99 Curthoys, 'Shut up, You Bourgeois Bitch', pp. 311–41.
100 Final letter from SA SOS, April 1972, SLSA, PRG 1561/92/1.
101 Potticary, 'Save Our Sons Remembered', in Miller and Marsden, *Years of Struggle*, p. 46.

Contributors

Steven Anderson is a Lecturer in the Department of History at the University of Adelaide. His doctoral thesis titled 'Death of a Spectacle: The Transition from Public to Private Executions in Colonial Australia' was shortlisted for the 2018 Serle Award, presented by the Australian Historical Association for the best postgraduate thesis in Australian History. In 2018 he won the History Council of South Australia's 'Emerging Historian' prize.

Philip Butterss is a Visiting Research Fellow in the Department of English and Creative Writing at the University of Adelaide. His book on the life and work of C.J. Dennis won the National Biography Award for 2015. He is currently writing a history of literary Adelaide from 1829 to the present.

Carolyn Collins is a Visiting Research Fellow in the Department of History at the University of Adelaide. Her doctoral thesis, titled '"Those Women with Banners": A History of the Save Our Sons Movement, 1965–1973', was awarded the University Doctoral Research Medal in 2016.

Jean Fornasiero is Emeritus Professor of French Studies at the University of Adelaide. Her research interests include the history of ideas in nineteenth-century France and French exploration and discovery. She is the co-author of *French Designs on Colonial New South Wales, 1803–1810* and *Encountering Terra Australis: The Australian Voyages of Nicolas Baudin and Matthew Flinders, 1800–1803*.

Robert Foster is Associate Professor and Head of the History Department at the University of Adelaide. His research interests focus on Australian and comparative Indigenous History. With Paul Sendziuk, he was co-convenor of the 2017 'Foundational Fictions' public lecture series and co-authored *A History of South Australia*, published by Cambridge University Press in 2018.

Jane Lydon is the Wesfarmers Chair in Australian History at the University of Western Australia. Her research interests include cultural history, human rights, humanitarianism and empire. Her books include *The Flash of Recognition: Photography and the Emergence of Indigenous Rights* (NewSouth, 2012), and *Photography, Humanitarianism, Empire* (Bloomsbury, 2016).

Stuart Macintyre is Emeritus Laureate Professor of History at the University of Melbourne. He has served as President of the Australian Academy of the Social Sciences and the Australian Historical Association, chair of the Humanities and Creative Arts panel of the Australian Research Council, and Dean of the Faculty of Arts at the University of Melbourne. He is the author of numerous critically acclaimed books, including *Australia's Boldest Experiment: War and Reconstruction in the 1940s*, which won the 2016 Ernest Scott Prize for the best book published in the field of Australian or New Zealand History.

Humphrey McQueen is a Canberra-based independent historian and cultural commentator. He previously taught history at the Australian National University. He has written nearly 20 books, including *Suspect History: Manning Clark and the Future of Australian History* (1997), *Temper Democratic: How Exceptional is Australia?* (1998) and, most recently, *We Built This Country: Builders' Labourers and Their Unions, 1787 to the Future* (2011). He is best known for his iconoclastic *A New Britannia: An Argument Concerning the Social Origins of Australian Radicalism* (1971).

Eric Richards was Emeritus Professor of History at Flinders University where he taught history for four decades before retiring in 2012. He published widely in the fields of British and Australian history, particularly on the themes of immigration and the Scottish Highlands. In 2014, he was Carnegie Trust Centenary Professor at the University of the Highlands and Islands in Scotland. His last book, *The Genesis of International Mass Migration: The British Case, 1750–1900* (Manchester University Press), was published in 2018.

Paul Sendziuk is an Associate Professor in the Department of History at the University of Adelaide, with expertise in Australian history, immigration history, and the history of disease and public health. His most recent book, co-authored with Robert Foster, is *A History of South Australia* (Cambridge University Press, 2018).

Lucy Treloar is the author a *Salt Creek* (2015), which won the Australian Book Industry's Matt Richell Award and the Dobbie Literary Award, and was shortlisted for prizes including the Miles Franklin Literary Award and the UK's Walter Scott Prize. Her short stories, published in *Overland*, *Best Australian Stories*, and elsewhere, have been similarly acclaimed.

John West-Sooby is Professor of French Studies at the University of Adelaide. He has a long-standing interest in the nineteenth-century French novel, and the literary and historical connections between France and Australia. He currently leads an Australian Research Council funded project, *Revolutionary Voyaging*, which examines state-sponsored scientific voyages undertaken during the French Revolution.

Index

A

abolition, 62, 165–69, 173–76
Aboriginal Affairs Act, 76
Aboriginal and Historic Relics Preservation Act, 76.
Aboriginal Lands Trust Act, 76
Aboriginal people, 2–3, 64, 66–69, 71, 73, 78, 98–99; Aboriginal-settler relations, 85–89, 105, 108; attitudes towards, 8–9, 65, 75, 79, 82, 86, 89, 94, 103, 106–7, 116; land title, 8, 65; frontier violence 2, 8, 44, 54 ,64–65, 79, 86, 88, 92, 126; reserves (see also North-West reserve), 8, 70, 72, 76; land rights, 11, 68–69, 77, 108; protesters, 64; rights and protections, 65–68, 70, 76, 78, 80; stereotypes, 84, 92; traditional life, 53, 76, 84, 109; welfare, 74; women, 5, 70, 76, 84, 113, 115; *see also* Indigenous peoples
Aborigines Protection League, 76
abortion, 5
Adams, Joseph, 121
Adelaide: 8–11, 26, 30, 53, 57, 59, 61, 63, 71, 79, 82–84, 86, 88, 92, 95–97, 118, 121–124, 126–134, 137–38, 149–50, 152, 154–57, 160–63, 167, 173–75, 178, 180, 182, 186–87, 190, 193
Adelaide Airport, 177, 178, 196
Adelaide and the Country, 10, 133–34

Adelaide Book Society, 120
Adelaide Circulating Library, 121
Adelaide Club, 149
Adelaide Critic, 123
Adelaide Electric Supply Company, 158
Adelaide High School, 146
Adelaide Hills, 61, 106
Adelaide Literary Society, 14
Adelaide Magistrates Court, 191
Adelaide Oval, 192
Adelaide Plains, 32, 155
Adelaide Railway Station, 189, 192
Adelaide Town Hall, 74, 146
Adelaide Young Men's Association, 120
Adelphi Planners, 30
Advertiser, 75, 122, 142–44, 147, 191
Africa, 58, 60
agriculture, 32, 41, 133, 136; *see also* farming
Anderson, Emma, 124
Angas, George Fife, 48–53, 58–60, 63
Angrave, Andy, 145
anti-discrimination laws, 5, 11
anti-war movement, 2, 178–179, 185–188, 190, 192, 195; *see also* Vietnam War and conscription
Anzac Day, 192
Anzac mythology, 3

architecture, 115, 131, 136, 162
Arnhem Land, 73
Arnold, Lynn, 178, 190
arts, 163, 192
Arunta, 54
Asia, 35, 156, 180, 183
Austin, Jane, 61
Australasian Critic, 128
Australian Democrats, 196
Australasian Federal Convention, 127
Australasian Home-Reading Union, 19, 120, 127
Australian Historical Novelists' Society, 99
Australian Labor Party (ALP), 159, 161, 178, 181, 187, 193, 196
Australian literature, 9
Australian Security and Intelligence Organisation (ASIO), 181–83
Australian Workers Union, 160

B
Baker, Arthur, 124
Baker, Richard, 138–40
Banking and finance, 8, 35, 46, 48–53, 140, 153, 186; Bank of Australasia, 52–53; National Provincial Bank, 52; Tamar Bank, 53; Union Bank, 50–52
Bank of South Australia, 50–53
Banks, Sir Joseph, 15, 112–113
Bannon, John, 138–39, 178
Barrow, Eliezer, 60
Barrow, Jacob, 60
Barrow, Joseph, 60
Barton, John, 103
Basedow, Herbert, 70-2, 74-5, 77
Bass Strait, 14, 17–18, 21–23
Baudin, Nicolas, 6, 13–26
Bauer, Ferdinand, 24
Beachport, 157
Bellchambers, T.P., 72

Bernhardt, Sarah, 122
Besant, Walter, 11
BHP, 152, 154, 156
Blackham, H.H., 124
Blackmore, Edwin Gordon, 139
Blackstone, William, 170, 171
Bode, Ettie, 124
Bohemian Club, 120
Bohemians, 118, 123, 127
Bolte, Henry, 192
bookshops, 9, 121, 131
Boothby, Guy, 128
Botany Bay, 43, 45, 113
Bradman, Sir Donald, 161
Bright, Robert, 189
Brighton, 147
Brisbane, 180, 188
Britain, 13, 19, 21–3, 25, 28, 34–36, 38, 41, 44, 45, 47, 48, 50, 58, 60, 88, 123, 126; see also England, Scotland, Wales
British, 13, 15–16, 22, 40, 67, 135; colonisation 35, 138, 67; cotton millers, 61, 104; economy 32; emigration, 33, 58, 156; empire,43, 46, 48, 51, 104, 129; fiction 131; Franco-British rivalry, 14, 23, 45; goods and ports, 59; government 7–8, 38–39, 57, 60, 67, 69; humanitarian lobby, 92, 173; Isles, 35–36, 38, 40; penal code, 176; sealers, 5; settlement, 3, 22, 25, 77; society and culture 31, 34, 82; soldiers, 11; see also English
British Society for the Diffusion of Information on the Subject of Capital Punishment, 173
British Tube Mills Ltd, 160
Broken Hill, 36
Brown, John, 68, 69
Brown, Robert, 16, 24
Bubble Act, 50
Builders' Labourers Union, 62; see also trade unions

Bulletin, 123
Burford, William, 11, 166–76
Burns, Robert, 123
Burnside, 146
Butler, Richard 151–53
Burra, 30
Buxton, Thomas Fowell, 69, 172

C

Cairns, Jim, 186, 192, 195
Callaghan, A.R., 145
Calwell, Arthur, 180
Campaign for Peace in Vietnam (CPV), 178, 190–196
Canada, 34, 38
Canberra, 131, 141–144, 186, 188, 192
Cape Banks, 14
Cape Jervis, 25
Cape Leeuwin, 20
capitalism, 43–52, 54, 56–8, 63
capitalist, 30, 32, 35, 39, 40, 43, 44, 61
capital punishment, 11, 165–170, 172–176; *see also* executions
car industry, 163
Carleton, Caroline, 129
Carlile, Richard, 62
Carlyle, Thomas, 92, 164
Cartledge, Jack, 154, 162
Catholic Church/Catholics, 38, 135, 160, 169, 182
Catholic Truth Society, 70
Cavanagh, James, 161
Cawthorne and Co., 121
Ceduna, 14
Centennial celebrations, 75
Chambers of Manufacturers, 161
Champ, Samuel, 62
Chandler, Alfred, 124
chattel-slavery, 44, 48, 58–59, 63; *see also* slavery, slaves

children, 40, 60, 80, 84, 103, 106, 115, 120, 123, 129, 186, 187
Children of Vietnam, 194
Chifley, Ben, 142, 147
Christianity and Christians, 70, 72, 75, 147, 168–69, 183–85
churches, 127, 135, 175, 185; Anglican, 135, 169; Baptist, 66, 169; Calvinists, 169; Churches of Christ, 167, 169; Congregationalist, 147, 169; Methodist, 71, 133, 147, 160, 182; *see also* Catholic Church/Catholics, Christianiy and Christians, Protestant Church
Civil Liberties Council, 188
Clarkson, Thomas, 63
class divisions 8, 11, 35, 54–56, 79, 93–95, 147, 162, 179; middle class, 3, 146, 47, 153, 181–82, 184, 195–96; propertied, 53, 58; working class, 62, 63, 127, 153, 184
Clay, Cassius (Muhammad Ali), 185
Cleland, J.B., 75, 77
Clemens, Samuel Langhorne, 1; *see also* Mark Twain
Clendinnen, Inga, 4, 99–102, 104–105, 111–12
climate, 26, 35, 43, 109
coal, 10, 150, 152, 158, 159
Cockburn, John, 139
Colonial Land and Emigration Commission (CLEC), 36, 37
colonial land revenue, 34
Colonial Office, 7, 29, 55, 67–69
Colonial Secretary, 56
colonies, 1, 5, 7, 22, 30–37, 39–41, 43–45, 48, 52–53, 55, 67–68, 88, 92, 94, 104, 130, 136–139, 169–170, 173, 175
Colonization Commission, 66, 67, 68, 167
Committee for Vietnam Protest (CVP), 178

Common Cause, 10, 144–149
Commonwealth Bill League, 139
Commonwealth Department of Defence, 158
Commonwealth Department of Labour and National Service, 191
Commonwealth Department of the War Organisation of Industry, 142
Commonwealth-state relations, 71, 73, 137–144, 148, 151, 153, 156–157, 159, 162, 179
communalism, 53–54
communism, 54, 145, 147, 179–183; anti-communist, 145
Communist Party of Australia, 145, 147, 159, 181–82
Comte de Fleurieu, 14
conscription, 11, 134, 177–197
Constitution, 5, 61, 73, 137–40, 143
Constitution Act, 161
Constitutional Convention, 143–44
consumer protection laws, 11
convicts, 5, 22, 55, 58, 65, 67, 86, 93–94, 126, 135, 167; convict labour, 5–6, 39; settlements, 22, 39; convict system, 36, 44–45, 134, transportation, 36
Cook, Maureen, 182
Cooke, Constance, 73–77
Coorong, 9, 25, 97–100, 103
Corelli, Marie, 121
Cornish, 49
cotton, 43, 63; cotton-millers, 61
Coxsedge, Joan, 196
Crawford, Sidney, 145
Crisp, Fin, 143
Crown lands, 31, 46
Cudmore, Collier, 159
Curtin, John, 142–144, 148

D

dairy industry, 150–51
Darling, Janet, 190, 194
Darling, Ralph, 22
Darling River and district, 54, 126, 139
Darwin, Charles, 70, 103–04
Davison, Graeme, 134
Deakin, Alfred, 137
de Bougainville, Hyacinthe, 16-18, 22
defence, 14; projects, 157; Department of, 158
democracy, 1, 7, 134; democratic institutions, 131; rights, 189
Dennis, C.J., 123, 128, 235
Department of Post-war Reconstruction, 145, 146, 148
depression, 47, 121, 131, 140, 151, 153, 160
Dickens, Charles, 35, 92, 121
Displaced Persons, 156
domestic servants, 40
Doyle, Conan, 121
drought, 75
Duguid, Charles, 145, 148
Dumas, Lloyd, 142, 144, 149
Duncan, Lindsay (Mrs T.C. Cloud), 111
Duncan, Sir Walter, 159
Dunstan, Don, 11, 64–65, 76–78, 165, 176, 178, 187, 192–193
Duperrey, Louis, 22
Dutch, 156

E

East India Company, 48, 50
economy, 32, 45, 47–48, 54, 59, 142, 148, 151–152, 156, 162
education, 40, 94, 119–20, 127, 129, 131, 133, 135, 146, 148, 163, 185
Education Act, 120
Edwards, Doris, 182
elections, 143, 148, 161, 183, 187–88, 192, 194–195
electricity, 152, 155, 158–59, 161–62

Electricity Trust of South Australia (ETSA), 159, 161
Elizabeth (suburb), 155–56, 162, 189
emigration, 30–39, 41, 57, 68; see also immigration, migrants
Empire, see British Empire
employment, 83, 142, 150, 160; see also unemployment
Encounter Bay, 6, 13–14, 126
Endeavour, 112
Engels, Friedrich, 45, 51
England: 6, 17, 23, 30, 34, 39, 41, 55, 82, 92, 103, 124, 135, 148, 167, 170, 172–174; see also Britain
English, 6, 13, 15–17, 30, 32–33, 38, 44, 51, 53, 99–100, 103–04, 118, 127, 145, 163, 171, 174, 181
English literature, 120–126, 129
environment, 3, 12, 105, 109, 162–163, 196
E.S. Wigg & Son bookshop, 121
Europe, 2, 14–15, 17, 25, 38, 42, 80, 135, 156, 163
European, 14, 22, 70, 89, 103–4, 106, 115, 126, 176; settlement, 7, 8, 45, 98, 103, 109, 167, 176; ideas, 68, 70
Evans, Matilda, 125
Evatt, Bert, 143
Ewart, William, 172
E.W. Cole bookshop, 21
executions, 56, 165–67, 169, 171–72, 175; see also capital punishment
exploration and explorers, 6, 17, 22–23, 25, 54, 102, 111; see also individual explorers
Eyre, Edward, 83, 89, 95
Eyre Peninsula, 23

F
factories, 141, 151, 155, 157–58, 160; factory employment, 10, 150

farming, 5, 9, 30, 32, 58–59, 70, 99, 109, 115, 133, 136, 138 (see also agriculture)
Federal Conventions, 127, 137
federal movement, 10, 136–138
Federal Parliament, 72–74, 142, 180, 185, 196
Federation, 136–140, 144, 147, 166, 174, 176
Fergusson, Sir James, 61
Festival of Arts, 163
Finsbury, 141, 157
First Fleet, 101
First World War, 145, 179, 180
Fleurieu Peninsula, 115
Flinders, Matthew, 6, 13–26
Ford, Reverend John J., 169–70
forestry, 151
foundational fictions: definition, 2
France, 6, 13, 21–26, 45, 145, 173
Freycinet, Henri, 20

G
Gandhi, 58
Garland, Tom, 145, 147, 149
Gasworkers Union, 145
Gawler, 130
Gawler, Governor, 57, 69, 74
Gellert, Leon, 128
General Motors-Holden, 141, 152, 155, 157
Genders, J.C., 72, 74, 77
Le Geographe, 16, 18–20
Germans, 45, 49–58, 70–71, 156–57; literature, 120; Germany, 58, 71
Giles, Isabella, 124
Gipps, Governor, 30, 32, 35
Glenelg, 64, 146, 155
Glenelg, Lord, 56, 67–68
Glorious Revolution, 48
Glynn, Patrick, 139

gold, 33, 41, 48, 136, 140
Golgerth, Joyce, 180
Gordon, Adam Lindsay, 121, 123–24, 129–31
Gordon, James, 61
Gouger, Robert, 28–29
governors, 21–2, 30–31, 35, 44, 51–52, 55, 57–58, 61, 64, 66–67, 69, 74–5, 78, 119, 128–131, 148, 175–76
Grant, James, 14
Greeks (migrants), 156
Greek Workers' Educational Association, 156
Grenville, Kate, 4, 9, 99–100, 104–5, 109, 112; novel *Secret River*, 4, 99–100, 102, 104, 109
Grey, George, 58, 83, 94
Griffith, Sir Samuel, 59
Gulf St Vincent, 24–25

H
Hall, Herbert, 127
Hamilton, George, 8–9, 79–96
Hannan, A.J., 148
Hawdon, Joseph, 83
Herodotus, 4
Hewett, Noreen, 181
High Court, 186, 188
Hill, Fidelia, 61
Hindmarsh, Governor John, 52, 55, 57, 64, 66, 71, 75
Hindmarsh Island, 104
Hirst, John, 10, 105, 133, 135–37, 139
historical fiction, 2, 4, 9, 98–101, 104–06, 109–10, 113, 115–17
history wars, 3, 4, 53, 62
Hoare, Hazel, 180
Hogben, Horace, 151, 153
Holden, Edward, 151, 159
Holdfast Bay City Council, 64, 78
Holt Government, 187

homosexuality, 5, 11
horses, 8, 51, 79–82, 92, 94, 115
House of Assembly, 5, 140, 159, 167, 175
House of Commons Select Committee, 30
housing, 141–42, 146–48, 150–51, 153–56, 161–62
Howard, John, 3
Howe, James, 139
Howell, John, 124
humanitarians, 8, 67–70, 76, 92, 96, 235
Hutchesson, Edna, 185

I
immigration, 4, 29, 31, 33, 34–38, 40–41, 155; *see also* emigration, migrants
Imperial Chemical Industries Ltd, 152
India, 23, 48, 50, 58, 80, 122
Indigenous peoples, 1, 3, 8, 26, 54, 57, 76–78, 83, 86, 88–89, 92, 95, 105–06, 114–16, 135, 148, 166–167, 175
industrialisation, 82, 141, 145, 150–52, 156–59, 160, 162–64
industry, 43, 45, 66, 139, 142, 151–53, 157
inequality, 127
Institute of Public Affairs, 143, 148
Investigator, 15, 135
Ireland, 38, 135; Irish, 38, 40, 135, 160; Irish Catholics, 60
Isles, Keith, 145, 147–49

J
Jamaica, 60–61
Japan, 141, 143, 163
Jennison, J.C., 71
Jewish community, 168, 175
John Martin's department store, 187
Johnson, Lyndon, 186
Jones, Doris Egerton, 128
Joplin, Thomas, 52
Jose, Arthur, 9, 118–19, 123, 126, 131

K

kangaroos, 18, 24
Kangaroo Island, 22–5, 49, 57, 66, 103
Kaurna, 72, 78, 96
Kaurna Heritage Committee, 78
Kendall, Henry, 121, 123
Kenwood, 155
Kilburn, 160
King, Philip Gidley, 21
Kingston, Charles, 137–40
Kingston SE, 157
Kipling, Rudyard, 62, 122–23
Knowles, Vernon, 128

L

labourers, 31, 33–34, 40, 44, 56–59, 62, 127
Lady Nelson, 14
laissez faire liberals, 11, 151
Lake Alexandrina, 54
land rights, 5, 11, 72, 74, 77, 78
Lane, William, 122
Lang, Jack, 144
Leane, Caroline Agnes, 124
Lefevre Peninsula, 152
Legislative Council (SA), 5, 61, 103, 139, 159, 173; Victorian Legislative Council, 196
Leigh Creek, 159, 160
Letters Patent, 8, 55, 65, 77, 78, 106
Lewin, Frances, 124
Lewis, Essington, 142, 156, 157
Liberal and Country League (LCL), 153
Liberal Party, 134, 159, 181–82
libraries, 9, 42, 62, 93, 121, 127, 131, 146–47, 162, 166–67, 169
Linger, Carl, 29
literary societies, 119–20, 127–28, 132, 175
Lockyer, Edmund, 22
Lord Hobart, 21

M

Mackintosh, James, 172
Makin, Norman, 142, 157
Malouf, David, 4, 102, 111
manufacturing, 41, 140–41, 150–52, 155–56
Maria Massacre, 166, 174
Martin, Catherine, 125–26
Martin, Chas, 189
Martin, Malachi, 98
Marryatville, 146
Marx, Karl, 32, 35, 43–49, 51, 54, 56, 58–59, 63
Masters and Servants Act, 56
McDonnell, Governor Richard, 176
McHenry, George, 124
McKenna, Mark, 100–01, 105, 112–14, 116–17
McLaren, David, 11, 166–76
McLean, Jean, 192
Medlin, Brian, 190
Melbourne, 1, 3, 9, 74, 83–84, 92, 97, 118–19, 121–22, 124, 126, 128, 137, 144, 153, 170, 174, 180, 187–89, 192, 194, 196
Melbourne City Council, 188
Menzies, Robert, 145, 180, 183, 185
migrants, 7, 29–31, 33, 36, 38–41, 155–56, *see also* emigration, immigration
Miller, Beryl, 83
Millicent, 154
Mills, Samuel, 61
Miners' Federation of Australia, 160
mining, 5, 13, 61–62, 133
missionaries, 73, 80
Mitchell, William, 118–20
Model Aboriginal State, 72–74
Montefiore, Moses, 60
moratoriums, 178–9, 190, 192–7
Mount Barker, 175
Mount Gambier, 14, 154

multiculturalism, 3, 134
munitions factories, 141–42, 157
Murdoch, Keith, 144, 147, 149
Murray Bridge, 157
Murray, John, 14
Murray, Stanley, 159
Myall Creek Massacre, 88

N
Napoleon, 20, 22–23, 26
Napoleonic Wars, 23
National Service Act, 178, 183, 186
Le Naturaliste, 16
New England, 129, 135
New Holland, 18, 25, 34, 45
Newland, Simpson, 107–09, 126
News, 144, 177, 183, 185
New South Wales, 6, 21–22, 30–32, 35, 37–39, 46, 55, 57–58, 60, 95, 104, 134, 137–38, 140–42, 144, 152, 158, 169, 173
newspapers, 62, 124, 128, 130–31, 143–44, 159, 174–75, 185
New Zealand, 28, 73
Ngarrindjeri, 55, 98, 105–06
Noack, Errol, 11
North Adelaide Presbyterian Church, 175
North America, 35, 38–40; *see also* United States, Canada
Northern Territory, 71, 98, 107, 137, 140
North-West Reserve, 72
Norwood, 146, 165
Nullarbor, 137
Nuriootpa, 147
Nuyts Archipelago, 14

O
Oehne, Keith, 190
O'Halloran, Mick, 160,
Outback, 30, 71
Overlander, 8, 79, 83, 86, 89–90, 92, 94

P
Palmer, Vance, 9, 118
Parkes, Henry, 169, 173
Peace Pledge Union, 178
Peel, Robert, 172
Peel, Thomas, 44
Pentreath, Reverend Guy, 145, 147–48
Péron, Francois, 18–20, 25–6
Perry, Frank, 151
Perth, 140–41, 180, 184
Peterborough, 157
Phillip, Governor, 44–45
Phillips, A.A., 9, 118
Philips Electrical Industries, 158
Pike, Douglas, 28–29, 31, 167
Pinnock, 155
Pinto, Sarah, 100, 105
Pitjantjatjara Land Rights Bill, 78
Plasterers' Society of South Australia, 145, 161
Playford, Thomas, 10, 11, 138, 142, 150–64
poetry, 118–19, 123–24, 127, 129–30, 132, 193
Poetry Recital Society, 127
police, 8, 54, 64, 79, 83, 89, 98, 134, 188, 190–92
Political Reform League, 153
Poor Law Amendment Act, 48
Port Adelaide 61, 129, 152, 175
Port Adelaide Congregational Church, 175
Port Augusta, 140, 154
Port Jackson, 14–15, 17, 20–21, 23
Port Lincoln, 24
Port Phillip, 21–22, 83–84, 86–87
Port Pirie, 136, 154, 157, 162
Portus, G.V., 145
post-war reconstruction, 10, 142
Potticary, Audrey, 182, 193, 196
poverty, 88, 92, 146

Pratt, W.N., 124
Pritchard, Ann, 191
Pritchard, Hal and Sadie, 184, 190–3, 196
Pritchard, Robert, 191
Proclamation Day, 2, 46, 64, 78, 136
Prohibition of Discrimination Act, 76
Prospect, 145–46
Protector of Aborigines, 66, 69, 71, 77, 89; *see also* Wyatt, William
Protestants, 135, 147, 160, 167, 169

Q
Quakers, 103, 135, 175, 178, 182; *see also* Society of Friends
Queensland, 126, 138, 141, 144, 154, 160, 188
Quick, John, 138

R
race, 1, 8, 79, 93, 95, 110
railways, 50–51, 137–41, 151, 157, 189, 192
Rainberd murders, 166
Ramsay, Alex, 145, 147–48, 154, 162
Reeve, Wybert, 121–2, 128
referendums, 139–140, 142–44, 148, 187
Reform Act, 48
regional development, 151
religion, 1, 110, 135; religious freedom, 1, 65; beliefs, 124, 127, 160, 182, 185; dissent, 168; *see also* church, Quakers, Catholic Church/Catholics
republicanism, 26, 51
Revolutionary wars, 14
Reynolds, Margaret, 196
Richards, R.S., 159
Ripon Regulations, 29, 55
River Murray, 86, 88–89, 95, 136, 139–40, 152, 157, 162–63, 167
Rodda, Charles, 128
Romilly, Samuel, 172

Roseworthy Agricultural College, 145
Rosman, Alice Grant, 128
Ross, Sir Robert Dalrymple, 61
Rothschild, Nathan, 60
Royal commissions, 140, 151, 159, 193
Royal Society, 75
Rufus River Massacre, 9, 79, 88–89, 95

S
SA Advisory Committee for Conscientious Objectors, 178
Sadler, James, 124
Salisbury, 155, 157
Salt Creek, 9, 98–99, 103, 105, 109, 112, 115, 117
Sams, W.A., 145
Savage Club, 120
Save Our Sons (SOS), 11–12, 178–193
schools, *see* education
Scotland, 51, 135, 136; Scots, 38, 164, 167, 169, 172
sealers, 15, 23
Second World War, 141–42, 153, 156, 158, 162, 176
serfdom, 53, 54, 56, 127; *see also* slavery
settlement: 2, 7–9, 13, 21–24, 26, 30, 32–33, 43–4, 63, 65, 67–68, 71, 78–79, 82–83, 98, 103, 133, 136–37, 142, 165–67, 176
settlers, 2, 7, 54–55, 66, 68, 89, 92, 107, 135–36
Sexton, John Henry, 72
Sharp, Cecil, 128
Sinnett, Percy, 124
Sladen, Douglas, 123
slavery, 8, 43–44, 48, 53–56, 58–59, 63; slaves, 36, 44–45, 56, 58, 60–63, 103
Smith, Adam, 47, 51, 56
Smith, Louis Laybourne, 147
Society for Democratic Action (SDA), 190

Society for the Abolition of Capital Punishment, 174
Society of Friends, 178, 185; *see also* Quakers
soldier settlement, 142
Song of Australia, 129
South Australian Committee for International Co-operation and Disarmament, 178, 185
South Australian Company, 7, 48, 50, 53, 56, 59, 61, 63, 167
South Australian Criminological Society, 175
South Australian Housing Trust, 146, 148, 153–56, 161–63
South Australian Literary Societies Union, 119, 127–28
South Australian Parliament, 175–76
South Australian Peace Committee, 182
Spain, 21, 59
Spence, Catherine Helen, 107, 121, 125, 130
Spencer Gulf, 24, 25
Spence, W.G., 127
squatters, 30, 55, 67, 135
Standard-Vacuum Refining Company (Australia) Pty Ltd, 152
Stanley, Effie, 125, 128
Stirling, Edward, 61
Storrie, William, 125
St Peters, 146
St Peter's College, 145, 148
Stretton, Hugh, 133
Stuart, Rupert Max, 165, 176
Sturt, Charles, 24, 54, 69
sugar, 61, 84
Swan River, 22, 44, 93
Sydney, 26, 28, 30, 34, 38, 82–84, 106, 112, 118–19, 123–24, 128, 130, 137, 141, 144, 153, 157–58, 174, 178, 180–81, 184–89, 192–94
Symon, Josiah, 127, 139
Symon, Lady Mary, 127

T

Taplin, George, 98
Tapp, Eulalie, 191
Tapp, John, 191
Tasmania, 16, 26; *see also* Van Diemen's Land
taxation, 34, 36, 142, 151–53, 160
Tennyson, Alfred, 129
Tennyson, Hallam, 119, 121, 128–31
Theatre Royal, 121–122
Thompson, A.B., 145
Thucydides, 4
tobacco, 61
Tolpuddle Martyrs, 57
Tomasetti, Glen, 187
Torrens, Robert, 29, 47, 55, 68
Townsend, Simon, 189
Townsville, 180, 196
Trades and Labour Council, 145
trade unions, 5, 57, 127, 144–45, 147, 160–61, 178, 181, 185
Twain, Mark, 1, 2, 5, 121–23; see also Clemens, Samuel Langhorne

U

Unaipon, David, 73
unemployment, 38, 41, 146, 148, 164; *see also* employment
Union of Australian Women (UAW), 178, 181–85, 195–97
United Kingdom, 48, 52, 58; *see also* England
United States, 35, 44, 135, 163, 173, 195; *see also* North America
University of Adelaide 2, 8, 10, 12, 107, 118–20, 133, 178, 185, 192
University Shakespeare Society, 120, 122, 127
Unley, 146, 181
Unley High School, 133
utopianism, 26, 30, 73

V

Valance, Glen Sabre, 165, 176
Van Diemen's Land, 6, 53–54, 67; see also Tasmania
Verne, Jules, 26
Victoria, 6, 14, 114–15, 123, 130, 136, 138, 141–44, 152, 154, 160, 167, 177, 192, 196
Vietnam Moratorium Campaign (VMC), 178, 190, 192–93, 196
Vietnam War, 11, 177–80, 184–85, 196
violence, 2, 8, 44, 54, 64, 66–67, 79, 86, 88, 92, 95, 101, 107, 126, 171, 193
volunteers, 10, 18, 196

W

Wainwright, J.W., 142, 145, 149, 151–53, 157–60, 162, 164
Wakefield, Edward Gibbon, 7, 24, 28–42, 44, 49, 56, 65, 133
Wales, 135, 173
Wallaroo Presbyterian Church, 175
Ward, Vilma, 188
Way, Samuel, 130
W.C. Rigby bookshop, 121
weapons and testing, 148, 157–58
Weapon's Research Establishment, 155
Weber, Max, 48–9, 57–8
Wedge, John Helder, 114
Welch, Sarah, 124
welfare, 37, 67–68, 72, 74, 162–63
Westall, William, 24
Western Australia, 22, 26, 71, 136–38, 140, 144, 154
West India, 61, 63

whales and whaling, 15, 106
Wharton, May, 181–3, 86–7
wheat industry, 29
Wheete Coolera, 114
Whigs, 48, 67
White, Bill, 187
White, S.A., 71–73
Whitlam, Gough, 161, 179, 188, 194
Whyalla, 150, 152, 154, 156–57, 162
Wilberforce, William, 63, 103
Williams, Roma, 146
Wilson, Keith, 151, 153
Wollongong, 180, 188, 192
Woman's Christian Temperance Union, 183, 185
Women's Centenary Committee, 75–76
Women's International League for Peace and Freedom (WILPF), 178, 185, 193, 196
Women's Non-Party Association, 73
Woodville, 146, 152, 157
Woolcock, Elizabeth, 166
wool industry, 30
writers' festivals, 110
Wyatt, William, 69

Y

Yorke Peninsula, 134
Younghusband, William, 172

Z

Zarb, John, 189

Turning Points
Chapters in South Australian history

EDITED BY ROBERT FOSTER AND PAUL SENDZIUK

How distinctive is South Australia after all?

South Australia has often been represented as 'different': free of convicts, more enlightened in its attitudes toward Aboriginal people, established on rational economic principles, and progressive in its social and political development. Some of this is true, some of it is not, but mostly the story is more complex.

In this book, eminent historians explore these themes by examining some key 'turning points' in South Australia's history. Henry Reynolds considers the question of Aboriginal rights to land. Bill Gammage illustrates the nature of Aboriginal land management. Paul Sendziuk unravels the myth of the colony's convict-free origins, while Robert Foster and Amanda Nettelbeck reveal a surprisingly strong sense of 'nationalism' in colonial South Australia. Susan Magarey traces the histories of two crucial events in the advancement of women. Neal Blewett examines the political innovations of Don Dunstan. Jill Roe looks at life in the country in twentieth-century South Australia, and Mark Peel life in the city, in particular the migrant experience after World War Two. Finally, John Hirst asks: 'How distinctive was South Australia after all?'

Wakefield Press is an independent publishing and
distribution company based in Adelaide, South Australia.
We love good stories and publish beautiful books.
To see our full range of books, please visit our website at
www.wakefieldpress.com.au
where all titles are available for purchase.
To keep up with our latest releases, news and events,
subscribe to our monthly newsletter.

Find us!

Facebook: www.facebook.com/wakefield.press
Twitter: www.twitter.com/wakefieldpress
Instagram: www.instagram.com/wakefieldpress

www.ingramcontent.com/pod-product-compliance
Lightning Source LLC
Chambersburg PA
CBHW030105170426
43198CB00009B/504